THE ANUNNAKI CHRONICLES

A Zecharia Sitchin Reader

EDITED AND INTRODUCED BY

JANET SITCHIN

Bear & Company
Rochester, Vermont • Toronto, Canada

Bear & Company
One Park Street
Rochester, Vermont 05767
www.BearandCompanyBooks.com

Bear & Company is a division of Inner Traditions International

Library of Congress Cataloging-in-Publication Data
Sitchin, Zecharia.
  The Anunnaki chronicles : a Zecharia Sitchin reader / edited and introduced by
Janet Sitchin.
     pages cm
  ISBN 978-1-59143-229-6 (hardback) — ISBN 978-1-59143-230-2 (ebook)
  1. Civilization, Ancient—Extraterrestrial influences. 2. Civilization—History. 3.
Human beings—Origin. 4. Extraterrestrial beings. 5. Human–alien encounters.
I. Sitchin, Janet. II. Title.
  CB156.S5723 2015
  001.942—dc23
                                                                 2015011075

Printed and bound in the United States by Lake Book Manufacturing, Inc.
The text stock is SFI certified. The Sustainable Forestry Initiative® program
promotes sustainable forest management.

10 9 8 7 6 5 4 3 2 1

Text design by Virginia Scott Bowman and layout by Debbie Glogover
This book was typeset in Garamond Premier Pro with Cochin, Ellington, Gill
Sans, and Myriad Pro used as display fonts
Map of the ancient Near East on page viii by Jim Wasserman

To send correspondence to the author of this book, mail a first-class letter to the
author c/o Inner Traditions • Bear & Company, One Park Street, Rochester, VT
05767, and we will forward the communication, or contact the author directly at
www.sitchin.com.

◇ ❖ ◇

Dedicated in memory of my uncle Zecharia,
who started this journey for the Sitchin family,
and in honor of my father,
Amnon Sitchin,
who first brought my attention to my uncle's work.

Contents

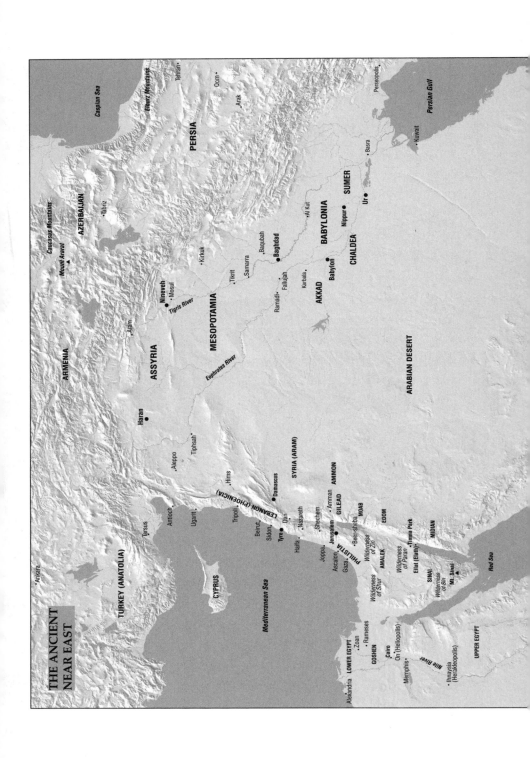

THE ANCIENT
NEAR EAST

TURKEY (ANATOLIA)

Ankara

CYPRUS

Mediterranean Sea

Tarsus
Antioch
Ugarit
Tripoli
LEBANON (PHOENICIA)
Beirut
Sidon
Tyre
Haifa
Joppa
Ascalon
Gaza
PHILISTIA

Aleppo
Tiphsah
Hims
Damascus
SYRIA (ARAM)
Dan
Nazareth
Shechem
Jerusalem
Amman
GILEAD
AMMON
Beer-sheba
Wilderness
of Zin
MOAB
EDOM

Haran

ASSYRIA

ARMENIA

MESOPOTAMIA

Euphrates River

Adam

Nineveh
Mosul
Tigris River

Caucasus Mountains
Mount Ararat

AZERBAIJAN

Tabriz

PERSIA

Elburz Mountains

Caspian Sea

Tehran

Qom

Arak

Tikrit
Samarra
Kirkuk

Ramadi
Fallujah
Karbala
AKKAD
Babylon

Baghdad
Baqubah
BABYLONIA
CHALDEA

Al Kut

Nippur
SUMER
Ur

Basra

Kuwait

Persepolis

Persian Gulf

ARABIAN DESERT

AMALEK
Wilderness
of Shur
Eilat (Elath)
Timna Park
Wilderness
of Paran
SINAI
Wilderness
of Sin
Mt. Sinai
MIDIAN

Red Sea

LOWER EGYPT
Alexandria
Rameses
Zoan
GOSHEN
Cairo
On (Heliopolis)
Memphis
Ihnasya
(Herakleopolis)
UPPER EGYPT
Nile River

Introduction

Those who had a chance to meet Zecharia Sitchin—at seminars, tours, book signings, or speaking engagements—were familiar with his modesty, warmth, understated intellect, dry humor, and his precisely chosen words, especially when he was speaking on a set of topics that he loved to discuss, on the subject of ancient civilizations, which included the ideas of ancient extraterrestrials coming to Earth. When he was engaged in a discussion of this nature, his demeanor was strong proof that the conversation was a serious one; his ideas were rooted in facts and not in wild speculation or fantasy.

My uncle Zecharia's first book, *The 12th Planet,* was published when I was a teen, but I did not actually read all the way through it until many more years had passed. Its first one hundred pages or so are filled with facts and proofs, and more proofs and more physical evidence, all of which support his theories. Reading this all those years ago, I was daunted and put the book down. The inclusion of all these facts and proofs was done deliberately by him in order to establish that he was presenting scholarly material, not sensationalized ideas. Especially in that first literary outing, he wanted to show that evidence exists to support his theories—and not just one piece of evidence, but many pieces of evidence. When I reread the book a few years ago, I was completely engrossed from page one.

My uncle's interest in the topic of ancient civilizations and human origins derived from his reading the Hebrew Bible, or Old Testament, in its original Hebrew, and then comparing what he had read to common

English translations that more times than not skewed the meaning. Most biblical scholars and archaeologists deem ancient writings to be allegory, myth, and/or legend, no matter whether the original source writings are from the Bible or are Sumerian, Akkadian, Assyrian, Egyptian, Greek, or Roman. Sitchin's premise was this: What if these ancient tales are not legend or myth or allegory; what if they are history?

The incident that sparked his interest in this compelling question occurred when he was a schoolboy in Israel during the time of the British Mandate. His interest had been sparked in one pivotal moment (which we will discuss later in the book)—and a life spent in research, the study of languages, travel, and museum visits would ensue. He accumulated so much fascinating evidence and developed so many fascinating theories and corollary ideas that his wife, Rina, encouraged him to "stop talking and start writing." As a result, he went on to author fourteen nonfiction volumes on the subject of ancient civilizations; the first of which, *The 12th Planet,* was published in 1976.

Sitchin led tours to see the places and the ancient artifacts he mentioned in his books and began conducting what he called "Sitchin Studies Seminars." I began attending the seminars to provide support to him, assisting with registration or doing whatever he needed me to do to ensure that things ran smoothly. At these seminars, I was fortunate to be able to hear him speak on the topics of his books and to hear the questions from his readers and the answers that he gave.

His words were always chosen carefully, given that he did not want to imply or put forward any idea for which he didn't have ample evidence and a firm conclusion in his mind about how the idea fit into the story of the Anunnaki ("Those Who from Heaven to Earth Came"). Well-meaning readers would frequently ask him to discuss various theories of other scholars, or to comment on aspects of ancient civilization that he hadn't researched or written about, or for which he did not yet have a solid conclusion or enough evidence. In these instances, he would invariably find a polite way to decline and say only what he knew to be true.

This integrity was a large part of his character and one of the reasons that he was well respected and believed. His goal in writing was to share the information he felt was vitally important for all of us, as a human family, to know about our origins. He said that he was a "reporter," writing the story of the Anunnaki as recorded by ancient peoples.

There were always the detractors and those who ascribed to him ideas that he had never discussed, let alone written about. However, there also existed readers and associates from all walks of life who were forthcoming with material that might help him with his research. Some of these behind-the-scenes contributors were professionals who were worried that by publicly endorsing his ideas their scientific or academic careers would be jeopardized or destroyed. Professional condemnation for thinking outside the established paradigm is the reason why more college professors, archaeologists, astronomers, and other scientists don't speak out more frequently on the possibility of extraterrestrials visiting Earth, and other related topics. However, it's interesting to note that many observatories are run by Jesuit priests; the Vatican has an interest in extraterrestrials; and NASA scientists have provided information to Sitchin.

In positing that the material from ancient writings and artifacts was, in fact, a recounting of historical events, and in seeing the same tales told in many different languages and yet involving the same personalities, Sitchin explored a new paradigm. This new paradigm also tacitly acknowledged that ancient accounts often described events and processes that were very technologically advanced. How *would* ancient people describe the launch of a NASA rocket? Perhaps in the same way that the tale of Gilgamesh discusses events that he, Gilgamesh, witnessed in ancient times. How *would* ancient people have explained a modern cell phone, especially a "smart phone"? They didn't have the technological language to explain exactly how a cell phone or a smart phone worked. Instead, to them, it operated as a provenance of the special magical powers of the gods. How *would* archaeologists of the nineteenth or early twentieth century—in an era where there were no cars or airplanes or computers—describe the things that the ancients had witnessed and that, indeed, were part and parcel of their everyday lives?

The stories of the ancients *must* be myth, because anything else would be beyond belief.

However, as our own society has advanced technologically, it's easier to envisage earlier cultures enjoying the benefits of technology too. In a time when man has landed on the moon, a celestial craft could more aptly be imagined and described. Old translations that previously made no sense can now be interpreted in this more modern way. This is another part of Sitchin's premise and also why he deviates in his interpretations of "the facts" that have been accepted by other scholars. He understood that *when* a particular set of events was interpreted had a direct bearing on its interpretation. Looking at the same events with a modern eye allows for a more expanded view of those events.

Translations are also subject to interpretation based on the experience, background, and worldview of the translator as well as being a product of the times in which the translator is operating. In Sitchin's research, he only wanted to draw upon material in its original language, so he wouldn't have to rely on a translation whose meaning might be skewed. He felt that reading a document in its original language provided access to nuances of meaning that otherwise might be lost or modified in translation.

Sumeria is known by historians as "the cradle of civilization." This land that is now Iraq, the land between the Tigris and Euphrates rivers and adjacent to the Persian Gulf, was where there were the first schools, the first courts, the first written language, the first arithmetic, and the first domesticated animals and cultivation of crops.*

The list of firsts is impressive. In the Sumerian's documents, they tell us that everything they know they learned from the Anunnaki. Much of the information that was known to ancient mankind and documented in drawings, cylinder seals, oral knowledge, and ancient texts has been rediscovered in modern times by our scientists. Almost daily there is more "new" information that corroborates knowledge that the Sumerians and other ancient peoples knew as fact. How could the Sumerians have known so much about the solar system without telescopes for viewing the heavens? The Anunnaki imparted this knowledge to them.

Sitchin's book series, The Earth Chronicles, and many companion

*Editor's note: Please refer to the map provided at the beginning of this chapter to orient yourself to the ancient locales as you continue your read.

volumes to this series, details ancient information about the Anunnaki and creates a coherent narrative about them. Who were they? Why did they come here? What did they do while they were here? Sitchin uses the evidence they left behind, and the ancient people—the Sumerians— left behind, to answer these and related questions. This book, *The Anunnaki Chronicles,* attempts to provide an overview of the information provided in the seven volumes of The Earth Chronicles and includes, for the first time, lectures, articles, letters, and other works by Zecharia Sitchin that have never been published in book form.

The Anunnaki Chronicles begins with a general discussion by Sitchin of the origins of our solar system and the planets in their courses, thus laying the groundwork for the ensuing conversation about the Anunnaki. In the first chapter he also outlines his conceptual cosmological timeline of events as they pertain to the Anunnaki and their presence on our planet. Chapter 2 examines the Sumerian culture in detail and inquires as to its genesis as a fully formed civilization, springing seemingly from nowhere. The next few chapters constitute an examination of early biblical accounts of visitors from space wherein Sitchin establishes the vital link between the fully formed Sumerian culture and these ancient visitors. At this point in our narrative, the Sumerian creation epic, the *Enuma Elish,* undergoes critical review by Sitchin, who illustrates, with passages from that venerated text, how real the events it was describing actually were.

Chapter 6 provides another critical examination, this time posing the question: Who was Yahweh, the God of the Heavens? Chapter 7 continues Sitchin's critical line of thinking with a study of the creation of "The Adam," early man who was created as a hybrid by the Anunnaki to work the gold mines on Earth, extracting this precious mineral that would be used to restore the atmosphere of their home planet, Nibiru. Chapters 8 and 9 detail the physical features of the ancient landscape that were of vital importance to the early inhabitants of our planet: the Great Pyramids of Giza and Mt. Sinai in the Sinai peninsula.

In the next three chapters our narrative turns its focus to the New World and reviews such fascinating topics as evidence of giants there and how they fit into the Sitchin cosmology. Following this, we turn to the formation of the calendar, what it meant over the ages, and how its development in our story reflects the ongoing power struggles between members of the Anunnaki family. Finally, our last chapter brings us back full circle, with an examination of Nibiru and a discussion about its imminent return to Earth. Additionally, two letters that Sitchin penned to the *New York Times* are included as appendices. They illustrate how careful Zecharia Sitchin was in the presentation of his research and why he was and is so highly regarded as a scholar of the ancient origins of mankind.

For those of you who are already readers of Sitchin's work, we hope that having a concise volume that covers the breadth of his oeuvre, as well as new material, will be a valuable resource for you. For new readers, we hope that this volume provides an overview of his cosmology. Further, we hope it piques your interest and that we'll be able to count you among those who believe that Zecharia Sitchin was onto something, and that you'll continue to read and explore these topics. For many of his readers, the information provided herein has answered lifelong questions that have never been fully explained until now. If true, which is something Sitchin believed, then this is some of the most important knowledge we have regarding our origins, and perhaps regarding our future.

JANET SITCHIN

JANET SITCHIN had the honor and unique experience of growing up amid the incredible knowledge and fascinating theories of her uncle, Zecharia Sitchin. His scholarly approach and adventurous spirit captured her imagination from a young age, drawing her in to the world of ancient civilizations and human origins. She served as one of Zecharia's lecture assistants from 1995 onward. She has been the webmaster for the official website of Zecharia Sitchin, www.sitchin.com, since 2000. A data-integration expert with a degree in computer science, she lives outside Miami, Florida.

1
Introducing
The 12th Planet

*Excerpt of the 1978 Prologue and an
Unpublished Article, Written in 1982,
"The 12th Planet: The Book as a Story"*

As Sitchin readers know, when it comes to explaining Zecharia Sitchin's area of interest—ancient aliens and ancient civilizations—which was the focus of his writing, it's a bit of a daunting task to do the topic justice in only a few short sentences. To many, the ideas he puts forward are fantastical and border on the outlandish. To others, his work is a breakthrough assembly of puzzle pieces into a coherent, plausible narrative, supported by physical evidence and age-old texts.

When I tell people that my uncle was an author and they ask what he wrote about, I start by saying that he wrote on the subject of ancient civilizations, and that he published fourteen books before he passed away in October 2010. They are always a bit impressed about that. I tell them that his first book, *The 12th Planet*, was especially scholarly, and although fascinating, it is a bit hard to get through its first hundred pages because of its very dense scholarly approach. I tell people that they should push through those first hundred pages, nevertheless, even if they are a bit more difficult to read, because after they make it through them, the material is so compelling that they won't want to put the book down. It becomes a page-turner, and for many, a life changer.

It is then that I begin to describe the premise of my uncle's life's work, to tell the story of the Nefilim (as he called them in the first book), who they were, why they came to Earth, and what they did here.

Appearing as the prologue to the 1978 paperback edition of *The 12th Planet* (published by Avon), the text that follows presents, in Sitchin's own words, a summary of the major topics in *The 12th Planet*. It will give you a window into his thinking, his cosmology, and as such, is a springboard for further ideas to come.

THE OLD TESTAMENT has filled my life from childhood. When the seed for this book was planted, nearly fifty years ago, I was totally unaware of the then raging Evolution versus Bible debates, but as a young schoolboy studying *Genesis* in its original Hebrew, I created a confrontation of my own. We were reading one day in Chapter VI that when God resolved to destroy Mankind by the Great Flood, "the sons of the deities," who married the daughters of men were upon the Earth. The Hebrew original named them *Nefilim;* the teacher explained it meant "giants"; but I objected: didn't it mean literally "Those Who Were Cast Down," who had descended to Earth? I was reprimanded and told to accept the traditional interpretation.

In the ensuing years, as I have learnt the languages and history and archaeology of the ancient Near East, the *Nefilim* became an obsession. Archaeological finds and the deciphering of Sumerian, Babylonian, Assyrian, Hittite, Canaanite, and other ancient texts and epic tales increasingly confirmed the accuracy of the biblical references to the kingdoms, cities, rulers, places, temples, trade routes, artifacts, tools, and customs of antiquity. Is it not now time, therefore, to accept the word of these same ancient records regarding the *Nefilim* as visitors to Earth from the heavens?

The Old Testament repeatedly asserted: "The throne of Yahweh is in heaven"—"from heaven did the Lord behold the Earth." The New Testament spoke of "Our Father, who art in Heaven." But the credibility of the Bible was shaken by the advent and general acceptance of Evolution. If Man evolved, then surely he could not have been created all at once by a Deity who, premeditating, had suggested "Let us make Adam in our image and after our likeness." All the ancient peoples believed in gods who had descended to Earth from the heavens and who could at will soar heavenwards. But these tales were never given credibility, having been branded by scholars from the very beginning as myths.

The writings of the ancient Near East, which include a profusion of astronomical texts, clearly speak of a planet from which these astronauts or "gods" had come. However, when scholars, fifty and one hundred years ago, deciphered and translated the ancient lists of celestial bodies, our astronomers were not yet aware of Pluto (which was only located in 1930). How then could they be expected to accept the evidence of yet one more member of our solar system? But now that we too are aware of the planets beyond Saturn, why not accept that ancient evidence for the existence of the Twelfth Planet?

As we ourselves venture into space, a fresh look and a literal acceptance of the ancient scriptures is more than timely. Now that astronauts have landed on the Moon, and unmanned spacecraft explore other planets, it is no longer impossible to believe that a civilization on another planet more advanced than ours was capable of landing its astronauts on the planet Earth sometime in the past.

Indeed, a number of popular writers have speculated that ancient artifacts such as the pyramids and giant stone sculptures must have been fashioned by advanced visitors from another planet—for surely primitive man could not have possessed by himself the required technology. How was it, for another example, that the civilization of Sumer seemed to flower so suddenly nearly 6,000 years ago without a precursor? But since these writers usually fail to show when, how and above all, from where such ancient astronauts did come—their intriguing questions remain unanswered speculations.

It has taken thirty years of research, of going back to the ancient sources, of accepting them literally, to re-create in my own mind a continuous and plausible scenario of prehistoric events. *The 12th Planet,* therefore, seeks to provide the reader with a narrative giving answers to the specific questions of When, How, Why, and Wherefrom. The evidence I adduce consists primarily of the ancient texts and pictures themselves.

In *The 12th Planet* I have sought to decipher a sophisticated cosmogony which explains, perhaps as well as modern scientific theories, how the solar system could have been formed, an invading planet caught into solar orbit, and Earth and other parts of the solar system brought into being.

The evidence I offer includes celestial maps dealing with space flight to Earth from that Planet, The Twelfth. Then, in sequence, it follows the dramatic establishment of the first settlements on Earth by the Nefilim. Their leaders are named; their relationships, loves, jealousies, achievements, and struggles are described; the nature of their "immortality" explained.

Above all, *The 12th Planet* aims to trace the momentous events that led to the creation of Man, and the advanced methods by which this was accomplished.

It then reveals the tangled relationship between Man and his lords and throws fresh light on the meaning of the events in the Garden of Eden, of the Tower of Babel, of the Great Flood. Finally, Man—endowed by his makers biologically and materially—ends up crowding his gods off the Earth.

This book suggests that we are not alone in our solar system. Yet it may enhance rather than diminish the faith in a Universal Almighty. For, if the *Nefilim* created Man on Earth, they may have only been fulfilling a vaster Master Plan.

Z. SITCHIN
NEW YORK, FEBRUARY 1977

Sitchin went into more detail on the subject matter of *The 12th Planet* in this article from 1982, "*The 12th Planet:* The Book as a Story." In this article he outlines major historical events beginning with the creation of the cosmos, our solar system, and planet Earth, and then proceeds to summarize the story of mankind's unfolding. Thoughout this book we will look more closely at specific topics that are touched upon in this outline, before coming full circle at book's end through our posing of the startling questions: Is the Twelfth Planet currently on its return orbit to Earth, and what does that mean for us? As we will learn, the Twelfth Planet returns to the vicinity of Earth every 3,600 years. The period of its return is said to be marked by general chaos and natural upheavals on Earth, which seems to be currently happening.

Let's now learn more about this Twelfth Planet, thereby setting the contextual stage for its possible return to Planet Earth in the very near future.

THE 12TH PLANET is based entirely on Mesopotamian text and pictorial evidence, traced back to the first known civilization in Sumer in the fourth millennium.

At the same, it constantly draws the parallels with the Old Testament, bringing the Book of Genesis to twentieth-century life.

Stripped of its extensive scientific discussion and proofs, *The 12th Planet* retells in space-age terms the information transmitted in the ancient writings:

The Creation of the Solar System: First the Sun, Mercury, and a planet called Tiamat; then Venus and Mars; then Jupiter and Saturn, Uranus and Neptune.

The Cataclysm or "Celestial Battle": The appearance from outer space of a large planet, drawn more and more into the Solar System until it collided with Tiamat, splitting her in two. The Asteroid Belt, the Comets, and Earth and Moon were thus created.

The Origin of Life: The invading planet—our Twelfth Planet—

was the bearer of life into the Solar System. Its collision with Tiamat imparted the Twelfth Planet's seed of life to Earth (Tiamat's half) circa 3.8 billion years ago.

Kingship of Heaven: Captured in Sun orbit, the Twelfth Planet orbits in a major comet-like orbit of 3,600 Earth-years, always returning to the "Place of the Crossing" between Mars and Jupiter (once every 3,600 years). It is a radiating planet, generating its own heat and atmosphere. Over the billions of years, life upon it evolved. A few million years ago, evolution culminated with producing intelligent, anthropomorphic beings on the Twelfth Planet.

A Civilization Outpaces Itself: Civilization(s) develop. There are cities, courts, palaces; science, technology, space exploration. Also the gamut of "human" emotion: love, hate, jealousy. A complex set of guidelines to the succession to the throne develops. Sons overthrow fathers, brother fights brother for the throne. There are all the material benefits/ evils of an advanced technology. Then some key minerals, some radioactive, but mostly gold on which the sophisticated electronics depend run short. Will civilization on the Twelfth Planet choke itself off?

A Goldmine Called "Earth": As a recurring struggle for the throne takes place, the Twelfth Planet nears "the crossing" between Jupiter and Mars. A deposed ruler saves his life by taking off in a spaceship— crashlanding on the nearby planet Earth. The group happily discovers that Earth also sustains life, less evolved but quite similar to that on the Twelfth Planet. They also find gold nuggets in Earth's riverbeds. Nine Twelfth-Planet years go by; the usurper is deposed. The escapees are rescued and return from Earth with great news: the essential mineral is available and within reach—on Earth.

Landing on Planet Earth: "Those who came crashing down before"—Genesis calls them just that, the Nefilim in Hebrew—return to Earth to obtain its gold. While their spaceships orbit Earth, the first group is lowered down in space capsules that splash into the Arabian Sea, off the Persian Gulf. Led by the chief engineer/scientist of the Nefilim, they wade ashore. Marching inland they reach the edge of the marshes. There they establish Earth Station I and name it ERIDU. The time is circa 445,000 years ago, when Earth is gripped by an Ice Age.

Cities of the Gods: While Earth orbits the Sun 3,600 times, the Twelfth Planet orbits the Sun just once. So while on Earth tens of thousands of years pass, for the Nefilim the wait is but of a short duration in their timescale. Soon the Ice Age gives way to a warmer climate. The Nefilim establish additional settlements: one as a spaceport, one as mission control center, one as a medical center, and one a center of metallurgical processing. They lay the "cities" out in a pattern that, from high above in the air, forms an arrowlike landing path.

The Seeds of Conflict: The decision to proceed with Mission Earth also plants the seed of conflict; for now the leader who was first to land and was therefore named EN.KI ("Lord Earth") is made subordinate to a brother of his (EN.LIL—"Lord of the Airspace") who arrives on Earth to take over the command. EN.KI is renamed E.A.—"Lord of the Waters"; as the chief scientist, he and his "fishmen" are given the task of extracting gold from the oceans' waters. The change of command lays the seeds of a conflict that henceforth constantly affects the fortunes of the Nefilim and mankind alike. Sex among the gods, both tender and violent, is geared to succession problems.

Mining in Southeastern Africa: The plan to extract gold from the oceans fails. There is only one choice left: to go and dig for the gold. The number of rank and file Nefilim is increased to 600, and some are sent to southeastern Africa (Rhodesia?) to dig for gold. Special "sunken boats"—submarines—transport the ore to southern Mesopotamia, where it is smelted and refined; then taken off Earth in shuttle craft that rise from the Spaceport and deliver their cargo to an orbiting Mother Ship then—once a year in the time scale of the Nefilim—on to the approaching Twelfth Planet.

Mutiny of the Anunnaki: Forty Nefilim-years after they had landed—circa 300,000 Earth years ago—the rank and file miners, the Anunnaki ("those who from Heaven to Earth came") mutinied. The occasion was a visit by EN.LIL to the mining lands (he was there once before—banished from Mesopotamia after he raped a young nurse, whom he later married). There was a court of inquiry. The ruler of the Twelfth Planet—the father of Enki and Enlil—came down to Earth, so serious was the crisis. Enlil demanded that the leader of the mutiny be executed. The others sided with the mutineers: the work in the mines was indeed too harsh, they concluded.

The Creation of Man: But the mining had to continue. A solution was offered: let NIN.TI—"she who gives life"—the female who was in charge of medicine—create "a primitive worker." She needed the help of the chief scientist. "The Being you want"—he said—"it already exists!" They extracted the genes of a young member of the Nefilim and fused them into the egg of a captured hominid, an Ape-woman. They implanted the fertilized egg in the ovum of a female member of the Nefilim. There was trial and error; imperfect beings came out. Finally a "perfect model of Man" was achieved. Similarly fertilized eggs were implanted in "batteries" of females of the Nefilim: Adams and Eves were thus created—the first *Homo sapiens*. They were at once put to do the hard work, in the mines of southern Africa.

The Garden of Eden: At first, Ea kept the new creatures in the Land of the Mines. Enlil needed to transport some of them to Mesopotamia to work in the fields there—in the "Orchard of Eden." To do this, he captured some of them by force, using sophisticated weapons. The new creature—a hybrid—could not procreate. Ea saw his chance to gain a new ally on Earth against his domineering and ruthless brother—Man. As the biblical serpent, he was the god who further manipulated Man genetically to enable him to procreate. (The biblical Hebrew "to know" meant to copulate for the purpose of having offspring.) Having obtained the Fruit of Knowing, Adam knew his wife Eve and she bore him Cain. Enraged, Enlil expelled them from the Garden of Eden, the Abode of the Gods.

Mankind Before the Deluge: But mankind, cast away to be on its own, took with it the knowledge it acquired: sheep raising, farming, metallurgy. There were cities built by Cain and his line east of Mesopotamia. But a series of murders doomed this line of mankind. Then a purer line was started with Seth; and in the days of his descendant Enosh, mankind was permitted to return to the land of the gods. It was then that temples and worship and the priesthood were started.

Prelude to Disaster: It was then—in the words of the Book of Genesis and its Sumerian origins—that the sons of the gods began to cohabit with the daughters of Man. Enlil was enraged by the defilement of the gods' racial purity. He saw his chance to get rid of mankind by the changing climate. A new Ice Age was developing, some 75,000 years ago. The climate became drier, harsher. Crops failed. There was hunger and Enlil decreed that food be withheld from the Earthlings. Ea clandestinely helped mankind, mostly with fish of the sea. But the hunger spread; there was cannibalism. Mankind was decimated—but not finished.

The Deluge—The Gods Flee Earth: As they were letting mankind perish, the Nefilim were themselves shaken by astounding news. Their scientific station in the southern hemisphere reported that the ice sheet over the Antarctic continent was beginning to shift, gliding on its own slush. The Anunnaki, in the orbiting mothercraft, confirmed the danger: as the Twelfth Planet neared Earth, its gravitational pull would give the ice sheet the fatal nudges; and as the ice sheet would slip into the ocean, a vast tidal wave would engulf the Earth!

Swearing to keep the coming calamity a secret from mankind, the Nefilim prepare to escape Earth in their shuttlecraft and let all flesh perish. Once again, Ea frustrates the plan by revealing the secret to a faithful Earthling, "Noah." He shows him how to build a submersible vessel; he is to enter it and seal it from within when the sky will be lit by the rising spacecraft at the spaceport to the north; he is to navigate the vessel to Ararat.

The Roles Reversed—The Gods Need Man: In their spacecraft, orbiting Earth, the gods view the desolation caused by the huge tidal wave and the ensuing rains—the Deluge. They cry; they repent having caused mankind to perish. As the waters abate, the peaks of Ararat emerge. The craft begin to land. To their surprise, the gods encounter Noah and his vessel full of surviving men, woman, children, and animals. Noah builds a fire, roasts some sheep—the favorite food of the gods. Enlil's craft lands too—and he blows his top. But the others point out to him that they might as well make the best of it. With all they had built on Earth wiped out, they do need mankind to help them survive. Enlil agrees, blesses Noah and his wife, takes them in his spaceship to the Mothercraft and thence to the Twelfth Planet. Noah's children are taught agriculture, husbandry, given tools (e.g. the plough), and seeds. Civilization—post-diluvial civilization—begins. It is about 11,000 B.C.

Back to Mesopotamia: But mankind, and the gods, must stay in the mountain lands; the valleys are filled with mud. As the Twelfth Planet nears Earth again, circa 7500 B.C., the gods consult and decide to go ahead with civilizing Man. They help him domesticate animals, build abodes, and teach him how to use clay for pottery and construction. Then circa 3800 B.C. the gods consult again, and the go-ahead is given: Mankind and the gods can return to southern Mesopotamia, to rebuild the ancient sites exactly as they were. The sudden civilization of Sumer blooms out almost overnight.

Mankind Reaches Skyward: How much "civilization"—science, technology—is mankind to be taught? In their rush to develop the new relationship, the Lofty Ones (the term we translate as "gods") teach man astronomy, mathematics, metallurgy, chemistry, the art of high-rise building. As cities are rebuilt, centered around rising temples or divine abodes, each ziggurat is provided with a restricted ("sacred") area where the Divine Birds or "Whirlwinds" (as the one seen by Ezekial) are housed. The gods roam Earth's skies, to visit spreading mankind. But mankind is unable to communicate as easily. The god of science then connives with his Sumerian followers an extreme scheme. In the center of Mesopotamia there still lies un-rebuilt the pre-diluvian spaceport, the primordial Bab-ili (Babylon—"Gateway of the Gods"). He coaches the Earthlings to rebuild the launch tower, the "Tower of Babel" and "raise a Shem," a spacerocket.

But the other gods, realizing the implications of the scheme, frustrate it. To forestall future unified efforts by the Earthlings, they confuse men's single language into many tongues. They disperse mankind and its habitats, giving Men the civilization of the Nile and then of the Indus River, spreading mankind to the four corners of the Earth.

Where is the Twelfth Planet now?

The ancient writings, including the Old Testament, described the return of the Twelfth Planet to Earth's vicinity as a time of earthquakes and havoc, followed by an era of peace and harmony. It was the called the "Day of the Lord" when the "Kingship of Heaven" would return to Earth.

The Twelfth Planet, by all calculations, is on its way back to our vicinity.

Have its people already launched their spacecraft toward Earth? Are the UFOs harbingers—advance scouts—of their future revisitation of Earth?

We will know the answer when our astronomers stop searching for answers in faraway galaxies, and instead train their telescopes on the parts of the Solar System indicated by the Sumerians!

2

The Sudden Civilization

Selection from
The 12th Planet *(Chapter 2)*

As archaeologists study the origins of mankind and our first civilizations, evidence points to Sumer in Mesopotamia as the place where advanced civilization began. And yet the ancient, extremely sophisticated culture of Sumeria is as startling as it is mysterious, for it seemed to appear fully formed as if from nowhere. How did this advanced society arise and what civilizations predated it? Zecharia Sitchin discusses this in chapter 2 of his first book, *The 12th Planet*.

We begin with the kingdoms of Babylon and Assyria, which evolved in ancient Mesopotamia well before the time of Christ. The Babylonian and Assyrian cultures flourished circa 1900 B.C. and lasted roughly 1,500 years. These two kingdoms were preceded by a kingdom named Akkad. The deeper that scholars delved, the more it became obvious that this kingdom of Akkad was a rich root culture, an element of which was a pre-Akkadian language—the first written language—that came to be called Sumerian.

In this chapter, Sitchin walks us through the various accomplishments and technological and artistic prowess of the Sumerian culture, which encompassed the disciplines of mathematics, architecture, metallurgy, and medicine and medical procedures, to name just a few. The level of unparalleled sophistication found across the board is inexplicable . . . unless one entertains the idea that these ancient peoples may have inherited their advanced knowledge from a very sophisticated culture or cultures that predated *them*. Using ancient texts to back up his ever-expanding line of questioning, Sitchin looks at the early, enigmatic origins of civilization in southern Mesopotamia.

FOR A LONG TIME, Western man believed that his civilization was the gift of Rome and Greece. But the Greek philosophers themselves wrote repeatedly that they had drawn on even earlier sources. Later on, travelers returning to Europe reported the existence in Egypt of imposing pyramids and temple-cities half-buried in the sands, guarded by strange stone beasts called sphinxes.

When Napoleon arrived in Egypt in 1799, he took with him scholars to study and explain these ancient monuments. One of his officers found near Rosetta a stone slab on which was carved a proclamation from 196 B.C. written in the ancient Egyptian pictographic writing (hieroglyphic) as well as in two other scripts.

The decipherment of the ancient Egyptian script and language, and the archaeological efforts that followed, revealed to Western man that a high civilization had existed in Egypt well before the advent of the Greek civilization. Egyptian records spoke of royal dynasties that began circa 3100 B.C.—two full millennia before the beginning of Hellenic civilization. Reaching its maturity in the fifth and fourth centuries B.C., Greece was a latecomer rather than an originator.

Was the origin of our civilization, then, in Egypt?

As logical as that conclusion would have seemed, the facts militated against it. Greek scholars did describe visits to Egypt, but the ancient sources of knowledge of which they spoke were found elsewhere. The pre-Hellenic cultures of the Aegean Sea—the Minoan on the island of Crete and the Mycenaean on the Greek mainland—revealed evidence that the Near Eastern, not the Egyptian, culture had been adopted. Syria and Anatolia, not Egypt, were the principal avenues through which an earlier civilization became available to the Greeks.

Noting that the Dorian invasion of Greece and the Israelite invasion of Canaan following the Exodus from Egypt took place at about the same time (circa the thirteenth century B.C.), scholars have been fascinated to discover a growing number of similarities between the Semitic and Hellenic civilizations. Professor Cyrus H. Gordon (*Forgotten Scripts: Evidence for the Minoan Language*) opened up a new field of study by showing that an early Minoan script, called Linear A, represented a Semitic language. He concluded that "the pattern (as distinct from the content) of the Hebrew and Minoan civilizations is the same to a remarkable extent," and pointed out that the island's name, Crete, spelled in Minoan *Ke-re-ta,* was the same as the Hebrew word *Ke-re-et* ("walled city") and had a counterpart in a Semitic tale of a king of Keret.

Even the Hellenic alphabet, from which the Latin and our own alphabets derive, came from the Near East. The ancient Greek historians themselves wrote that a Phoenician named Kadmus ("ancient") brought them the alphabet, comprising the same number of letters, in the same order, as in Hebrew; it was the only Greek alphabet when the Trojan War took place. The number of letters was raised to twenty-six by the poet Simonides of Ceos in the fifth century B.C.

That Greek and Latin writing, and thus the whole foundation of our Western culture, were adopted from the Near East can easily be demonstrated by comparing the order, names, signs, and even numerical values of the original Near Eastern alphabet with the much later ancient Greek and the more recent Latin (Fig. 4).

The scholars were aware, of course, of Greek contacts with the Near East in the first millennium B.C., culminating with the defeat of the Persians by Alexander the Macedonian in 331 B.C. Greek records contained much information about these Persians and their lands (which roughly paralleled today's Iran). Judging by the names of their kings—Cyrus, Darius, Xerxes—and the names of their deities, which appear to belong to the Indo-European linguistic stem, scholars reached the conclusion that they were part of the Aryan ("lordly") people that

Hebrew name	CANAANITE-PHOENICIAN	EARLY GREEK	LATER GREEK	Greek name	LATIN
Aleph	⳥ ⳥	Δ	Λ	Alpha	A
Beth	⅁ ⅁	S ⴒ	B	Beta	B
Gimel	⅂	⅂	⎾	Gamma	C G
Daleth	◿ ◿	Δ	Δ	Delta	D
He	⅌ ⅌	⅂	Ɛ	E(psilon)	E
Vau	Ɏ	Ɏ	Ⱶ	Vau	F V
Zayin	ⵣ ⵣ	I	I	Zeta	
Heth (1)	Ⴂ H	B	B	(H)eta	H
Teth	⊗	⊗	⊗	Theta	
Yod	ⱬ	⁊	⟨	Iota	I
Khaph	Ⱶ Ɏⱴ	⋊	k	Kappa	
Lamed	⳼ ⳼	∨⊣⅂	L ∧	Lambda	L
Mem	ⱳ ⱳ	ⱱ	⋔	Mu	M
Nun	ⱴ ⱶ	⋎	N	Nu	N
Samekh	⅌ ⅍⅍	ⵣ	ⵣ	Xi	X
Ayin	o O	o	o	O(nicron)	O
Pe	⁊Ɉ)	⁊	⎾	Pi	P
Ṣade (2)	ⱴ ⱶⱴ	M	M	San	
Koph	ⳊⳊⳗ	φ	ϙ	Koppa	Q
Resh	⅁	◁	Ρ	Rho	R
Shin	W	⟨	⟨	Sigma	S
Tav	✕	T	T	Tau	T

(1) "H", commonly transliterated as "H" for simplicity, is pronounced in the Sumerian and Semitic languages as "CH" in the Scottish or German "loch".

(2) "Ṣ", commonly transliterated as "S" for simplicity, is pronounced in the Sumerian and Semitic languages as "TS".

Fig. 4

appeared from somewhere near the Caspian Sea toward the end of the second millennium B.C. and spread westward to Asia Minor, eastward to India, and southward to what the Old Testament called the "lands of the Medes and Parsees."

Yet all was not that simple. In spite of the assumed foreign origin of these invaders, the Old Testament treated them as part and parcel of biblical events. Cyrus, for example, was considered to be an "Anointed of Yahweh"—quite an unusual relationship between the Hebrew God and a non-Hebrew. According to the biblical Book of Ezra, Cyrus acknowledged his mission to rebuild the Temple in Jerusalem, and stated that he was acting upon orders given by Yahweh, whom he called "God of Heaven."

Cyrus and the other kings of his dynasty called themselves Achaemenids—after the title adopted by the founder of the dynasty, which was Hacham-Anish. It was not an Aryan but a perfect Semitic title, which meant "wise man." By and large, scholars have neglected to investigate the many leads that may point to similarities between the Hebrew God Yahweh and the deity Achaemenids called "Wise Lord," whom they depicted as hovering in the skies within a Winged Globe, as shown on the royal seal of Darius (Fig. 5).

It has been established by now that the cultural, religious, and historic roots of these Old Persians go back to the earlier empires of Babylon

Fig. 5

and Assyria, whose extent and fall is recorded in the Old Testament. The symbols that make up the script that appeared on the Achaemenid monuments and seals were at first considered to be decorative designs. Engelbert Kampfer, who visited Persepolis, the Old Persian capital, in 1686, described the signs as "cuneates," or wedge-shaped impressions. The script has since been known as cuneiform.

As efforts began to decipher the Achaemenid inscriptions, it became clear that they were written in the same script as inscriptions found on ancient artifacts and tablets in Mesopotamia, the plains and highlands that lay between the Tigris and Euphrates rivers. Intrigued by the scattered finds, Paul Emile Botta set out in 1843 to conduct the first major purposeful excavation. He selected a site in northern Mesopotamia, near present-day Mosul, now called Khorsabad. Botta was soon able to establish that the cuneiform inscriptions named the place Dur Sharru Kin. They were Semitic inscriptions, in a sister language of Hebrew, and the name meant "walled city of the righteous king." Our textbooks call this king Sargon II.

This capital of the Assyrian king had as its center a magnificent royal palace whose walls were lined with sculptured bas-reliefs, which, if placed end to end, would stretch for over a mile. Commanding the city and the royal compound was a step pyramid called a ziggurat; it served as a "stairway to Heaven" for the gods (Fig. 6).

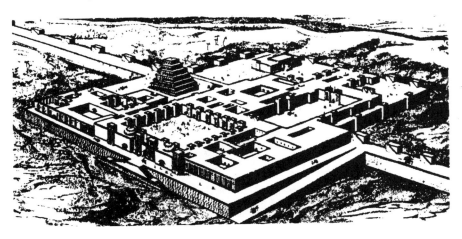

Fig. 6

The layout of the city and the sculptures depicted a way of life on a grand scale. The palaces, temples, houses, stables, warehouses, walls, gates, columns, decorations, statues, artworks, towers, ramparts, terraces, gardens—all were completed in just five years. According to Georges Contenau (*La Vie Quotidienne à Babylone et en Assyrie*), "the imagination reels before the potential strength of an empire which could accomplish so much in such a short space of time," some 3,000 years ago.

Not to be outdone by the French, the English appeared on the scene in the person of Sir Austen Henry Layard, who selected as his site a place some ten miles down the Tigris River from Khorsabad. The natives called it Kuyunjik; it turned out to be the Assyrian capital of Nineveh.

Biblical names and events had begun to come to life. Nineveh was the royal capital of Assyria under its last three great rulers: Sennacherib, Esarhaddon, and Ashurbanipal. "Now, in the fourteenth year of king Hezekiah, did Sennacherib king of Assyria come up against all the walled cities of Judah," relates the Old Testament (II Kings 18:13), and when the Angel of the Lord smote his army, "Sennacherib departed and went back, and dwelt in Nineveh."

The mounds where Nineveh was built by Sennacherib and Ashurbanipal revealed palaces, temples, and works of art that surpassed those of Sargon. The area where the remains of Esarhaddon's palaces are believed to lie cannot be excavated, for it is now the site of a Muslim mosque erected over the purported burial place of the prophet Jonah, who was swallowed by a whale when he refused to bring Yahweh's message to Nineveh.

Layard had read in ancient Greek records that an officer in Alexander's army saw a "place of pyramids and remains of an ancient city"—a city that was already buried in Alexander's time! Layard dug it up, too, and it turned out to be Nimrud, Assyria's military center. It was there that Shalmaneser II set up an obelisk to record his military expeditions and conquests. Now on exhibit at the British Museum, the obelisk lists, among the kings who were made to pay tribute, "Jehu, son of Omri, king of Israel."

Again, the Mesopotamian inscriptions and biblical texts supported each other!

Astounded by increasingly frequent corroboration of the biblical narratives by archaeological finds, the Assyriologists, as these scholars came to be called, turned to the tenth chapter of the Book of Genesis. There Nimrod—"a mighty hunter by the grace of Yahweh"—was described as the founder of all the kingdoms of Mesopotamia.

> And the beginning of his kingdom:
> Babel and Erech and Akkad, all in the Land of Shin'ar.
> Out of that Land there emanated Ashur where
>   Nineveh was built, a city of wide streets;
> and Khalah, and Ressen—the great city which is
>   between Nineveh and Khalah.

There were indeed mounds the natives called Calah, lying between Nineveh and Nimrud. When teams under W. Andrae excavated the area from 1903 to 1914, they uncovered the ruins of Ashur, the Assyrian religious center and its earliest capital. Of all the Assyrian cities mentioned in the Bible, only Ressen remains to be found. The name means "horse's bridle"; perhaps it was the location of the royal stables of Assyria.

At about the same time as Ashur was being excavated, teams under R. Koldewey were completing the excavation of Babylon, the biblical Babel—a vast place of palaces, temples, hanging gardens, and the inevitable ziggurat. Before long, artifacts and inscriptions unveiled the history of the two competing empires of Mesopotamia: Babylonia and Assyria, the one centered in the south, the other in the north.

Rising and falling, fighting and coexisting, the two constituted a high civilization that encompassed some 1,500 years, both rising circa 1900 B.C. Ashur and Nineveh were finally captured and destroyed by the Babylonians in 614 and 612 B.C., respectively. As predicted by the biblical prophets, Babylon itself came to an inglorious end when Cyrus the Achaemenid conquered it in 539 B.C.

Though they were rivals throughout their history, one would be hard put to find any significant differences between Assyria and

Babylonia in cultural or material matters. Even though Assyria called its chief deity Ashur ("all-seeing") and Babylonia hailed Marduk ("son of the pure mound"), the pantheons were otherwise virtually alike.

Many of the world's museums count among their prize exhibits the ceremonial gates, winged bulls, bas-reliefs, chariots, tools, utensils, jewelry, statues, and other objects made of every conceivable material that have been dug out of the mounds of Assyria and Babylonia. But the true treasures of these kingdoms were their written records: thousands upon thousands of inscriptions in the cuneiform script, including cosmologic tales, epic poems, histories of kings, temple records, commercial contracts, marriage and divorce records, astronomical tables, astrological forecasts, mathematical formulas, geographic lists, grammar and vocabulary school texts, and, not least of all, texts dealing with the names, genealogies, epithets, deeds, powers, and duties of the gods.

The common language that formed the cultural, historical, and religious bond between Assyria and Babylonia was Akkadian. It was the first known Semitic language, akin to but predating Hebrew, Aramaic, Phoenician, and Canaanite. But the Assyrians and Babylonians laid no claim to having invented the language or its script; indeed, many of their tablets bore the postscript that they had been copied from earlier originals.

Who, then, invented the cuneiform script and developed the language, its precise grammar and rich vocabulary? Who wrote the "earlier originals"? And why did the Assyrians and Babylonians call the language Akkadian?

Attention once more focuses on the Book of Genesis. "And the beginning of his kingdom: Babel and Erech and Akkad." Akkad—could there really have been such a royal capital, preceding Babylon and Nineveh?

The ruins of Mesopotamia have provided conclusive evidence that once upon a time there indeed existed a kingdom by the name of Akkad, established by a much earlier ruler, who called himself a *sharrukin* ("righteous ruler"). He claimed in his inscriptions that his empire stretched, by the grace of his god Enlil, from the Lower Sea (the Persian Gulf) to the Upper Sea (believed to be the Mediterranean). He boasted that "at the wharf of Akkad, he made moor ships" from many distant lands.

The scholars stood awed: They had come upon a Mesopotamian empire in the third millennium B.C.! There was a leap—backward—of some 2,000 years from the Assyrian Sargon of Dur Sharrukin to Sargon of Akkad. And yet the mounds that were dug up brought to light literature and art, science and politics, commerce and communications—a full-fledged civilization—long before the appearance of Babylonia and Assyria. Moreover, it was obviously the predecessor and the source of the later Mesopotamian civilizations; Assyria and Babylonia were only branches off the Akkadian trunk.

The mystery of such an early Mesopotamian civilization deepened, however, as inscriptions recording the achievements and genealogy of Sargon of Akkad were found. They stated that his full title was "King of Akkad, King of Kish"; they explained that before he assumed the throne, he had been a counselor to the "rulers of Kish." Was there, then—the scholars asked themselves—an even earlier kingdom, that of Kish, which preceded Akkad?

Once again, the biblical verses gained in significance.

> And Kush begot Nimrod;
> He was first to be a Hero in the Land. . . .
> And the beginning of his kingdom:
> Babel and Erech and Akkad.

Many scholars have speculated that Sargon of Akkad was the biblical Nimrod. If one reads "Kish" for "Kush" in the above biblical verses, it would seem Nimrod was indeed preceded by Kish, as claimed by Sargon. The scholars then began to accept literally the rest of his inscriptions: "He defeated Uruk and tore down its wall . . . he was victorious in the battle with the inhabitants of Ur . . . he defeated the entire territory from Lagash as far as the sea."

Was the biblical Erech identical with the Uruk of Sargon's inscriptions? As the site now called Warka was unearthed, that was found to be the case. And the Ur referred to by Sargon was none other than the biblical Ur, the Mesopotamian birthplace of Abraham.

Not only did the archaeological discoveries vindicate the biblical records; it also appeared certain that there must have been kingdoms and cities and civilizations in Mesopotamia even before the third millennium B.C. The only question was: How far back did one have to go to find the *first* civilized kingdom?

The key that unlocked the puzzle was yet another language.

Scholars quickly realized that names had a meaning not only in Hebrew and in the Old Testament but throughout the ancient Near East. All the Akkadian, Babylonian, and Assyrian names of persons and places had a meaning. But the names of rulers that preceded Sargon of Akkad did not make sense at all: The king at whose court Sargon was a counselor was called Urzababa; the king who reigned in Erech was named Lugalzagesi; and so on.

Lecturing before the Royal Asiatic Society in 1853, Sir Henry Rawlinson pointed out that such names were neither Semitic nor Indo-European; indeed, "they seemed to belong to no known group of languages or peoples." But if names had a meaning, what was the mysterious language in which they had the meaning?

Scholars took another look at the Akkadian inscriptions. Basically, the Akkadian cuneiform script was syllabic: Each sign stood for a complete syllable (*ab, ba, bat,* etc.). Yet the script made extensive use of signs that were not phonetic syllables but conveyed the meanings "god," "city," "country," or "life," "exalted," and the like. The only possible explanation for this phenomenon was that these signs were remains of an earlier writing method which used pictographs. Akkadian, then, must have been preceded by another language that used a writing method akin to the Egyptian hieroglyphs.

It was soon obvious that an earlier language, and not just an earlier form of writing, was involved here. Scholars found that Akkadian inscriptions and texts made extensive use of loanwords—words borrowed intact from another language (in the same way that a modern Frenchman would borrow the English word *weekend*). This was especially true where scientific or technical terminology was involved, and also in matters dealing with the gods and the heavens.

One of the greatest finds of Akkadian texts was the ruins of a library assembled in Nineveh by Ashurbanipal; Layard and his colleagues carted away from the site 25,000 tablets, many of which were described by the ancient scribes as copies of "olden texts." A group of twenty-three tablets ended with the statement: "23rd tablet: language of Shumer not changed." Another text bore an enigmatic statement by Ashurbanipal himself:

> The god of scribes has bestowed on me the gift of the
>   knowledge of his art.
> I have been initiated into the secrets of writing.
> I can even read the intricate tablets in Shumerian;
> I understand the enigmatic words in the stone carvings
>   from the days before the Flood.

The claim by Ashurbanipal that he could read intricate tablets in "Shumerian" and understand the words written on tablets from "the days before the Flood" only increased the mystery. But in January 1869 Jules Oppert suggested to the French Society of Numismatics and Archaeology that recognition be given to the existence of a pre-Akkadian language and people. Pointing out that the early rulers of Mesopotamia proclaimed their legitimacy by taking the title "King of Sumer and Akkad," he suggested that the people be called "Sumerians," and their land, "Sumer."

Except for mispronouncing the name—it should have been S*h*umer, not Sumer—Oppert was right. Sumer was not a mysterious, distant land, but the early name for southern Mesopotamia, just as the Book of Genesis had clearly stated: The royal cities of Babylon and Akkad and Erech were in "the Land of Shin'ar." (Shinar was the biblical name for Shumer.)

Once the scholars had accepted these conclusions, the flood gates were opened. The Akkadian references to the "olden texts" became meaningful, and scholars soon realized that tablets with long columns of words were in fact Akkadian-Sumerian lexicons and dictionaries, prepared in Assyria and Babylonia for their own study of the first written language, Sumerian.

Without these dictionaries from long ago, we would still be far from being able to read Sumerian. With their aid, a vast literary and cultural treasure opened up. It also became clear that the Sumerian script, originally pictographic and carved in stone in vertical columns, was then turned horizontally and, later on, stylized for wedge writing on soft clay tablets to become the cuneiform writing that was adopted by the Akkadians, Babylonians, Assyrians, and other nations of the ancient Near East (Fig. 7).

The decipherment of the Sumerian language and script, and the realization that the Sumerians and their culture were the fountainhead of the Akkadian–Babylonian–Assyrian achievements, spurred archaeological searches in southern Mesopotamia. All the evidence now indicated that the beginning was there.

The first significant excavation of a Sumerian site was begun in 1877 by French archaeologists; and the finds from this single site were so extensive that others continued to dig there until 1933 without completing the job.

Called by the natives Telloh ("mound"), the site proved to be an early Sumerian city, the very Lagash of whose conquest Sargon of Akkad had boasted. It was indeed a royal city whose rulers bore the same title Sargon had adopted, except that it was in the Sumerian language: EN.SI ("righteous ruler"). Their dynasty had started circa 2900 B.C. and lasted for nearly 650 years. During this time, forty-three *ensi's* reigned without interruption in Lagash: Their names, genealogies, and lengths of rule were all neatly recorded.

The inscriptions (Fig. 8) provided much information. Appeals to the gods "to cause the grain sprouts to grow for harvest . . . to cause the watered plant to yield grain," attest to the existence of agriculture and irrigation. A cup inscribed in honor of a goddess by "the overseer of the granary" indicated that grains were stored, measured, and traded.

An *ensi* named Eannatum left an inscription on a clay brick which makes it clear that these Sumerian rulers could assume the throne only with the approval of the gods. He also recorded the conquest of another city, revealing to us the existence of other city-states in Sumer at the beginning of the third millennium B.C.

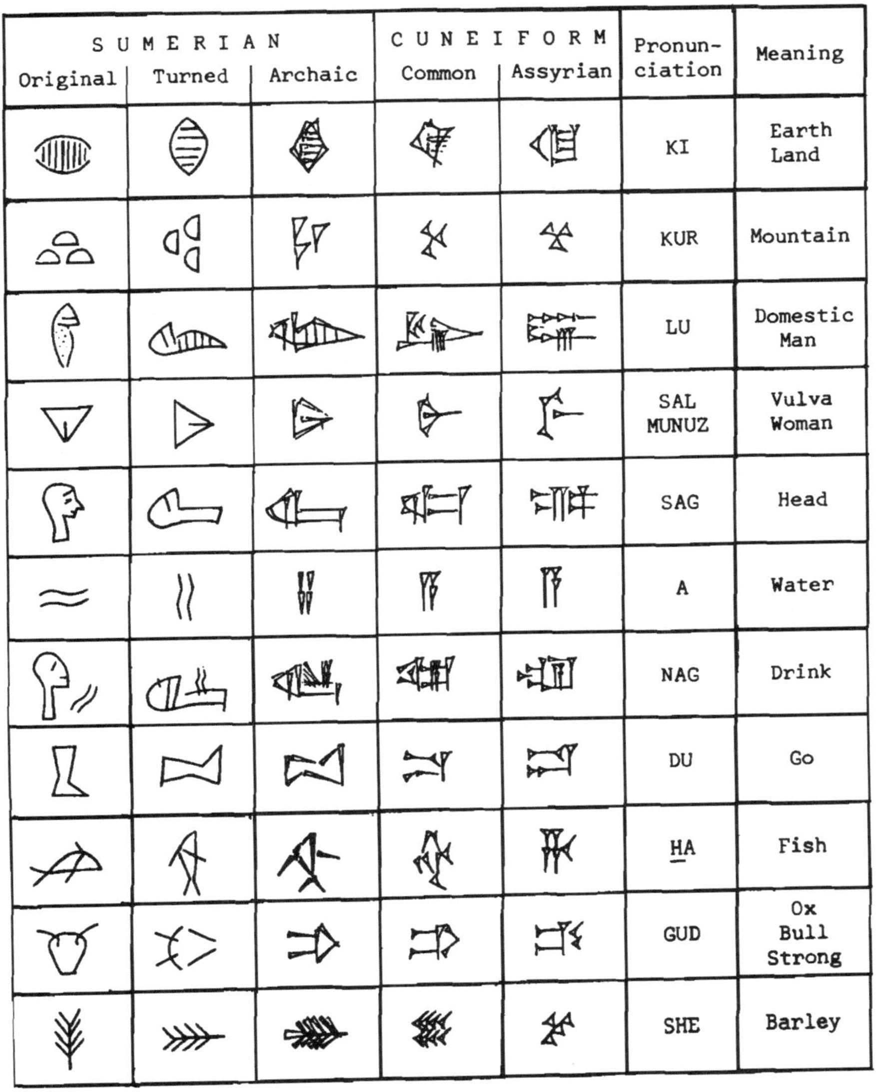

| SUMERIAN | | | CUNEIFORM | | Pronun-ciation | Meaning |
Original	Turned	Archaic	Common	Assyrian		
					KI	Earth Land
					KUR	Mountain
					LU	Domestic Man
					SAL MUNUZ	Vulva Woman
					SAG	Head
					A	Water
					NAG	Drink
					DU	Go
					HA	Fish
					GUD	Ox Bull Strong
					SHE	Barley

Fig. 7

Eannatum's successor, Entemena, wrote of building a temple and adorning it with gold and silver, planting gardens, enlarging brick-lined wells. He boasted of building a fortress with watchtowers and facilities for docking ships.

One of the better-known rulers of Lagash was Gudea. He had a large number of statuettes made of himself, all showing him in a votive

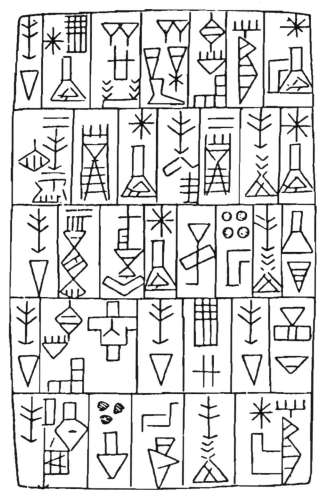

Fig. 8

stance, praying to his gods. This stance was no pretense: Gudea had indeed devoted himself to the adoration of Ningirsu, his principal deity, and to the construction and rebuilding of temples.

His many inscriptions reveal that, in the search for exquisite building materials, he obtained gold from Africa and Anatolia, silver from the Taurus Mountains, cedars from Lebanon, other rare woods from Ararat, copper from the Zagros range, diorite from Egypt, carnelian from Ethiopia, and other materials from lands as yet unidentified by scholars.

When Moses built for the Lord God a "Residence" in the desert, he did so according to very detailed instructions provided by the Lord. When King Solomon built the first Temple in Jerusalem, he did so after the Lord had "given him wisdom." The prophet Ezekiel was shown very detailed plans for the Second Temple "in a Godly vision" by a "person who had the appearance of bronze and who held in his hand a flaxen string and a measuring rod." Ur-Nammu, ruler of Ur, depicted in an earlier millennium how his god, ordering him to build for him a temple and giving him the pertinent instructions, handed him the measuring rod and rolled string for the job (Fig. 9).

Twelve hundred years before Moses, Gudea made the same claim. The instructions, he recorded in one very long inscription, were given to him in a vision. "A man that shone like the heaven," by whose side stood "a divine bird," "commanded me to build his temple." This "man," who "from the crown on his head was obviously a god," was later identified as the god Ningirsu. With him was a goddess who "held the tablet of her favorable star of the heavens"; her other hand "held a holy stylus," with which she indicated to Gudea "the favorable planet." A third man,

Fig. 9

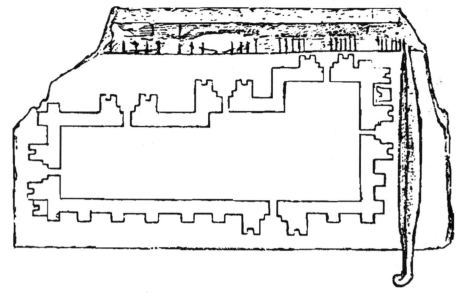

Fig. 10

also a god, held in his hand a tablet of precious stone; "the plan of a temple it contained." One of Gudea's statues shows him seated, with this tablet on his knees; on the tablet the divine drawing can clearly be seen (Fig. 10).

Wise as he was, Gudea was baffled by these architectural instructions, and he sought the advice of a goddess who could interpret divine messages. She explained to him the meaning of the instructions, the plan's measurements, and the size and shape of the bricks to be used. Gudea then employed a male "diviner, maker of decisions" and a female "searcher of secrets" to locate the site, on the city's outskirts, where the god wished his temple to be built. He then recruited 216,000 people for the construction job.

Gudea's bafflement can readily be understood, for the simple-looking "floor plan" supposedly gave him the necessary information to build a complex ziggurat, rising high by seven stages. Writing in *Der Alte Orient* in 1900, A. Billerbeck was able to decipher at least part of the divine architectural instructions. The ancient drawing, even on the partly damaged statue, is accompanied at the top by groups of vertical lines whose number diminishes as the space between them increases.

Fig. 11

The divine architects, it appears, were able to provide, with a single floor plan, accompanied by seven varying scales, the complete instructions for the construction of a seven-stage high-rise temple.

It has been said that war spurs Man to scientific and material breakthroughs. In ancient Sumer, it seems, temple construction spurred the people and their rulers into greater technological achievements. The ability to carry out major construction work according to prepared architectural plans, to organize and feed a huge labor force, to flatten land and raise mounds, to mold bricks and transport stones, to bring rare metals and other materials from afar, to cast metal and shape utensils and ornaments—all clearly speak of a high civilization, already in full bloom in the third millennium B.C. (Fig. 11).

As masterful as even the earliest Sumerian temples were, they represented but the tip of the iceberg of the scope and richness of the material achievements of the first great civilization known to Man.

In addition to the invention and development of writing, without which a high civilization could not have come about, the Sumerians

Fig. 12

should also be credited with the invention of printing. Millennia before Johann Gutenberg "invented" printing by using movable type, Sumerian scribes used ready-made "type" of the various pictographic signs, which they used as we now use rubber stamps to impress the desired sequence of signs in the wet clay.

They also invented the forerunner of our rotary presses—the cylinder seal. Made of extremely hard stone, it was a small cylinder into which the message or design had been engraved in reverse; whenever the seal was rolled on the wet clay, the imprint created a "positive" impression on the clay. The seal also enabled one to assure the authenticity of documents; a new impression could be made at once to compare it with the old impression on the document (Fig. 12).

Many Sumerian and Mesopotamian written records concerned themselves not necessarily with the divine or spiritual but with such daily tasks as recording crops, measuring fields, and calculating prices. Indeed, no high civilization would have been possible without a parallel advanced system of mathematics.

The Sumerian system, called sexagesimal, combined a mundane 10

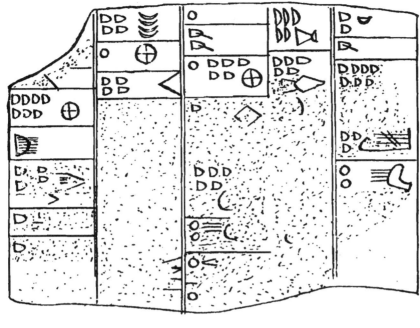

Fig. 13

with a "celestial" 6 to obtain the base figure 60. This system is in some respects superior to our present one; in any case, it is unquestionably superior to later Greek and Roman systems. It enabled the Sumerians to divide into fractions and multiply into the millions, to calculate roots or raise numbers several powers. This was not only the first-known mathematical system but also one that gave us the "place" concept: Just as, in the decimal system, 2 can be 2 or 20 or 200, depending on the digit's place, so could a Sumerian 2 mean 2 or 120 (2 × 60), and so on, depending on the "place" (Fig. 13).

The 360-degree circle, the foot and its 12 inches, and the "dozen" as a unit are but a few examples of the vestiges of Sumerian mathematics still evident in our daily life. Their concomitant achievements in astronomy, the establishment of a calendar, and similar mathematical-celestial feats will receive much closer study in coming chapters.

Just as our own economic and social system—our books, court and tax records, commercial contracts, marriage certificates, and so on—depends on paper, Sumerian/Mesopotamian life depended on clay.

Temples, courts, and trading houses had their scribes ready with tablets of wet clay on which to inscribe decisions, agreements, letters, or calculate prices, wages, the area of a field, or the number of bricks required in a construction.

Clay was also a crucial raw material for the manufacture of utensils for daily use and containers for storage and transportation of goods. It was also used to make bricks—another Sumerian "first," which made possible the building of houses for the people, palaces for the kings, and imposing temples for the gods.

The Sumerians are credited with two technological breakthroughs that made it possible to combine lightness with tensile strength for all clay products: reinforcing and firing. Modern architects have discovered that reinforced concrete, an extremely strong building material, can be created by pouring cement into molds containing iron rods; long ago, the Sumerians gave their bricks great strength by mixing the wet clay with chopped reeds or straw. They also knew that clay products could be given tensile strength and durability by firing them in a kiln. The world's first high-rise buildings and archways, as well as durable ceramic wares, were made possible by these technological breakthroughs.

The invention of the kiln—a furnace in which intense but controllable temperatures could be attained without the risk of contaminating products with dust or ashes—made possible an even greater technological advance: the Age of Metals.

It has been assumed that man discovered that he could hammer "soft stones"—naturally occurring nuggets of gold as well as copper and silver compounds—into useful or pleasing shapes, sometime about 6000 B.C. The first hammered-metal artifacts were found in the highlands of the Zagros and Taurus mountains. However, as R. J. Forbes (*The Birthplace of Old World Metallurgy*) pointed out, "in the ancient Near East, the supply of native copper was quickly exhausted, and the miner had to turn to ores." This required the knowledge and ability to find and extract the ores, crush them, then smelt and refine them—processes that could not have been carried out without kiln-type furnaces and a generally advanced technology.

The art of metallurgy soon encompassed the ability to alloy copper with other metals, resulting in a castable, hard, but malleable metal we call bronze. The Bronze Age, our first metallurgical age, was also a Mesopotamian contribution to modern civilization. Much of ancient commerce was devoted to the metals trade; it also formed the basis for the development in Mesopotamia of banking and the first money—the silver *shekel* ("weighed ingot").

The many varieties of metals and alloys for which Sumerian and Akkadian names have been found and the extensive technological terminology attest to the high level of metallurgy in ancient Mesopotamia. For a while this puzzled the scholars because Sumer, as such, was devoid of metal ores, yet metallurgy most definitely began there.

The answer is energy. Smelting, refining, and alloying, as well as casting, could not be done without ample supplies of fuels to fire the kilns, crucibles, and furnaces. Mesopotamia may have lacked ores, but it had fuels in abundance. So the ores were brought to the fuels, which explains many early inscriptions describing the bringing of metal ores from afar.

The fuels that made Sumer technologically supreme were bitumens and asphalts, petroleum products that naturally seeped up to the surface in many places in Mesopotamia. R. J. Forbes (*Bitumen and Petroleum in Antiquity*) shows that the surface deposits of Mesopotamia were the ancient world's prime source of fuels from the earliest times to the Roman era. His conclusion is that the technological use of these petroleum products began in Sumer circa 3500 B.C.; indeed, he shows that the use and knowledge of the fuels and their properties were greater in Sumerian times than in later civilizations.

So extensive was the Sumerian use of these petroleum products—not only as fuel but also as road-building materials, for waterproofing, caulking, painting, cementing, and molding—that when archaeologists searched for ancient Ur they found it buried in a mound that the local Arabs called "Mound of Bitumen." Forbes shows that the Sumerian language had terms for every genus and variant of the bituminous substances found in Mesopotamia. Indeed, the names of bituminous and petroleum materials in other languages—Akkadian, Hebrew, Egyptian,

Coptic, Greek, Latin, and Sanskrit—can clearly be traced to the Sumerian origins; for example, the most common word for petroleum—*naphta*—derives from *napatu* ("stones that flare up").

The Sumerian use of petroleum products was also basic to an advanced chemistry. We can judge the high level of Sumerian knowledge not only by the variety of paints and pigments used and such processes as glazing but also by the remarkable artificial production of semiprecious stones, including a substitute for lapis lazuli.

Bitumens were also used in Sumerian medicine, another field where the standards were impressively high. The hundreds of Akkadian texts that have been found employ Sumerian medical terms and phrases extensively, pointing to the Sumerian origin of all Mesopotamian medicine.

The library of Ashurbanipal in Nineveh included a medical section. The texts were divided into three groups—*bultitu* ("therapy"), *shipir bel imti* ("surgery") and *urti mashmashshe* ("commands and incantations"). Early law codes included sections dealing with fees payable to surgeons for successful operations, and penalties to be imposed on them in case of failure: A surgeon, using a lancet to open a patient's temple, was to lose his hand if he accidentally destroyed the patient's eye.

Some skeletons found in Mesopotamian graves bore unmistakable marks of brain surgery. A partially broken medical text speaks of the surgical removal of a "shadow covering a man's eye," probably a cataract; another text mentions the use of a cutting instrument, stating that "if the sickness has reached the inside of the bone, you shall scrape and remove."

Sick persons in Sumerian times could choose between an A.ZU ("water physician") and an IA.ZU ("oil physician"). A tablet excavated in Ur, nearly 5,000 years old, names a medical practitioner as "Lulu, the doctor." There were also veterinarians—known either as "doctors of oxen" or as "doctors of asses."

A pair of surgical tongs is depicted on a very early cylinder seal, found at Lagash, that belonged to "Urlugale-dina, the doctor." The seal also shows the serpent on a tree—the symbol of medicine to this day

Fig. 14

(Fig. 14). An instrument that was used by midwives to cut the umbilical cord was also frequently depicted.

Sumerian medical texts deal with diagnosis and prescriptions. They leave no doubt that the Sumerian physician did not resort to magic or sorcery. He recommended cleaning and washing; soaking in baths of hot water and mineral solvents; application of vegetable derivatives; rubbing with petroleum compounds.

Medicines were made from plant and mineral compounds and were mixed with liquids or solvents appropriate to the method of application. If taken by mouth, the powders were mixed into wine, beer, or honey; if "poured through the rectum"—administered in an enema—they were mixed with plant or vegetable oils. Alcohol, which plays such an important role in surgical disinfection and as a base for many medicines, reached our languages through the Arabic *kohl,* from the Akkadian *kuhlu.*

Models of livers indicate that medicine was taught at medical schools with the aid of clay models of human organs. Anatomy must have been an advanced science, for temple rituals called for elaborate dissections of sacrificial animals—only a step removed from comparable knowledge of human anatomy.

Several depictions on cylinder seals or clay tablets show people lying on some kind of surgical table, surrounded by teams of gods or people. We know from epics and other heroic texts that the Sumerians and their successors in Mesopotamia were concerned with matters of life, sickness, and death. Men like Gilgamesh, a king of Erech, sought the "Tree of Life" or some mineral (a "stone") that could provide eternal youth. There were also references to efforts to resurrect the dead, especially if they happened to be gods:

> Upon the corpse, hung from the pole,
> they directed the Pulse and the Radiance;
> Sixty times the Water of Life,
> Sixty times the Food of Life,
> they sprinkled upon it;
> And Inanna arose.

Were some ultramodern methods, about which we can only speculate, known and used in such revival attempts? That radioactive materials were known and used to treat certain ailments is certainly suggested by a scene of medical treatment depicted on a cylinder seal dating to the very beginning of Sumerian civilization. It shows, without question, a man lying on a special bed; his face is protected by a mask, and he is being subjected to some kind of radiation (Fig. 15).

One of Sumer's earliest material achievements was the development of textile and clothing industries.

Our own Industrial Revolution is considered to have commenced with the introduction of spinning and weaving machines in England in the 1760s. Most developing nations have aspired ever since to develop a textile industry as the first step toward industrialization. The evidence shows that this has been the process not only since the eighteenth century but ever since man's first great civilization. Man could not have made woven fabrics before the advent of agriculture, which provided him with flax, and the domestication of animals, creating a source for wool. Grace M. Crowfoot (*Textiles, Basketry and Mats in Antiquity*) expressed the scholastic consensus by stating that

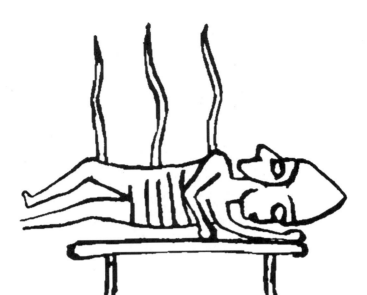

Fig. 15

textile weaving appeared first in Mesopotamia, around 3800 B.C.

Sumer, moreover, was renowned in ancient times not only for its woven fabrics, but also for its apparel. The Book of Joshua (7:21) reports that during the storming of Jericho a certain person could not resist the temptation to keep "one good coat of Shin'ar," which he had found in the city, even though the penalty was death. So highly prized were the garments of Shinar (Sumer), that people were willing to risk their lives to obtain them.

A rich terminology already existed in Sumerian times to describe both items of clothing and their makers. The basic garment was called TUG—without doubt, the forerunner in style as well as in name of the Roman toga. Such garments were TUG.TU.SHE, which in Sumerian meant "garment which is worn wrapped around" (Fig. 16).

The ancient depictions reveal not only an astonishing variety and opulence in matters of clothing, but also elegance, in which good taste and coordination among clothes, hairdos, headdresses, and jewelry prevailed (Figs. 17, 18).

Fig. 16

Fig. 17

Fig. 18

* * *

Another major Sumerian achievement was its agriculture. In a land with only seasonal rains, the rivers were enlisted to water year-round crops through a vast system of irrigation canals.

Mesopotamia—the Land Between the Rivers—was a veritable food basket in ancient times. The apricot tree, the Spanish word for which is *damasco* ("Damascus tree"), bears the Latin name *armeniaca*, a loan-word from the Akkadian *armanu*. The cherry—*kerasos* in Greek, *kirsche* in German—originates from the Akkadian *karshu*. All the evidence suggests that these and other fruits and vegetables reached Europe from Mesopotamia. So did many special seeds and spices: Our word *saffron* comes from the Akkadian *azupiranu*, *crocus* from *kurkanu* (via *krokos* in Greek), *cumin* from *kamanu*, *hyssop* from *zupu*, *myrrh* from *murru*. The list is long; in many instances, Greece provided the physical and etymological bridge by which these products of the land reached Europe. Onions, lentils, beans, cucumbers, cabbage, and lettuce were common ingredients of the Sumerian diet.

What is equally impressive is the extent and variety of the ancient Mesopotamian food-preparation methods, their cuisine. Texts and pictures confirm the Sumerian knowledge of converting the cereals they had grown into flour, from which they made a variety of leavened and unleavened breads, porridges, pastries, cakes, and biscuits. Barley was also fermented to produce beer; "technical manuals" for beer production have been found among the texts. Wine was obtained from grapes and from date palms. Milk was available from sheep, goats, and cows; it was used as a beverage, for cooking, and for converting into yogurt, butter, cream, and cheeses. Fish was a common part of the diet. Mutton was readily available, and the meat of pigs, which the Sumerians tended in large herds, was considered a true delicacy. Geese and ducks may have been reserved for the gods' tables.

The ancient texts leave no doubt that the haute cuisine of ancient Mesopotamia developed in the temples and in the service of the gods. One text prescribed the offering to the gods of "loaves of barley bread . . . loaves of emmer bread; a paste of honey and cream; dates, pastry . . . beer, wine, milk . . . cedar sap, cream." Roasted meat was offered with libations of "prime beer, wine, and milk." A specific cut of a bull was prepared according to a strict recipe, calling for "fine flour . . . made to a dough in water, prime beer, and wine," and mixed with animal fats, "aromatic ingredients made from hearts of plants," nuts, malt, and spices. Instructions for "the daily sacrifice to the gods of the city of Uruk" called for the serving of five different beverages with the meals, and specified what "the millers in the kitchen" and "the chef working at the kneading trough" should do.

Our admiration for the Sumerian culinary art certainly grows as we come across poems that sing the praises of fine foods. Indeed, what can one say when one reads a millennia-old recipe for "coq au vin":

> In the wine of drinking,
> In the scented water,
> In the oil of unction
> This bird have I cooked,
> and have eaten.

A thriving economy, a society with such extensive material enterprises could not have developed without an efficient system of transportation. The Sumerians used their two great rivers and the artificial network of canals for waterborne transportation of people, goods, and cattle. Some of the earliest depictions show what were undoubtedly the world's first boats.

We know from many early texts that the Sumerians also engaged in deep-water seafaring, using a variety of ships to reach faraway lands in search of metals, rare woods and stones, and other materials unobtainable in Sumer proper. An Akkadian dictionary of the Sumerian language was found to contain a section on shipping, listing 105 Sumerian terms for various ships by their size, destination, or purpose (for cargo, for passengers, or for the exclusive use of certain gods). Another 69 Sumerian terms connected with the manning and construction of ships were translated into the Akkadian. Only a long seafaring tradition could have produced such specialized vessels and technical terminology.

Fig. 19

For overland transportation, the wheel was first used in Sumer. Its invention and introduction into daily life made possible a variety of vehicles, from carts to chariots, and no doubt also granted Sumer the distinction of having been the first to employ "ox power" as well as "horse power" for locomotion (Fig. 19).

In 1956 Professor Samuel N. Kramer, one of the great Sumerologists of our time, reviewed the literary legacy found beneath the mounds of Sumer. The table of contents of *From the Tablets of Sumer* is a gem in itself, for each one of the twenty-five chapters described a Sumerian "first," including the first schools, the first bicameral congress, the first historian, the first pharmacopoeia, the first "farmer's almanac," the first cosmogony and cosmology, the first "Job," the first proverbs and sayings, the first literary debates, the first "Noah," the first library catalogue; and Man's first Heroic Age, his first law codes and social reforms, his first medicine, agriculture, and search for world peace and harmony.

This is no exaggeration.

The first schools were established in Sumer as a direct outgrowth of the invention and introduction of writing. The evidence (both archaeological, such as actual school buildings, and written, such as exercise tablets) indicates the existence of a formal system of education by the beginning of the third millennium B.C. There were literally thousands of scribes in Sumer, ranging from junior scribes to high scribes, royal scribes, temple scribes, and scribes who assumed high state office. Some acted as teachers at the schools, and we can still read their essays on the schools, their aims and goals, their curriculum and teaching methods.

The schools taught not only language and writing but also the sciences of the day—botany, zoology, geography, mathematics, and theology. Literary works of the past were studied and copied, and new ones were composed.

The schools were headed by the *ummia* ("expert professor"), and the faculty invariably included not only a "man in charge of drawing" and a "man in charge of Sumerian," but also a "man in charge of the whip." Apparently, discipline was strict; one school alumnus described on a clay tablet how he had been flogged for missing school, for insufficient neatness, for loitering, for not keeping silent, for misbehaving, and even for not having neat handwriting.

An epic poem dealing with the history of Erech concerns itself with the rivalry between Erech and the city-state of Kish. The epic text relates how the envoys of Kish proceeded to Erech, offering a peaceful settlement of their dispute. But the ruler of Erech at the time, Gilgamesh, preferred to fight rather than negotiate. What is interesting is that he had to put the matter to a vote in the Assembly of the Elders, the local "Senate":

> The lord Gilgamesh,
> Before the elders of his city put the matter,
> Seeks out the decision:
> "Let us not submit to the house of Kish,
> let us smite it with weapons."

The Assembly of the Elders was, however, for negotiations. Undaunted, Gilgamesh took the matter to the younger people, the Assembly of the Fighting Men, who voted for war. The significance of the tale lies in its disclosure that a Sumerian ruler had to submit the question of war or peace to the first bicameral congress, some 5,000 years ago.

The title of First Historian was bestowed by Kramer on Entemena, king of Lagash, who recorded on clay cylinders his war with neighboring Umma. While other texts were literary works or epic poems whose themes were historical events, the inscriptions by Entemena were straight prose, written solely as a factual record of history.

Because the inscriptions of Assyria and Babylonia were deciphered well before the Sumerian records, it was long believed that the first code of laws was compiled and decreed by the Babylonian king Hammurabi, in circa 1900 B.C. But as Sumer's civilization was uncovered, it became clear that the "firsts" for a system of laws, for concepts of social order, and for the fair administration of justice belonged to Sumer.

Well before Hammurabi, a Sumerian ruler of the city-state of Eshnunna (northeast of Babylon) encoded laws that set maximum prices for foodstuffs and for the rental of wagons and boats so that the poor could not be oppressed. There were also laws dealing with offenses against person and property, and regulations pertaining to family matters and to master-servant relations.

Even earlier, a code was promulgated by Lipit-Ishtar, a ruler of Isin. The thirty-eight laws that remain legible on the partly preserved tablet (a copy of an original that was engraved on a stone stela) deal with real estate, slaves and servants, marriage and inheritance, the hiring of boats, the rental of oxen, and defaults on taxes. As was done by Hammurabi after him, Lipit-Ishtar explained in the prologue to his code that he acted on the instructions of "the great gods," who had ordered him "to bring well-being to the Sumerians and the Akkadians."

Yet even Lipit-Ishtar was not the first Sumerian law encoder. Fragments of clay tablets that have been found contain copies of laws encoded by Urnammu, a ruler of Ur circa 2350 B.C.—more than half a millennium before Hammurabi. The laws, enacted on the authority of the god Nannar, were aimed at stopping and punishing "the grabbers of the citizens' oxen, sheep, and donkeys" so that "the orphan shall not fall prey to the wealthy, the widow shall not fall prey to the powerful, the man of one shekel shall not fall prey to a man of 60 shekels." Urnammu also decreed "honest and unchangeable weights and measurements."

But the Sumerian legal system, and the enforcement of justice, go back even farther in time.

By 2600 B.C. so much must already have happened in Sumer that the *ensi* Urukagina found it necessary to institute reforms. A long inscription by him has been called by scholars a precious record of man's first social reform based on a sense of freedom, equality, and justice—a "French Revolution" imposed by a king 4,400 years before July 14, 1789.

The reform decree of Urukagina listed the evils of his time first, then the reforms. The evils consisted primarily of the unfair use by supervisors of their powers to take the best for themselves; the abuse of official status; the extortion of high prices by monopolistic groups.

All such injustices, and many more, were prohibited by the reform decree. An official could no longer set his own price "for a good donkey or a house." A "big man" could no longer coerce a common citizen. The rights of the blind, poor, widowed, and orphaned were restated. A divorced woman—nearly 5,000 years ago—was granted the protection of the law.

How long had Sumerian civilization existed that it required a major reform? Clearly, a long time, for Urukagina claimed that it was his god Ningirsu who called upon him "to restore the decrees of former days." The clear implication is that a return to even older systems and earlier laws was called for.

The Sumerian laws were upheld by a court system in which the proceedings and judgments as well as contracts were meticulously recorded and preserved. The justices acted more like juries than judges; a court was usually made up of three or four judges, one of whom was a professional "royal judge" and the others drawn from a panel of thirty-six men.

While the Babylonians made rules and regulations, the Sumerians were concerned with justice, for they believed that the gods appointed the kings primarily to assure justice in the land.

More than one parallel can be drawn here with the concepts of justice and morality of the Old Testament. Even before the Hebrews had kings, they were governed by judges; kings were judged not by their conquests or wealth but by the extent to which they "did the righteous thing." In the Jewish religion, the New Year marks a ten-day period during which the deeds of men are weighed and evaluated to determine their fate in the coming year. It is probably more than a coincidence that the Sumerians believed that a deity named Nanshe annually judged Mankind in the same manner; after all, the first Hebrew patriarch—Abraham—came from the Sumerian city of Ur, the city of Ur-Nammu and his code.

The Sumerian concern with justice or its absence also found expression in what Kramer called "the first 'Job.'" Matching together fragments of clay tablets at the Istanbul Museum of Antiquities, Kramer was able to read a good part of a Sumerian poem which, like the biblical Book of Job, dealt with the complaint of a righteous man who, instead of being blessed by the gods, was made to suffer all manner of loss and disrespect. "My righteous word has been turned into a lie," he cried out in anguish.

In its second part, the anonymous sufferer petitions his god in a manner akin to some verses in the Hebrew Psalms:

> My god, you who are my father,
> who Begot me—lift up my face. . . .
> How long will you neglect me,
> leave me unprotected . . .
> leave me without guidance?

Then follows a happy ending. "The righteous words, the pure words uttered by him, his god accepted; . . . his god withdrew his hand from the evil pronouncement."

Preceding the biblical Book of Ecclesiastes by some two millennia, Sumerian proverbs conveyed many of the same concepts and witticisms.

> If we are doomed to die—let us spend;
> If we shall live long—let us save.

> When a poor man dies, do not try to revive him.

*

He who possesses much silver, may be happy;
He who possesses much barley, may be happy;
But who has nothing at all, can sleep!

Man: For his pleasure: Marriage;
On his thinking it over: Divorce.

It is not the heart which leads to enmity;
it is the tongue which leads to enmity.

In a city without watchdogs,
the fox is the overseer.

The material and spiritual achievements of the Sumerian civilization were also accompanied by an extensive development of the performing arts. A team of scholars from the University of California at Berkeley made news in March 1974 when they announced that they had deciphered the world's oldest song. What professors Richard L. Crocker, Anne D. Kilmer, and Robert R. Brown achieved was to read and actually play the musical notes written on a cuneiform tablet from circa 1800 B.C., found at Ugarit on the Mediterranean coast (now in Syria).

"We always knew," the Berkeley team explained, "that there was music in the earlier Assyrio-Babylonian civilization, but until this deciphering we did not know that it had the same heptatonic-diatonic scale that is characteristic of contemporary Western music, and of Greek music of the first millennium B.C." Until now it was thought that Western music originated in Greece; now it has been established that our music—as so much else of Western civilization—originated in Mesopotamia. This should not be surprising, for the Greek scholar Philo had already stated that the Mesopotamians were known to "seek world-wide harmony and unison through the musical tones."

There can be no doubt that music and song must also be claimed as a Sumerian "first." Indeed, Professor Crocker could play the ancient tune only by constructing a lyre like those which had been found in the ruins

Fig. 20

of Ur. Texts from the second millennium B.C. indicate the existence of musical "key numbers" and a coherent musical theory; and Professor Kilmer herself wrote earlier (*The Strings of Musical Instruments: Their Names, Numbers, and Significance*) that many Sumerian hymnal texts had "what appear to be musical notations in the margins." "The Sumerians and their successors had a full musical life," she concluded. No wonder, then, that we find a great variety of musical instruments—as well as of singers and dancers performing—depicted on cylinder seals and clay tablets (Fig. 20).

Like so many other Sumerian achievements, music and song also originated in the temples. But, beginning in the service of the gods, these performing arts soon were also prevalent outside the temples. Employing the favorite Sumerian play on words, a popular saying commented on the fees charged by singers: "A singer whose voice is not sweet is a 'poor' singer indeed."

Many Sumerian love songs have been found; they were undoubtedly sung to musical accompaniment. Most touching, however, is a lullaby that a mother composed and sang to her sick child:

Come sleep, come sleep, come to my son.
Hurry sleep to my son;
Put to sleep his restless eyes. . . .
You are in pain, my son;
I am troubled, I am struck dumb,
I gaze up to the stars.
The new moon shines down on your face;
Your shadow will shed tears for you.
Lie, lie in your sleep. . . .

May the goddess of growth be your ally;
May you have an eloquent guardian in heaven;
May you achieve a reign of happy days. . . .
May a wife be your support;
May a son be your future lot.

What is striking about such music and songs is not only the conclusion that Sumer was the source of Western music in structure and
harmonic composition. No less significant is the fact that as we hear
the music and read the poems, they do not sound strange or alien at
all, even in their depth of feeling and their sentiments. Indeed, as we
contemplate the great Sumerian civilization, we find that not only are
our morals and *our* sense of justice, *our* laws and architecture and arts
and technology rooted in Sumer, but the Sumerian institutions are so
familiar, so close. At heart, it would seem, we are all Sumerians.

After excavating at Lagash, the archaeologist's spade uncovered Nipper,
the onetime religious center of Sumer and Akkad. Of the 30,000 texts
found there, many remain unstudied to this day. At Shuruppak, school-
houses dating to the third millennium B.C. were found. At Ur, scholars
found magnificent vases, jewelry, weapons, chariots, helmets made of
gold, silver, copper, and bronze, the remains of a weaving factory, court
records—and a towering ziggurat whose ruins still dominate the landscape. At Eshnunna and Adab the archaeologists found temples and
artful statues from pre-Sargonic times. Umma produced inscriptions

speaking of early empires. At Kish monumental buildings and a ziggurat from at least 3000 B.C. were unearthed.

Uruk (Erech) took the archaeologists back into the fourth millennium B.C. There they found the first colored pottery baked in a kiln, and evidence of the first use of a potter's wheel. A pavement of limestone blocks is the oldest stone construction found to date. At Uruk the archaeologists also found the first ziggurat—a vast man-made mound, on top of which stood a white temple and a red temple. The world's first inscribed texts were also found there, as well as the first cylinder seals. Of the latter, Jack Finegan (*Light from the Ancient Past*) said, "The excellence of the seals upon their first appearance in the Uruk period is amazing." Other sites of the Uruk period bear evidence of the emergence of the Metal Age.

In 1919, H. R. Hall came upon ancient ruins at a village now called El-Ubaid. The site gave its name to what scholars now consider the first phase of the great Sumerian civilization. Sumerian cities of that period—ranging from northern Mesopotamia to the southern Zagros foothills—produced the first use of clay bricks, plastered walls, mosaic decorations, cemeteries with brick-lined graves, painted and decorated ceramic wares with geometric designs, copper mirrors, beads of imported turquoise, paint for eyelids, copper-headed "tomahawks," cloth, houses, and, above all, monumental temple buildings.

Farther south, the archaeologists found Eridu—the first Sumerian city, according to ancient texts. As the excavators dug deeper, they came upon a temple dedicated to Enki, Sumer's God of Knowledge, which appeared to have been built and rebuilt many times over. The strata clearly led the scholars back to the beginnings of Sumerian civilization: 2500 B.C., 2800 B.C., 3000 B.C., 3500 B.C.

Then the spades came upon the foundations of the first temple dedicated to Enki. Below that, there was virgin soil—nothing had been built before. The time was circa 3800 B.C. That is when civilization began.

It was not only the first civilization in the true sense of the term. It was a most extensive civilization, all-encompassing, in many ways more advanced than the other ancient cultures that had followed it. It was undoubtedly the civilization on which our own is based.

Having begun to use stones as tools some 2,000,000 years earlier, Man achieved this unprecedented civilization in Sumer circa 3800 B.C. And the perplexing fact about this is that to this very day the scholars have no inkling who the Sumerians were, where they came from, and how and why their civilization appeared.

For its appearance was sudden, unexpected, and out of nowhere.

H. Frankfort (*Tell Uqair*) called it "astonishing." Pierre Amiet (*Elam*) termed it "extraordinary." A. Parrot (*Sumer*) described it as "a flame which blazed up so suddenly." Leo Oppenheim (*Ancient Mesopotamia*) stressed "the astonishingly short period" within which this civilization had arisen. Joseph Campbell (*The Masks of God*) summed it up in this way: "With stunning abruptness . . . there appears in this little Sumerian mud garden . . . the whole cultural syndrome that has since constituted the germinal unit of all the high civilizations of the world."

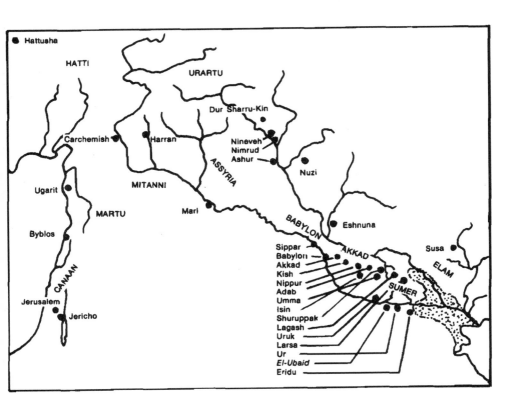

Napoleon conquers Europe
American Revolution

Columbus discovers America
Byzantine empire falls to Turks
Inca empire arises in South America
Aztec civilization in Mexico
Magna Carta granted by King John
Norman conquest of England

Charlemagne forms Holy Roman Empire

Muhammed proclaims Islam

Sack of Rome

Maya civilization in Central America

Jerusalem falls to Roman legions

Jesus of Nazareth

Hannibal challenges Rome
Great Wall begun in China
Alexander defeats Darius
Greek Classical age begins
Roman republic founded
Buddha rises in India
Cyrus captures Babylon
Fall of Nineveh

David king in Jerusalem
Dorian invasion of Greece
Israelite Exodus from Egypt

Mycenaean culture begins
Aryans migrate to India
Hittite empire rises
Abraham migrates from Ur
Hammurabi king in Babylon
Rise of Babylon & Assyria

Chinese civilization begins
Indus valley civilization
Hurrians arrive in Near East
Gudea rules in Lagash
Ur-Nammu rules in Ur

Sargon first king of Akkad
Minoan Civilization in Crete
Gilgamesh rules in Erech

Etana rules in Kish
Egyptian civilization begins

Kingship begins in Kish

Sumerian civilization begins in Eridu

| 2000 AD | 1000 AD | 0 | 1000 BC | 2000 BC | 3000 BC | 4000 BC |

3

UFOs, Pyramids, and the Twelfth Planet

*Lecture at the UFO Conference at
the Great Pyramid, January 1992*

Over the years, Zecharia Sitchin has often been asked to speak at various conferences. In January 1992, he spoke at the UFO Conference at its meeting at the site of the Great Pyramid in Giza, Egypt. In this talk, he explains how his interest in what would become his lifelong passion began. He talks about how, early on, he learned to forge a trail of discovery that would further solidify the development of his theories about the Anunnaki: the ancient visitors who came to Earth roughly 445,000 years ago and, in so doing, changed the course of human evolution. One facet of this story presented here involves the legends of the Greek gods, while another discusses the famous Alexander the Great, in what is an examination by Sitchin of who Alexander really was. We then turn to photos taken by NASA in 1986 and 1989 that provide very real evidence that accounts in the ancient texts describing our planets in their courses and their formation—heretofore deemed to be myth—were based on actual fact.

At every step of the way, Sitchin's careful scrutiny of the archaic texts of Mesopotamia corroborates the biblical records, including—and as further articulated in this chapter—accounts of UFOs. Sitchin also explains who built the Giza Pyramids and what their real function was. Part and parcel of this discussion is the exposing of scholarly frauds by Sitchin, frauds that were perpetrated by some of the pyramids' early investigators who were in search of fame and glory for themselves and not necessarily the truth.

WHENEVER I AM ASKED ABOUT UFOS—what do I think about UFOs, do I believe they exist, do I believe the people who encountered them—I am ready with my own UFO story.

It is one about a young man who was hiking from his hometown to another place. As it got dark at the end of the day, he lay down to sleep in the field. In the middle of the night he was awakened—not by noises, but by bright lights. Half-asleep, half-blinded by the bright light, he saw a UFO. It was hovering above the ground. A ladder or steps were coming down from an open hatch or doorway, reaching to the ground. Some of the occupants of the UFO were going up and down this ladder. He could see their commander, standing in the open door, silhouetted against the light inside. And, overcome with awe and fear, the young man fainted.

When he came to, the UFO was gone. But the young man knew what he had seen. Here is what he had realized: "Indeed," he said to himself, "the Lord is present in this place, and I knew it not. . . . How awesome is this place! It must be the place of the gods, and this is their gateway to heaven!"

Now, what should we make of this story? What would you think if the young man would have rushed in here and told us all that? What would the media make of it? Would they ridicule it, or report it as a truthful experience?

As it happens, the tale has been reported in a publication that I consider very, very reliable. It is called the Bible. And, as some of you might have guessed, the story that I told you is the so-called Jacob's dream. It is one UFO encounter about which I have no doubts, because I am a great believer in the veracity of the Hebrew Bible.

This UFO report, in chapter 28 of Genesis, contains a great deal of important information. It shows us that in biblical times people were awed, but not mystified, by the phenomenon which nowadays is called the UFO enigma. To Jacob what he had seen was not a UFO, an UN-identified Flying Object, but one that he did identify at once. He knew what it was, and he realized at once that he had inadvertently chosen as his rest place for the night a spot that was adjacent to a UFO base. He knew that the vehicle was operated by "the gods"; and he realized that "this was their gateway to heaven."

Jacob's vision is not the only biblical tale of flying craft coming from and disappearing into the skies. There is the story of the fiery chariot that carried the Prophet Elijah to heaven, and the story of the flying machine that the Prophet Ezekiel had seen. Such stories illustrate the point that I wish to impress upon you: If you believe in the Bible, you must accept the possibility of UFOs.

As a matter of fact, it is thanks to the Bible that I am addressing you today. I am sure that each one of us can recall an event, a moment to which they can trace their interest in the subject that has brought us together here, at the foot of the Great Pyramid. Mine was an incident when I was a schoolboy, studying the Old Testament in its original Hebrew language. We reached chapter 6 of Genesis, the story of the Deluge, the Great Flood. The tale of Noah and the ark is preceded by several very enigmatic verses; they tell us of the days preceding the Deluge. We read that "those were the days when the sons of the gods"—"sons" in the plural, "gods" in the plural—were upon the Earth. They married the daughters of Man, and had offspring by them. Those enigmatic "sons of the gods" are called in those verses Nefilim; and the teacher explained that the term meant "giants."

But young Sitchin raised his hand and asked the teacher: Why do you say "giants" when the word Nefilim means in Hebrew "those who came or descended" to Earth—presumably from the heavens?

Instead of commending me for my linguistic perception, the teacher reprimanded me. "Sitchin, sit down!" he said, "You don't question the Bible!"

The reprimand hurt me, for I was not questioning the Bible. On the contrary, I was trying to point out the true meaning of the Bible's words. And it was that childhood incident that kept churning within me and that, as I grew up, prompted me to search for the identity of the Nefilim.

Who were those people? Why did the Bible describe them by a term that indicated they were not of this Earth, but had come down to us from the heavens? Why was such a great distinction made between them and the females called "the daughters of Man?" Why were they called the "sons of the gods?" And how could the Bible, preaching belief in one great and omnipotent god, speak of many sons of many gods?

My first steps in a lifelong search were into the field of biblical scholarship. I found the first important clue, quite unexpectedly, in the commentaries of a nineteenth-century scholar in Russia. This is what he said regarding the Nefilim:

"In ancient times the rulers of countries were the sons of deities who arrived upon the Earth from the heavens, and they ruled the Earth and married wives from among the daughters of Man. They were the sons of deities who, in the earliest times, came down from the heavens upon the Earth, and that is why they called themselves Nefilim, meaning 'Those who fell down.'"

The scholar, known as Malbim, quickly added that these were tales of pagan gods, which should be of no interest to a devout person who believes in a one and only God.

This Malbim, I found out, was basing his commentary on what we call mythology. And what is better known than the mythology of the Greeks, with their tales of those wonderful Olympian gods—twelve of them—and their sons and daughters who *did* cavort with the offspring of Men? What a wonderful bunch they were, on the one hand so divine, seemingly immortal, able to roam the skies, armed with weapons that emit beams or shake the Earth with lightning bolts; and on the other hand so humanlike—loving and hating, sleeping and mating. . . .

One of the most important sacred places of ancient Greece was

Delphi, dedicated to the god Apollo and site of the most known oracle goddesses. Nowadays, the visitors walk up what is called the Sacred Way and can see the ancient Omphalus stone and stand where the ancient priests and worshippers stood—but hardly any one of the modern visitors stops to think that 2,500 years ago those who went there were not curiosity seekers but *believers:* they were people to whom those ancient gods were not a myth but a *reality;* people who were certain that they were worshipping actual divine beings, gods who indeed from Heaven to Earth came. And the way they had come here, to Earth, was in flying machines that we nowadays, out of ignorance of what history teaches us, call UN-identified Flying Objects, UFOs. . . .

In the land where we are now, in ancient Egypt, the same beliefs prevailed. The Egyptians also believed in gods who had come to Earth from another planet, a planet called in Egyptian hieroglyphic texts "Planet of Millions of Years." They called those gods *Neteru,* a word that meant "the Guardians." And they wrote in their histories that before the pharaohs, the human kings, Egypt was ruled by demigods, the offspring of intercourse between the gods and human females. And before that, only gods ruled in the valley of the Nile. These were beliefs that were uncannily similar to the biblical references to the Nefilim!

One who was certain that the tales were true was the famed Greek conqueror, Alexander the Great. In the fourth century B.C. he came to these lands in search of immortality. He did so because he was convinced that he was entitled to live as long as the gods; and the reason was the rumors in the Macedonian court that the real father of Alexander was not his father Phillip, but an Egyptian god who, disguised, came one night into Alexander's mother's quarters and there fathered the future conqueror. The name of that Egyptian god was Amon-Ra, meaning "RA, the Hidden One."

Fighting his way through Asia Minor (today's Turkey) and the lands that are now Syria, Lebanon, and Israel, Alexander reached Egypt. His first stop, his very first stop, was at a city called by the Egyptians ANU, and known to us from the Hebrew Bible by the name ON. The Greeks called it "City of the Sun," Heliopolis. There, in a shrine dedicated to the great god, there was on display the actual object in which the god had come to Earth from the heavens, his so-called "celestial boat." It was a well-known shrine, and once a year its Holy of Holies was opened to admit the pharaoh to see the sacred object. Thousands of pilgrims were gathered at Heliopolis at that time, not unlike the thousands who come once a year to Mecca to venerate the *Ka'aba,* the sacred black stone.

No one knows where that object, the celestial boat, had vanished to, or when it disappeared. Indeed, one theory is that it was taken to Mecca and that it was placed within the large boxlike structure that houses the Ka'aba and which no one can ever enter. But we do know how that object looked, because a small stone replica of it was discovered by archaeologists. What Alexander went to see and what he did see was a UFO. . . . Except that for him, as for Jacob 1,500 years earlier, it was not an UN-identified Flying Object, but the remains of a very identifiable command module of a spacecraft.

Where was this shrine with its own "space museum;" where was Heliopolis? *Right here,* within easy reach of where we are now. Today its name is retained only as that of an eastern suburb of Cairo, a faint echo of what was once a glorified and venerated sacred place. And as now, then too it was in the proximity of the plateau of Giza and its three unique pyramids and the no less unique Sphinx.

Before we turn our attention to the pyramids and the Sphinx, we have to follow in the footsteps of Alexander in our, and his, search for the identity of the gods and the meaning and purpose of the monuments they had left behind. As detailed in my second book, *The Stairway to Heaven,* Alexander went from Heliopolis to a shrine in the western desert where he heard an oracle confirm his semidivine lineage. But in order to gain the immortality to which he felt entitled, he was to find the Gateway of the Gods.

The directions given him by the Egyptian priests led him to the Sinai peninsula. There he followed a maze of subterranean passages and encountered amazing artifacts and sights. But when he reached a place of a mysterious radiance, his way was blocked by an angel. The angel told him the meaning of the oracle's words. The Gateway of the Gods,

Alexander was told, was the literal meaning of the name of the city called Babylon; its ancient name, BAB-IL, meant exactly that: Gateway of the Gods. It will be there, the angel told Alexander, that he would find the god RA who, in Babylon, was known as *Marduk*.

Finally arriving in Babylon, Alexander did come face to face with the god who, according to the rumors, was his real father. But the great god who was supposed to grant Alexander immortality *was dead*. What Alexander had found was the god embalmed in his tomb. And only then did Alexander understand the true oracle: He, like the gods, was fated to die in the end. He would become immortal—but only by being remembered. So, to assure that, he built cities called Alexandria wherever he went.

The Greeks, one discovers in studying their tales, indeed asserted that their gods came from across the Mediterranean Sea. Their gods, they admitted, were no different from those of the Egyptians and the Phoenicians, of the Canaanites and of the Hittites. Indeed, as archaeologists have uncovered the remains of those ancient Near Eastern civilizations and cultures and scholars were able to decipher their writings, it became evident that all the tales we call "mythologies" are renderings and versions of much earlier tales that were first recorded on clay tablets in a land called in the Bible *Shin'ar;* scholars call it by the name it was called in the clay tablets: SHUMER. It meant, literally, "Land of the Guardians"—the very term that in Egyptian, *Neteru,* was applied to the gods. The name is written in English "Sumer" rather than the more accurate "SHumer." Mythology, tales of the gods of Heaven and Earth, all began there.

When archaeologists began to unearth the ancient cities of Mesopotamia (today's Iraq), they found Nineveh, that was the capital of Assyria, and Babylon, capital of the Babylonians—both first known to us from the Bible—and of other ancient places. Those discoveries took the scholars back 3,000 and 4,000 years, to the first and second millennia B.C. But the Bible explicitly spoke of cities and civilizations that *preceded* Assyria and Babylon, and the scholars of the time just could not believe that was possible.

Once again the veracity of the Bible was questioned. But as we now know, after some 150 years of archaeological progress, the Bible was proven right. The more archaeologists moved south in the great plain between the Tigris and Euphrates rivers, toward the Persian Gulf, the older were the remains they dug up. They also came upon inscriptions in a language that preceded that of Assyria and Babylon. Then the earliest cities mentioned in the Bible, like Erech and Ur (the city of Abraham), were discovered. And so it was that Sumer was brought back to light—mankind's first great civilization. It blossomed out an incredible *six thousand* years ago.

We tend to think of human progress as a gradual process. The fact that puzzles all scholars is that in Shumer (or Sumer) a high civilization blossomed out suddenly, unexpectedly, out of nowhere. Without a precedent or a gradual process, there sprang out great cities, high-rise temples, palaces, courts of justice, commerce, shipping, irrigation, metallurgy, mathematics, and medicine. All of a sudden, as if waved in by a magic wand, there appeared kings and priests, judges and doctors, dancers, musicians, artists, and artisans. And above all, a written language: scribes, schools, a literature, epic tales, poems, proverbs, libraries. Every aspect of a high civilization that we can think of had its "first," its beginning, in Sumer.

Of the hundreds of illustrations in my five books to date, I offer up a few here. The first to use bricks and kilns in which to dry and harden them, the Sumerians built step pyramids, called ziggurats, that rose by stages to great heights.*

Inventing the first "rotary press," the Sumerian craftsmen cut from hard stone small cylinders on which they engraved in reverse various depictions; when these were rolled on wet clay, a "positive" of the drawing was impressed on the clay and became a permanent "picture" from antiquity.†

Thousands of such cylinder seals have been found, giving us an accurate graphic record of the Sumerians, their daily lives, their religion,

---

*Editor's note: Please see illustration "A" on facing page for an example of a ziggurat, as well as Fig. 6 found in chapter 2 on page 23.
†Editor's note: Please see Fig. 12 in chapter 2 on page 36 for an illustration of a cylindrical seal.

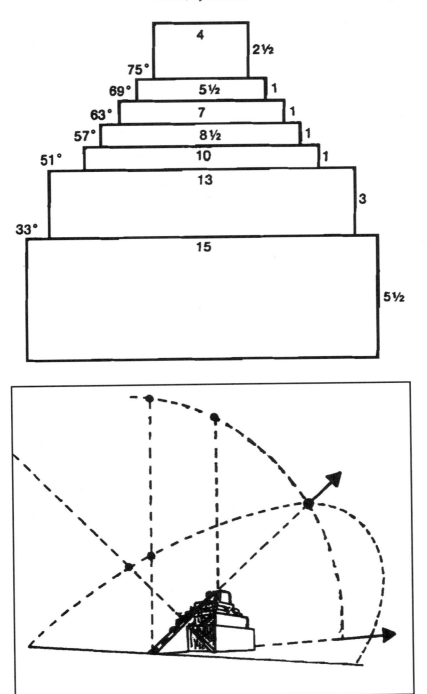

Illustration A

Illustration B

and the way they and their gods looked. Many statues and statuettes, exquisitely crafted, depict for us both gods and their worshippers. In illustration "B" you can see how a Sumerian lady looked, how elegantly she was dressed, how noble her demeanor was. Above all, the most important legacy were the tens of thousands of inscribed tablets ("C" is an example) that recorded commercial and marital contracts, payments of taxes, temple inventories—or, on the other hand, recorded lists of gods and kings and historical and prehistorical events, or provided advanced scientific texts indicating an amazingly sophisticated knowledge.

Most amazing of all was the Sumerian knowledge of astronomy. The astonishing fact is that all the principles of a spherical astronomy, which is the basis of modern astronomy, were inherited by us from the Sumerians. The concept of a celestial sphere, an axis, the plane of orbit, the circle of 360 degrees, the grouping of stars into constellations, the

Illustration C

division of the skies into twelve houses of the zodiac—even the names and pictorial depictions of the zodiacs—all that comes to us from the Sumerians. We learn at school that the first one to suggest that the Sun, not the Earth, was in the center of our solar system was Copernicus, in 1543. *Not so.* Not only did the Sumerians know the true nature of our solar system, they even depicted it!*

How could the Sumerians have known all that, 6,000 years ago?

We have learnt in school that the ancient peoples knew only of the Sun, Moon, and five planets—that they were not aware of any planets beyond Saturn simply because they could not see them. Well, here we find the Sumerians depicting not only Uranus and Neptune, which are way beyond Saturn, but even the farthest-out: Pluto. This is truly astounding, because we ourselves did not know more than the Greeks or Romans until the invention of the telescope. Uranus was discovered

---

*Editor's note: The following chapter includes further information about these depictions; see Fig. 45 on page 89.

in 1781, some two hundred years ago; Neptune in 1846, a hundred and fifty years ago. It is a measure of how far behind ancient knowledge we have been if it is realized that when Neptune was discovered, archaeologists had already unearthed the Mesopotamian tablets with the astronomical information that included not only Uranus and Neptune but also Pluto—and . . .

We discovered Pluto only in 1930, just some sixty years ago. . . .

Let me increase the puzzle. In August 1977—a year after my first book, *The 12th Planet,* was published—NASA, the U.S. space agency, launched two spacecraft named Voyager-1 and Voyager-2 toward Jupiter, Saturn, and beyond. In 1986 Voyager-2 flew by Uranus and sent back Man's first-ever photos and other close-up data on Uranus, which is two billion miles away from us. In August 1989, Voyager-2 reached Neptune, and again provided us with the first-ever breathtaking pictures and other data of the planet, twice as distant from us as Uranus.

In both instances, as I watched the NASA televised transmissions, I literally jumped out of my seat, and shouted: "Oh, my God! That is exactly how the Sumerians had described the two planets 6,000 years ago! Blue green, twinlike, watery . . ." On page 243 of the original English edition of *The 12th Planet*—published a year before the spacecraft were even launched—I quote the Sumerian texts describing each planet, and the ancient text fits perfectly with the astounding NASA discoveries.

Once again the question is: How could the Sumerians know all that?

The answer lies in the number *twelve.* I have already mentioned that ancient pantheons were headed by twelve "Olympian" gods. But the celestial number twelve also applied to the twelve tribes of Israel, the twelve apostles of Jesus, the twelve zodiacs, the twelve months of the year, and so on. Why twelve? To match the number of the members of the solar system, the Sumerians explained. Besides the Sun and Moon there are not nine but ten other planets, they insisted. They called that twelfth member of the solar system, Nibiru; its name meant "Planet of the Crossing" and its symbol was the cross.

A long text known by its opening line, *Enuma Elish,* details the Sumerian cosmogony; describes the process by which planets formed around the Sun; details the arrival of an invader from outer space; a celestial collision; the formation of our Earth; and the origin of the Moon. In my latest book, *Genesis Revisited,* I show that the Sumerian text provides answers to many aspects of the solar system that still puzzle our scientists—and that much of what we have found out in the last decades actually is no more than catching up with ancient knowledge.

Many astronomers are convinced that such an additional planet does, in fact, exist. They call it "Planet X"; some admit that there is not much more to do but let the fact be known and name the planet. I, on my part, believe that the first confirmation took place in 1983 and have written to the International Astronomical Union in Paris insisting that the planet be called by its Sumerian name, Nibiru.

The existence of Nibiru explains the source of the amazing Sumerian knowledge. As if to pre-empt the questions, the Sumerians themselves repeatedly stated: All that we know, they said, was taught to us by the ANUNNAKI.

The name literally meant "Those Who from Heaven to Earth Came"—the exact meaning of the Hebrew term *Nefilim* that the Bible used. And the Sumerians, in text after text, described how those Anunnaki had in fact come to Earth—traveling in space from Nibiru, coming and going between their planet and ours every 3,600 years when Nibiru, in its great elliptical orbit around the Sun, passes between Mars and Jupiter.

The saga of the arrival of the Anunnaki on Earth 450,000 years ago and their activities here read as science-fiction. As noted previously, scholars call these detailed texts "myths." But I have asked myself "What if?" *What if these are not imagined stories but rather accurate records of actual happenings?* In my books, which have the overall title of The Earth Chronicles, I have re-created from those texts a compelling scenario of the ancient events, illustrated with hundreds of depictions found in archaeological discoveries.

I can give you here only a very brief summary of that history and prehistory of Earth and mankind. The first group of fifty visitors to Earth, led by a brilliant scientist called ENKI, splashed down in the Persian Gulf, waded ashore, and established near the present-day city of Basra (Iraq) their first settlement. They called it ERIDU, meaning "Home in the Faraway." It is the source of the name by which we call our planet, *Erde* in the Indo-European languages, *Erets* in the Semitic languages, *Ertha-Earth* in English, and so on.

The Anunnaki came to Earth for gold. Not to be used in jewelry or ornaments, but in order to create, on their own planet, a shield of suspended gold particles with which to protect their dwindling atmosphere. The first plan, to extract the gold from the waters of the Persian Gulf, did not succeed. So they went to southeast Africa and began to obtain the gold by mining it.

At some point—the time is exactly stated in the Sumerian texts—the Anunnaki assigned to the mines mutinied. What were their leaders to do? Enki, the chief scientist, had a solution. From a being that already exists on Earth—let us call it an Ape-man—a more intelligent "primitive worker" could be created, he said. And the text then describes a process of genetic engineering whereby the genes of a young Anunnaki were mixed with the egg of a female Ape-woman, to create "The Adam". . . . The Anunnaki "jumped the gun" on evolution, and created us, *Homo sapiens,* through genetic engineering.

This happened some 250,000 years ago. It should not surprise you to learn that the latest scientific studies in genetics confirm that all the people living today stem from a single "Eve" who lived in southeastern Africa 250,000 years ago. . . .

As time passed, there began the intermarriage between the Anunnaki/Nefilim and the daughters of the Adam, which the Book of Genesis mentions. This brings us to the time of the Deluge, the Great Flood, about 13,000 years ago. As scholars have recognized more than a century ago, the biblical tale of the Deluge, of Noah and how mankind was saved, is only an abbreviated version of a much longer and much more detailed Sumerian text. In that text, as in all the tales that the Bible chose to include, the deeds attributed by the Bible to a single entity called "Elohim" (a plural term, by the way!) are the actions and words of many of the Anunnaki. In those texts, the main participants in the happenings are Enki and his half brother Enlil, their half sister Ninharsag, and their sons and daughters.

In the aftermath of the Deluge, the Anunnaki divided the Earth among themselves. To Enki and his offspring the African lands were given. To Enlil and his offspring were given the lands of the Semites and Indo-Europeans. In those parts of Earth three regions of civilization were granted to mankind—the civilizations of Sumer in Mesopotamia circa 3800 B.C., of the Egyptians circa 3100 B.C., and of the Indus Valley circa 2900 B.C. The fourth region was a "sacred" region, exclusive for the use of the Anunnaki themselves—as their post-Diluvial spaceport. It was the domain of Ninharsag, who did her best to keep the peace between the two quarrelling clans of Enki and Enlil.

This division of the Earth, and the resulting establishment of the post-Diluvial spaceport in the Sinai peninsula, were key decisions that shaped the ensuing events on Earth. Among those results was the building of the three pyramids at Giza, and a series of wars that I have named in my books the Pyramid Wars.

Before the Deluge the spaceport was in Mesopotamia, in Sumer. It involved three elements: the mission control center, which was in Nippur, Enlil's center; the spaceport itself, which was in a place called Sippar; and a landing corridor, which was anchored at its point on the twin-peaked Mount Ararat [illustration "D," top]. In the aftermath of the avalanche of water, the valley between the two great rivers made Mesopotamia uninhabitable for a long time. So the spaceport was shifted to the neutral zone in the Sinai peninsula, where the hard soil of the flat central valley made it perfect for the purpose. As before, the mission control center was at some distance away, and I have suggested that it was in what was later known as Jerusalem. The landing corridor's point was again anchored on Mount Ararat's twin peaks. But on what were the two ends of the landing corridor to be anchored?

I show the layout of the spaceport and its approaches in illustration "D" [bottom]. You can see that one end of the corridor's two lines could be anchored in twin peaks in the Sinai's mountains. But where were two more peaks to be used for anchoring the other line? The answer of

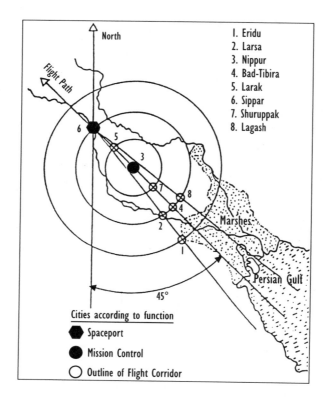

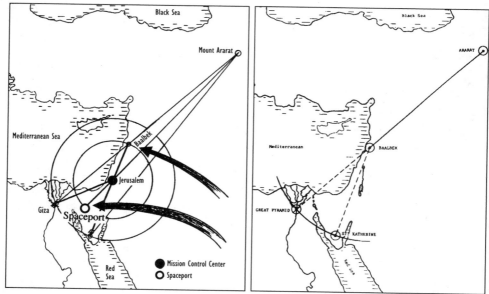

Illustration D

the Anunnaki was to create, to artificially build, two such visible markers: *the two great pyramids of Giza.*

A little-known fact about what is called the Second Pyramid is that although it is somewhat smaller than its neighbor, the Great Pyramid, it rises to the *same height* because it is built on somewhat higher ground. In my books, I have reproduced Sumerian illustrations and texts that leave no doubt of their familiarity with these pyramids. The Great Pyramid was called by the same term as the ziggurat of Enlil in Nippur: E.KUR—"House which is like a mountain," and like it, was equipped with radiating crystals that emitted various directional beams. These were placed in specially cut niches along what is called the Grand Gallery (see illustration "E"), in a hollowed-out stone chest that still stands in the chamber called the "King's Chamber" and in a long vertical niche in what is called the "Queen's Chamber." You can still see these chambers and niches, but not the radiating crystals and other wonderful equipment: it was deliberately destroyed when the most ferocious Pyramid War ended with a victory of the Enlilites.

This is all described in several long Sumerian texts that I fully quote in my writings. The final and most awesome war took place in the days of Abraham, the first Hebrew patriarch; it is recalled in the Bible as the upheavaling of Sodom and Gomorrah. It was then, in 2024 B.C., that the Anunnaki used nuclear weapons to destroy the spaceport in the Sinai and deny to Marduk, alias RA, supremacy on Earth.

This, in brief, is the story of the Anunnaki from their first splashdown in the Persian Gulf some 445,000 years ago until the first use of nuclear weapons on Earth some 4,000 years ago. Many find it so well documented that they join me in believing that in my books, for the first time since antiquity, the true story of Earth and mankind and its gods is being put together in a plausible scenario.

Others find it all very difficult to accept. If we turn from the Sumerian-Mesopotamian and biblical evidence to the Egyptian sources, we find that the ancient Egyptians had no problem with these conclusions. In the tomb of an Egyptian governor of the Sinai, in a series of color drawings depicting his life and achievements, one section shows very clearly a rocketship in an underground silo. If you look at

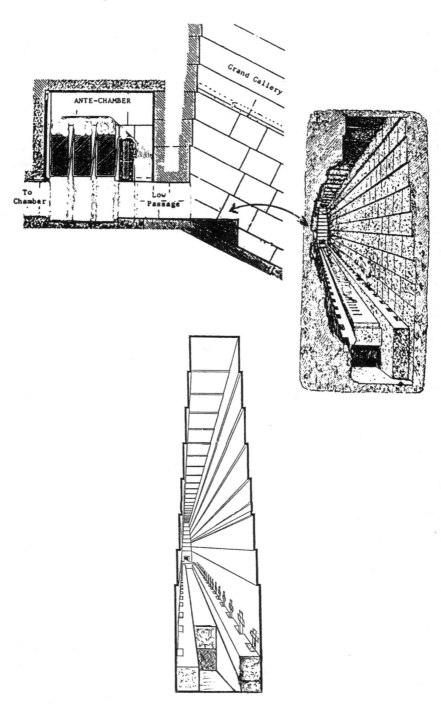

Illustration E

Illustration F

illustration "F" you will see that it is shown with two operators inside it, below ground; while the command module is aboveground, where palm trees grow and giraffes roam.

The pharaohs, so was the royal tradition, could join the gods in an afterlife by journeying from their tombs eastward, to the Sinai peninsula, and there, sitting between two astronauts, soar heavenward in a rocketship. The pyramids that the pharaohs built were accordingly called "stairways to heaven," which I took to be the title of my second book.

But while ancient Egyptians had no problem with all that, modern Egyptologists do. In the course of your visit to Egypt you will hear that the pyramids were all built by the pharaohs, including the three unique ones at Giza. You will hear that they were all built as tombs in which the pharaohs were buried. And you will be told that the Great Pyramid was built by a pharaoh called *Khufu* (we call him *Cheops*); the large one next to it, the so-called Second Pyramid, by his successor *Chefra* (we call him *Chefren*); and the third, smaller one, by his successor *Menka-ra* whom we call by his Greek name *Mycerinus*.

This custom of each pharaoh building himself a pyramid, you will be told, began with the father of Khufu-Cheops who was called *Sneferu*, the founder of what is known as the Fourth Dynasty whose kings reigned from about 2600 to about 2500 B.C. To Menkara/Mycerinus another minor feat, that of creating the Sphinx, is also attributed.

There are about thirty major pyramids in Egypt, and all of them—*except the three at Giza*—were indeed built by the pharaohs—not necessarily one each, and not as tombs to be buried in, but rather as cenotaphs, symbolic monuments for someone buried—elsewhere. While the other pyramids are elaborately decorated and covered on their inside walls with quotes from the Book of the Dead and other ancient incantations known as the Pyramid Texts, there is absolutely no decoration, no painting, no inscription whatsoever in the three Giza pyramids. They are unique in their size and durability; they are unique in their elaborate stone masonries; they are unique—and especially the Great Pyramid—in their internal construction of chambers and corridors, whose incredible alignments reveal a sophisticated knowledge of mathematics, geometry, engineering, geography, and astronomy. The total mass of the Great Pyramid alone, estimated at 93 million cubic feet and weighing 7 million tons, has been calculated to exceed that of all the cathedrals, churches, and chapels combined that have been built in England since the beginning of Christianity. . . .

One can go on and on extolling the uniquely impressive features of the Great Pyramid and its companions at Giza. Our key question is this: Were they built, as Egyptologists believe, in the twenty-sixth century B.C. by Egyptian kings—Khufu, Chefra, and Menkara—or were they built by the Anunnaki thousands of years earlier? Were these pyramids built as royal tombs, or—as I have shown—as beacons in a landing corridor for a spaceport in the Sinai?

If you press the Egyptologists for evidence that the pharaohs were actually buried inside their pyramids, they will have none. They did have one example until several decades ago; that was the Small Pyramid, here at Giza. In July 1837 an Englishman by the name of Howard Vyse, who was excavating in the area, reported that he had found near a stone sarcophagus inside this pyramid fragments—of the cover of a mummy case with a royal inscription on it, together with part of the skeleton of the king's name. The name spelled out MEN-KA-RA—the "Mycerinus" in the Greek language to whom this pyramid was attributed. It was a unique discovery, because not only did it show the pyramid to have been a royal tomb, but also unquestionably evidenced the pharaoh's name.

It was, as I said, the one and only instance. It also proved to have been an archaeological fraud. Scholars at the time already had some doubts about the age of the mummy case due to its style. And when a few decades ago radiocarbon dating was developed, it was established without doubt that the mummy-case cover belonged not to the fourth but to the twenty-fifth dynasty, not to 2600 B.C. but to 700 B.C., and that the skeletal remains were not even from the pre-Christian times, but from the first centuries of the Christian era. Someone, in other words, took a piece of wooden coffin found elsewhere, and a skeleton from a common grave, and put them into a pile of rubble inside the Small Pyramid (which had been entered before many, many times) and announced: Look what I found!

When I was writing my first book, I was not aware of this forgery, because textbooks dealing with ancient Egypt just gloss over it. Earlier textbooks repeat the tale of the discovery as conclusive evidence that Menkara built this pyramid and was buried in it. My conclusions regarding the Anunnaki and their spaceport were based on Sumerian, not Egyptian, sources at the time. But when I began to continue the story of The Earth Chronicles and started to examine the Egyptian sources, I faced a dilemma. As I saw it, the Anunnaki and not the pharaohs had built the Giza pyramids and carved out the Sphinx, and they did it not circa 2600 B.C. but circa 9000 B.C. But that is not what Egyptologists were saying. So I had to examine the evidence that the Egyptologists had.

That evidence was twofold. That found in the Small or Third Pyramid, which I have just reviewed for you, and an inscription with the royal name of Cheops found inside the Great Pyramid. Whereas the evidence found in the Third Pyramid was in chambers that had been entered many times before, the evidence in the Great Pyramid was in a chamber that had apparently never been entered since its original construction.

The story again involves the same Englishman, Howard Vyse, and I tell it in titillating detail in my second book, *The Stairway to Heaven*. The black sheep of a famous English family, Howard Vyse became fascinated with the archaeological discoveries in Egypt and decided to use his family's money to attain fame for himself. He began by searching for a legendary secret chamber inside the Great Pyramid, which, according to rumors, held all the riches of the Pharaoh Cheops. After much work and almost running out of funds, he began to use gunpowder inside the pyramid to blow his way into narrow spaces above the King's Chamber. The first one was discovered in 1765 by an explorer named Nathaniel Davison. Vyse discovered four more, one above the other—see illustration "G."

The Great Pyramid, as I have stated, is totally devoid of any decoration or inscription. So was the chamber discovered by Davison. But in the three chambers discovered by Vyse, uncharacteristically, there *were* inscriptions: masons' markings and royal names, all made with red paint. And one of the inscriptions clearly spelled "Khufu." Vyse, in other words, offered proof from a chamber that had been sealed all these millennia that it was Khufu (Cheops) whose masons had built this pyramid. He called the British and Austrian consuls in Cairo to witness the inscription. They copied it on cloth-paper, signed it, and sent it to the British Museum for safekeeping. There it lay undisturbed for almost a century and a half; and textbook after textbook told its students that yes, this inscription identified the Pharaoh Khufu as the builder of the Great Pyramid.

So, what about my Anunnaki as builders? What about the spaceport, and flying vehicles, and Nibiru?

As I was researching the ancient evidence, something odd struck

"Wellington's Chamber"

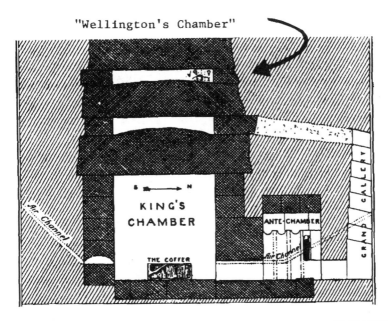

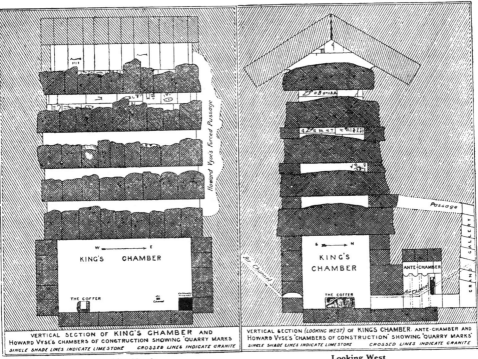

Looking North   Looking West

Illustration G

me. According to the Egyptological theory of a succession of Pharaohs building a succession of pyramids, the Sphinx was built (by carving the native stone) by Chephren, the supposed builder of the Second Pyramid. He was the fourth king of the Fourth Dynasty. Yet, Egyptian drawings on tablets from the *first* Dynasty already showed the Sphinx (illustration "H")! In other words, the very first pharaohs, six hundred years before Chephren, already saw the Sphinx standing at Giza!

Illustration H

Moreover, a well-known stone stela discovered in the 1850s and known as the "Inventory Stela" bears an inscription by Khufu (Cheops) in which he mentions not only the Sphinx but also the Great Pyramid as already existing in his time—about a century *before* his successor Chephren has supposedly carved out the Sphinx. . . .

So, I asked myself—What is going on here?

When I came across the fact that the so-called "evidence" from the Third Pyramid was a forgery, something rang a bell. The forger was in that case Colonel Vyse. But was he not also the discoverer of the Khufu/Cheops evidence in the Great Pyramid?

As I read and reread his diaries and other data concerning the activities in Egypt and Egyptology at that time, I could not shake off the feeling that the red-paint inscriptions Vyse claimed to have found in the narrow chambers were also a forgery. With much behind the scenes diplomacy and with a bit of luck, I was able to find, in the dusty archives of the British Museum in London, the cloth-bound testament left there by Vyse 150 years earlier. "You are the first one in more than a century that is asking to see this," the curator of the Egyptian Department of the museum told me.

The minute I opened the folded sheets, I knew I had found the evidence for the forgery. In a nutshell, here it is: Due to poor knowledge at the time of Egyptian hieroglyphics, the assistant of Vyse, a Mr. Hill, who climbed into the chambers and with brush and red paint drew the crucial cartouches with the royal name, spelled KH-U-F-U the way I show in illustration "I." But what he wrote or painted was not Khufu but RA-U-F-U (illustration "J"), invoking in vain the name of RA, Egypt's supreme god. The correct way to write it is the way I show in illustration "I"; this is how you will see it written on the Inventory Stela when you visit the Cairo Museum.

I submitted this and other evidence in my book *The Stairway to Heaven*. A few months after the book was published I received a letter from an engineer living in Pittsburgh. What you say about the forgery, he wrote, has been known in my family for the past 150 years! I called him at once. It turned out that his great-grandfather was the master mason whom Vyse had hired to use gunpowder inside the pyramid, and

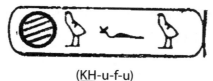

(K̲H-u-f-u)

Illustration I

(R̲A-u-f-u)

Illustration J

he wrote back home about the night Mr. Hill went into the pyramid with brush and paint and perpetrated the forgery. After 150 years, an eye-witness emerged to corroborate my conclusions. . . .

Astronomers now concur that there indeed is one more planet in our solar system. Other scientists—in geology, biology, genetics, and mathematics—corroborate other aspects of ancient knowledge. I detail all that in the other books of The Earth Chronicles series and in the latest book, *Genesis Revisited*. In that latest book I also follow step by step one of the most shocking incidents in the modern space program. This is what the truth is about the spacecraft called Phobos-2 that was launched by the Soviets with international participation to probe Mars and its moonlet Phobos. The spacecraft was hit in March 1989 by, quote, "something that should not be there." I show in my book one of the last photographs transmitted by the spacecraft showing that "something." What is claimed to be a subsequent photo-frame has since been shown by a Russian source: it shows an elongated alien object closing in on the spacecraft.

There are amazing features on Mars, not just the famous face but also actual structures. They include what looks like the layout of a spaceport. According to the Sumerian texts, the Anunnaki used Mars as a station on the way from Nibiru to Earth. That ancient spaceport has been *re-activated!*

And, if I am right about this conclusion, then this will explain where UFOs and their android occupants come from.

Earth is being scouted again; and after the android messengers, the Anunnaki themselves will follow—fulfilling all the prophecies about the Return of the Kingdom of Heaven to Earth.

In confirming the conclusions about the twelfth member of our solar system and the Anunnaki, we also solve the enigma of the UFO phenomenon. Some of the most compelling evidence is right here: the three pyramids of Giza and the Sphinx.

4

The Stairway to Heaven and the Epic of Creation

Selections from
The Stairway to Heaven *(Chapter 5) and*
The 12th Planet *(Chapter 7)*

The existence of the Twelfth Planet—Nibiru—is germane to Sitchin's cosmology, for it was from there the Anunnaki originated. Some questions about Nibiru thus must be asked: Where is it? Why don't we know about it? How did the Sumerians know about it? When is it coming next? This last question is more fully answered in Zecharia Sitchin's book *The End of Days.* The others may be answered, at least partially, by understanding the Sumerian creation epic the *Enuma Elish,* as explained by Zecharia Sitchin in several of his books, and by understanding what the Sumerians knew about Nibiru's orbit, as told to them by the Anunnaki themselves.

My father, Amnon Sitchin (Zecharia Sitchin's brother), who has a Ph.D. in aeronautical and mechanical engineering, assisted in the calculations of that planet's orbit. Some things to note about the orbit are that it is elliptical; it is in a clockwise direction (most of the other planets in our solar system rotate counterclockwise around the Sun); and it is not on the same ecliptic as these other planets, making it hard to spot since there is a vast area in which it might be located. Amnon Sitchin notes that "Except for the period and the length of the orbit of Nibiru, the inclination and tilt to the ecliptic is almost identical to that of Haley's Comet."

This excerpt from chapter 5 of *The Stairway to Heaven* gives a quick overview of the events described in the *Enuma Elish* and throws some scholarly light on the mysterious planet Nibiru.

FROM THE SUMERIAN COSMOLOGICAL TALES and epic poems, from texts that served as autobiographies of these gods, from lists of their functions and relationships and cities, from chronologies and histories called King Lists, and a wealth of other texts, inscriptions, and drawings, we have pieced together a cohesive drama of what had happened in prehistoric times, and how it all began.

Their story begins in primeval times, when our Solar System was still young. It was then that a large planet appeared from outer space and was drawn into the Solar System. The Sumerians called the invader NIBIRU—"Planet of the Crossing"; the Babylonian name for it was Marduk. As it passed by the outer planets, Marduk's course curved in, to a collision course with an old member of the Solar System—a planet named Tiamat. As the two came together, the satellites of Marduk split Tiamat in half. Its lower part was smashed into bits and pieces, creating the comets and the asteroid belt—the "celestial bracelet" of planetary debris that orbits between Jupiter and Mars. Tiamat's upper part, together with its chief satellite, were thrown into a new orbit, to become Earth and the Moon.

Marduk itself, intact, was caught in a vast elliptical orbit around the Sun, returning to the site of the "celestial battle" between Jupiter and Mars once in 3,600 Earth-years (Fig. 44). It was thus that the Solar System ended up with *twelve* members—the Sun, the Moon (which the Sumerians considered a celestial body in its own right), the nine planets we know of, and one more—the twelfth: Marduk.

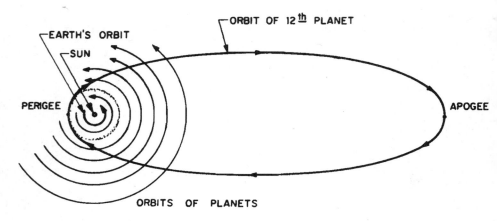

Fig. 44

When Marduk invaded our Solar System, it brought with it the seed of life. In the collision with Tiamat, some of the seed of life was transferred to its surviving part—Planet Earth. As life evolved on Earth, it emulated evolution on Marduk. And so it was that when on Earth the human species just began to stir, on Marduk intelligent beings had already achieved high levels of civilization and technology.

It was from that twelfth member of the Solar System, the Sumerians said, that astronauts had come to Earth—the "Gods of Heaven and Earth." It was from such Sumerian beliefs, that all the other ancient peoples acquired their religions and gods. These gods, the Sumerians said, created Mankind and eventually gave it civilization—all knowledge, all sciences, including an incredible level of a sophisticated astronomy.

This knowledge encompassed recognition of the Sun as the central body of the Solar System, cognizance of all the planets we know of today—even the outer planets Uranus, Neptune, and Pluto, which are relatively recent discoveries of modern astronomy—planets which could not have been observed and identified with the naked eye. And, in planetary texts and lists, as well as in pictorial depictions, the Sumerians insisted that there was one more planet—NIBIRU, *Marduk*—which, when nearest Earth, passed between Mars and Jupiter, as shown on this 4,500-year-old cylinder seal (Fig. 45).

Fig. 45

Chapter 7 of *The 12th Planet* puts forth hard evidence for the existence of Nibiru based on the depiction on the ancient Sumerian cylinder seal that is 4,500 years old (Fig. 45 above and Fig. 99 detail on page 90). This seal depicts our solar system, with twelve celestial bodies: ten planets and the sun and moon. If this ancient seal is an accurate depiction of our solar system as it existed at that time, it helps to disprove the heretofore prevalent theory that posits that the moon was formed when a piece of Earth fell away and formed its own body. More recent scientific evidence about the chemical makeup of the moon seems to corroborate the Sumerian perspective that the Earth and the moon were formed at the same time of roughly the same materials. If the seal is accurate in its depiction of the moon as a body separate from the Earth, might it also be correct in its inclusion of the planet that may be Nibiru?

This selection from chapter 7 also articulates the contents of the Sumerian *Enuma Elish* (the Epic of Creation), one of the world's most important works. Sitchin walks us, line by line, through a good portion of the narrative and keys it to real time events having to do with the formation of the cosmos, and that of our own solar system. The creation myth *Enuma Elish* was also a hallowed text for the Babylonians, used as part of their religious rituals celebrating the New Year and, in honoring it, they celebrated the extraordinary genesis of the world as they knew it to be. The *Enuma Elish* explains enigmas in the movement and orientation of the planets, the comets, and the satellites of planets.

ON MOST OF THE ANCIENT CYLINDER SEALS that have been found, symbols that stand for certain celestial bodies, members of our Solar System, appear above the figures of gods or humans.

An Akkadian seal from the third millennium B.C., now at the Vorderasiatische Abteilung of the State Museum in East Berlin (catalogued VA/243), departs from the usual manner of depicting the celestial bodies. It does not show them individually but rather as a group of eleven globes encircling a large, rayed star. It is clearly a depiction of the Solar System as it was known to the Sumerians: a system consisting of *twelve* celestial bodies (Fig. 99).

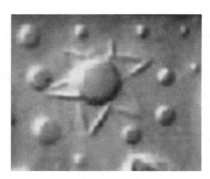

Fig. 99

We usually show our Solar System schematically as a line of planets stretching away from the Sun in ever-increasing distances. But if we depicted the planets, not in a line, but one after the other in a *circle* (the closest, Mercury, first, then Venus, then Earth, and so on), the result would look something like Fig. 100. (All drawings are schematic and not to scale; planetary orbits in the drawings that follow are circular rather than elliptical for ease of presentation.)

If we now take a second look at an enlargement of the Solar System depicted on cylinder seal VA/243, we shall see that the "dots" encircling the star are actually globes whose sizes and order conform to that of the Solar System in Fig. 100. The small Mercury is followed by a larger Venus. Earth, the same size as Venus, is accompanied by the small Moon. Continuing in a counterclockwise direction, Mars is shown correctly as smaller than Earth but larger than the Moon or Mercury (Fig. 101).

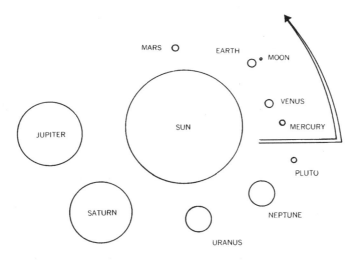

Fig. 100

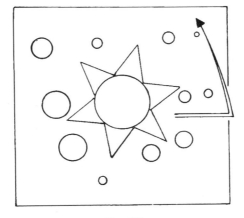

Fig. 101

The ancient depiction then shows a planet unknown to us—considerably larger than Earth, yet smaller than Jupiter and Saturn, which clearly follow it. Farther on, another pair perfectly matches our Uranus and Neptune. Finally, the smallish Pluto is also there, but not where we now place it (after Neptune); instead, it appears between Saturn and Uranus.

Treating the Moon as a proper celestial body, the Sumerian depiction fully accounts for all of our known planets, places them in the correct order (with the exception of Pluto), and shows them by size.

The 4,500-year-old depiction, however, also insists that there was—or has been—another major planet between Mars and Jupiter. It is, as we shall show, the Twelfth Planet, the planet of the Nefilim.

If this Sumerian celestial map had been discovered and studied two centuries ago, astronomers would have deemed the Sumerians totally uninformed, foolishly imagining more planets beyond Saturn. Now, however, we know that Uranus and Neptune and Pluto are really there. Did the Sumerians imagine the other discrepancies, or were they properly informed by the Nefilim that the Moon was a member of the Solar System in its own right, Pluto was located near Saturn, and there was a Twelfth Planet between Mars and Jupiter?

The long-held theory that the Moon was nothing more than "a frozen golf ball" was not discarded until the successful conclusion of several U. S. Apollo Moon missions. The best guesses were that the Moon was a chunk of matter that had separated from Earth when Earth was still molten and plastic. Were it not for the impact of millions of meteorites, which left craters on the face of the Moon, it would have been a faceless, lifeless, history-less piece of matter that solidified and forever follows Earth.

Observations made by unmanned satellites, however, began to bring such long-held beliefs into question. It was determined that the chemical and mineral makeup of the Moon was sufficiently different from that of Earth to challenge the "breakaway" theory. The experiments conducted on the Moon by the American astronauts and the study and analysis of the soil and rock samples they brought back have established beyond doubt that the Moon, though presently barren, was once a "living planet." Like Earth it is layered, which means that it solidified from its own original molten stage. Like Earth it generated heat, but whereas Earth's heat comes from its radioactive materials, "cooked" inside Earth under tremendous pressure, the Moon's heat comes, apparently, from layers of radioactive materials lying very near the surface. These materials, however, are too heavy to have floated up. What, then, deposited them near the Moon's surface?

The Moon's gravity field appears to be erratic, as though huge chunks of heavy matter (such as iron) had not evenly sunk to its core but were scattered about. By what process or force, we might ask? There is evidence that the ancient rocks of the Moon were magnetized. There is also evidence that the magnetic fields were changed or reversed. Was it by some unknown internal process, or by an undetermined outside influence?

The Apollo 16 astronauts found on the Moon rocks (called breccias) that result from the shattering of solid rock and its rewelding together by extreme and sudden heat. When and how were these rocks shattered, then refused? Other surface materials on the Moon are rich in rare radioactive potassium and phosphorus, materials that on Earth are deep down inside.

Putting such findings together, scientists are now certain that the Moon and Earth, formed of roughly the same elements at about the same time, evolved as separate celestial bodies. In the opinion of the scientists of the U. S. National Aeronautics and Space Administration (NASA), the Moon evolved "normally" for its first 500 million years. Then, they said (as reported in the *New York Times*),

> The most cataclysmic period came 4 billion years ago, when celestial bodies the size of large cities and small countries came crashing into the Moon and formed its huge basins and towering mountains.
>
> The huge amounts of radioactive materials left by the collisions began heating the rock beneath the surface, melting massive amounts of it and forcing seas of lava through cracks in the surface.
>
> Apollo 15 found a rockslide in the crater Tsiolovsky six times greater than any rockslide on Earth. Apollo 16 discovered that the

collision that created the Sea of Nectar deposited debris as much as 1,000 miles away.

Apollo 17 landed near a scarp eight times higher than any on Earth, meaning it was formed by a moon-quake eight times more violent than any earthquake in history.

The convulsions following that cosmic event continued for some 800 million years, so that the Moon's makeup and surface finally took on their frozen shape some 3.2 billion years ago.

The Sumerians, then, were right to depict the Moon as a celestial body in its own right. And, as we shall soon see, they also left us a text that explains and describes the cosmic catastrophe to which the NASA experts refer.

The planet Pluto has been called "the enigma." While the orbits around the Sun of the other planets deviate only somewhat from a perfect circle, the deviation ("eccentricity") of Pluto is such that it has the most extended and elliptical orbit around the Sun. While the other planets orbit the Sun more or less within the same plane, Pluto is out of kilter by a whopping seventeen degrees. Because of these two unusual features of its orbit, Pluto is the only planet that cuts across the orbit of another planet, Neptune.

In size, Pluto is indeed in the "satellite" class: Its diameter, 3,600 miles, is not much greater than that of Triton, a satellite of Neptune, or Titan, one of the ten satellites of Saturn. Because of its unusual characteristics, it has been suggested that this "misfit" might have started its celestial life as a satellite that somehow escaped its master and went into orbit around the Sun on its own.

This, as we shall soon see, is indeed what happened—according to the Sumerian texts.

And now we reach the climax of our search for answers to primeval celestial events: the existence of the Twelfth Planet. Astonishing as it may sound, our astronomers have been looking for evidence that indeed such a planet once existed between Mars and Jupiter.

Toward the end of the eighteenth century, even before Neptune had been discovered, several astronomers demonstrated that "the planets were placed at certain distances from the Sun according to some definite law." The suggestion, which came to be known as Bode's Law, convinced astronomers that a planet ought to revolve in a place where hitherto no planet had been known to exist—that is, between the orbits of Mars and Jupiter.

Spurred by these mathematical calculations, astronomers began to scan the skies in the indicated zone for the "missing planet." On the first day of the nineteenth century, the Italian astronomer Giuseppe Piazzi discovered at the exact indicated distance a very small planet (485 miles across), which he named Ceres. By 1804 the number of asteroids ("small planets") found there rose to four; to date, nearly 3,000 asteroids have been counted orbiting the Sun in what is now called the asteroid belt. Beyond any doubt, this is the debris of a planet that had shattered to pieces. Russian astronomers have named it Phayton ("chariot").

While astronomers are certain that such a planet existed, they are unable to explain its disappearance. Did the planet self-explode? But then its pieces would have flown off in all directions and not stayed in a single belt. If a collision shattered the missing planet, where is the celestial body responsible for the collision? Did it also shatter? But the debris circling the Sun, when added up, is insufficient to account for even one whole planet, to say nothing of two. Also, if the asteroids comprise the debris of two planets, they should have retained the axial revolution of two planets. But all the asteroids have a single axial rotation, indicating they come from a single celestial body. How then was the missing planet shattered, and what shattered it?

The answers to these puzzles have been handed down to us from antiquity.

About a century ago the decipherment of the texts found in Mesopotamia unexpectedly grew into a realization that there—in Mesopotamia—texts existed that not only paralleled but also preceded portions of the Holy Scriptures. *Die Kielschriften und das alte Testament* by Eberhard Schräder in 1872 started an avalanche of books, articles, lectures, and debates that lasted half a century. Was there a link, at some early time, between Babylon and the Bible? The headlines provocatively affirmed, or denounced: BABEL UND BIBEL.

Among the texts uncovered by Henry Layard in the ruins of the library of Ashurbanipal in Nineveh, there was one that told a tale of Creation not unlike the one in the Book of Genesis. The broken tablets, first pieced together and published by George Smith in 1876 (*The Chaldean Genesis*), conclusively established that there indeed existed an Akkadian text, written in the Old Babylonian dialect, that related how a certain deity created Heaven and Earth and all upon Earth, including Man.

A vast literature now exists that compares the Mesopotamian text with the biblical narrative. The Babylonian deity's work was done, if not in six "days," then over the span of six tablets. Parallel to the biblical God's seventh day of rest and enjoyment of his handiwork, the Mesopotamian epic devotes a seventh tablet to the exaltation of the Babylonian deity and his achievements. Appropriately, L. W. King named his authoritative text on the subject *The Seven Tablets of Creation*.

Now called "The Creation Epic," the text was known in antiquity by its opening words, *Enuma Elish* ("When in the heights"). The biblical tale of Creation begins with the creation of Heaven and Earth; the Mesopotamian tale is a true cosmogony, dealing with prior events and taking us to the beginning of time:

> *Enuma elish la nabu shamamu*
>   When in the heights Heaven had not been named
> *Shaplitu ammatitm shuma la zakrat*
>   And below, firm ground [Earth] had not been called

It was then, the epic tells us, that two primeval celestial bodies gave birth to a series of celestial "gods." As the number of celestial beings increased, they made great noise and commotion, disturbing the Primeval Father. His faithful messenger urged him to take strong measures to discipline the young gods, but they ganged up on him and robbed him of his creative powers. The Primeval Mother sought to take revenge. The god who led the revolt against the Primeval Father had a new suggestion: Let his young son be invited to join the Assembly of the Gods and be given supremacy so that he might go to fight single-handed the "monster" their mother turned out to be.

Granted supremacy, the young god—Marduk, according to the Babylonian version—proceeded to face the monster and, after a fierce battle, vanquished her and split her in two. Of one part of her he made Heaven, and of the other, Earth.

He then proclaimed a fixed order in the heavens, assigning to each celestial god a permanent position. On Earth he produced the mountains and seas and rivers, established the seasons and vegetation, and created Man. In duplication of the Heavenly Abode, Babylon and its towering temple were built on Earth. Gods and mortals were given assignments, commandments, and rituals to be followed. The gods then proclaimed Marduk the supreme deity and bestowed on him the "fifty names"—the prerogatives and numerical rank of the Enlilship.

As more tablets and fragments were found and translated, it became evident that the text was not a simple literary work: It was the most hallowed historical-religious epic of Babylon, read as part of the New Year rituals. Intended to propagate the supremacy of Marduk, the Babylonian version made him the hero of the tale of Creation. This, however, was not always so. There is enough evidence to show that the Babylonian version of the epic was a masterful religious-political forgery of earlier Sumerian versions, in which Anu, Enlil, and Ninurta were the heroes.

No matter, however, what the actors in this celestial and divine drama were called, the tale is certainly as ancient as Sumerian civilization. Most scholars see it as a philosophic work—the earliest version of the eternal struggle between good and evil—or as an allegorical tale of nature's winter and summer, sunrise and sunset, death and resurrection.

But why not take the epic at face value, as nothing more nor less than the statement of cosmologic facts as known to the Sumerians, as told them by the Nefilim? Using such a bold and novel approach, we find that the "Epic of Creation" perfectly explains the events that probably took place in our Solar System.

The stage on which the celestial drama of *Enuma Elish* unfolds is the primeval universe. The celestial actors are the ones who create as well as the ones being created. Act I:

> When in the heights Heaven had not been named,
> And below, Earth had not been called;
> Naught, but primordial APSU, their Begetter,
> MUMMU, and TIAMAT—she who bore them all;
> Their waters were mingled together.
>
> No reed had yet formed, no marshland had
>   appeared.
> None of the gods had yet been brought into being,
> None bore a name, their destinies were
>   undetermined;
> Then it was that gods were formed in their midst.

With a few strokes of the reed stylus upon the first clay tablet—in nine short lines—the ancient poet-chronicler manages to seat us in front row center, and boldly and dramatically raise the curtain on the most majestic show ever: the Creation of our Solar System.

In the expanse of space, the "gods"—the planets—are yet to appear, to be named, to have their "destinies"—their orbits—fixed. Only three bodies exist: "primordial AP.SU" ("one who exists from the beginning"); MUM.MU ("one who was born"); and TIAMAT ("maiden of life"). The "waters" of Apsu and Tiamat were mingled, and the text makes it clear that it does not mean the waters in which reeds grow, but rather the primordial waters, the basic life-giving elements of the universe.

Apsu, then, is the Sun, "one who exists from the beginning."

Nearest him is Mummu. The epic's narrative makes clear later on that Mummu was the trusted aide and emissary of Apsu: a good description of Mercury, the small planet rapidly running around his giant master. Indeed, this was the concept the ancient Greeks and Romans had of the god-planet Mercury: the fast messenger of the gods.

Farther away was Tiamat. She was the "monster" that Marduk later shattered—the "missing planet." But in primordial times she was the very first Virgin Mother of the first Divine Trinity. The space between her and Apsu was not void; it was filled with the primordial elements of Apsu and Tiamat. These "waters" "commingled," and a pair of celestial gods—planets—were formed in the space between Apsu and Tiamat.

> Their waters were mingled together. . . .
> Gods were formed in their midst:
> God LAHMU and god LAHAMU were
>   brought forth;
> By name they were called.

Etymologically, the names of these two planets stem from the root *LHM* ("to make war"). The ancients bequeathed to us the tradition that Mars was the God of War and Venus the Goddess of both Love and War. LAHMU and LAHAMU are indeed male and female names, respectively; and the identity of the two gods of the epic and the planets Mars and Venus is thus affirmed both etymologically and mythologically. It is also affirmed astronomically: As the "missing planet," Tiamat was located beyond Mars. Mars and Venus are indeed located in the space between the Sun (Apsu) and "Tiamat." We can illustrate this by following the Sumerian celestial map (Figs. 102, 103).

The process of the formation of the Solar System then went on. Lahmu and Lahamu—Mars and Venus—were brought forth, but even

> Before they had grown in age
> And in stature to an appointed size—
> God ANSHAR and god KISHAR were formed,
> Surpassing them [in size].
> As lengthened the days and multiplied the years,
> God ANU became their son—of his ancestors a rival.
> Then Anshar's firstborn, Anu,
> As his equal and in his image begot NUDIMMUD.

With a terseness matched only by the narrative's precision, Act I of the epic of Creation has been swiftly played out before our very eyes.

We are informed that Mars and Venus were to grow only to a limited size; but even before their formation was complete, another pair of planets was formed. The two were majestic planets, as evidenced by their

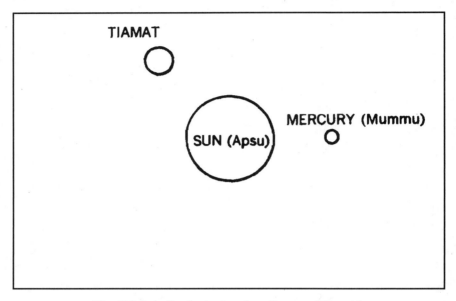

Fig. 102. I. In the Beginning: Sun, Mercury, "Tiamat."

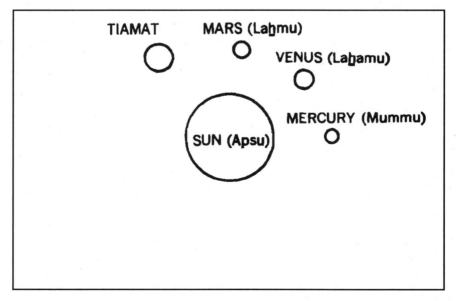

Fig. 103. II. The Inner Planets—the "gods in the midst"—come forth.

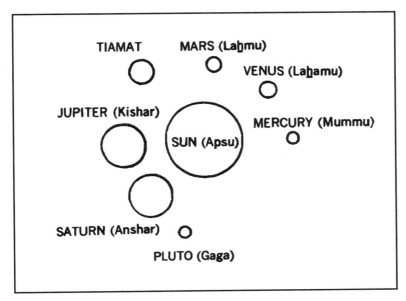

Fig. 104. III. The SHAR's—the giant planets—are created,
together with their "emissary."

names—AN.SHAR ("prince, foremost of the heavens") and KI.SHAR ("foremost of the firm lands"). They overtook in size the first pair, "surpassing them" in stature. The description, epithets, and location of this second pair easily identify them as Saturn and Jupiter (Fig. 104).

Some time then passed ("multiplied the years"), and a third pair of planets was brought forth. First came ANU, smaller than Anshar and Kishar ("their son"), but larger than the first planets ("of his ancestors a rival" in size). Then Anu, in turn, begot a twin planet, "his equal and in his image." The Babylonian version names the planet NUDIMMUD, an epithet of Ea/Enki. Once again, the descriptions of the sizes and locations fit the next known pair of planets in our Solar System, Uranus and Neptune.

There was yet another planet to be accounted for among these outer planets, the one we call Pluto. The "Epic of Creation" has already referred to Anu as "Anshar's firstborn," implying that there was yet another planetary god "born" to Anshar/Saturn. The epic catches up with this celestial deity later on, when it relates how Anshar sent out his emissary GAGA on various missions to the other planets. Gaga appears in function and

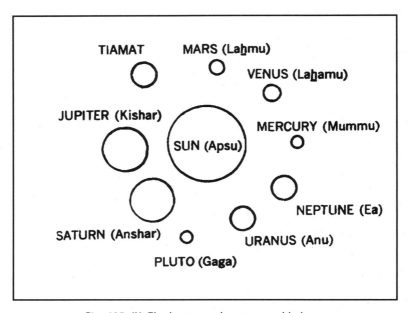

Fig. 105. IV. The last two planets are added—
equal, in each other's image.

stature equal to Apsu's emissary Mummu; this brings to mind the many similarities between Mercury and Pluto. Gaga, then, was Pluto; but the Sumerians placed Pluto on their celestial map not beyond Neptune, but next to Saturn, whose "emissary," or satellite, it was (Fig. 105).

As Act I of the "Epic of Creation" came to an end, there was a Solar System made up of the Sun and nine planets:

SUN—*Apsu,* "one who existed from the beginning."
MERCURY—*Mummu,* counselor and emissary of Apsu.
VENUS—*Lahamu,* "lady of battles."
MARS—*Lahmu,* "deity of war."
??—*Tiamat,* "maiden who gave life."
JUPITER—*Kishar,* "foremost of firm lands."
SATURN—*Anshar,* "foremost of the heavens."
PLUTO—*Gaga,* counselor and emissary of Anshar.
URANUS—*Anu,* "he of the heavens."
NEPTUNE—*Nudimmud (Ea),* "artful creator."

Where were Earth and the Moon? They were yet to be created, products of the forthcoming cosmic collision.

With the end of the majestic drama of the birth of the planets, the authors of the Creation epic now raise the curtain on Act II, on a drama of celestial turmoil. The newly created family of planets was far from being stable. The planets were gravitating toward each other; they were converging on Tiamat, disturbing and endangering the primordial bodies.

> The divine brothers banded together;
> They disturbed Tiamat as they surged back and forth.
> They were troubling the "belly" of Tiamat
> By their antics in the dwellings of heaven.
> Apsu could not lessen their clamor;
> Tiamat was speechless at their ways.
> Their doings were loathsome. . . .
> Troublesome were their ways.

We have here obvious references to erratic orbits. The new planets "surged back and forth"; they got too close to each other ("banded together"); they interfered with Tiamat's orbit; they got too close to her "belly"; their "ways" were troublesome. Though it was Tiamat that was principally endangered, Apsu, too, found the planets' ways "loathsome." He announced his intention to "destroy, wreck their ways." He huddled with Mummu, conferred with him in secret. But "whatever they had plotted between them" was overheard by the gods, and the plot to destroy them left them speechless. The only one who did not lose his wits was Ea. He devised a ploy to "pour sleep upon Apsu." When the other celestial gods liked the plan, Ea "drew a faithful map of the universe" and cast a divine spell upon the primeval waters of the Solar System.

What was this "spell" or force exerted by "Ea" (the planet Neptune)—then the outermost planet—as it orbited the Sun and circled all the other planets? Did its own orbit around the Sun affect the Sun's magnetism and thus its radioactive outpourings? Or did Neptune itself emit, upon its creation, some vast radiations of energy? Whatever the effects were, the epic likened them to a "pouring of sleep"—a calming effect—upon Apsu (the Sun). Even "Mummu, the Counsellor, was powerless to stir."

As in the biblical tale of Samson and Delilah, the hero—overcome by sleep—could easily be robbed of his powers. Ea moved quickly to rob Apsu of his creative role. Quenching, it seems, the immense outpourings of primeval matter from the Sun, Ea/Neptune "pulled off Apsu's tiara, removed his cloak of aura." Apsu was "vanquished." Mummu could no longer roam about. He was "bound and left behind," a lifeless planet by his master's side.

By depriving the Sun of its creativity—stopping the process of emitting more energy and matter to form additional planets—the gods brought temporary peace to the Solar System. The victory was further signified by changing the meaning and location of the Apsu. This epithet was henceforth to be applied to the "Abode of Ea." Any additional planets could henceforth come only from the new Apsu—from "the Deep"—the far reaches of space that the outermost planet faced.

How long was it before the celestial peace was broken once more? The epic does not say. But it does continue, with little pause, and raises the curtain on Act III:

> In the Chamber of Fates, the place of Destinies,
> A god was engendered, most able and wisest of gods;
> In the heart of the Deep was MARDUK created.

A new celestial "god"—a new planet—now joins the cast. He was formed in the Deep, far out in space, in a zone where orbital motion—a planet's "destiny"—had been imparted to him. He was attracted to the Solar System by the outermost planet: "He who begot him was Ea" (Neptune). The new planet was a sight to behold:

> Alluring was his figure, sparkling the lift of his eyes;
> Lordly was his gait, commanding as of olden times. . . .
> Greatly exalted was he above the gods, exceeding
>   throughout. . . .

He was the loftiest of the gods, surpassing was his
    height;
His members were enormous, he was exceedingly tall.

Appearing from outer space, Marduk was still a newborn planet, belching fire and emitting radiation. "When he moved his lips, fire blazed forth."

As Marduk neared the other planets, "they heaped upon him their awesome flashes," and he shone brightly, "clothed with the halo of ten gods." His approach thus stirred up electrical and other emissions from the other members of the Solar System. And a single word here confirms our decipherment of the Creation epic: *Ten* celestial bodies awaited him—the Sun and only nine other planets.

The epic's narrative now takes us along Marduk's speeding course. He first passes by the planet that "begot" him, that pulled him into the Solar System, the planet Ea/Neptune. As Marduk nears Neptune, the latter's gravitational pull on the newcomer grows in intensity. It rounds out Marduk's path, "making it good for its purpose."

Marduk must still have been in a very plastic stage at that time. As he passed by Ea/Neptune, the gravitational pull caused the side of Marduk to bulge, as though he had "a second head." No part of Marduk, however, was torn off at this passage; but as Marduk reached the vicinity of Anu/Uranus, chunks of matter began to tear away from him, resulting in the formation of four satellites of Marduk. "Anu brought forth and fashioned the four sides, consigned their power to the leader of the host." Called "winds," the four were thrust into a fast orbit around Marduk, "swirling as a whirlwind."

The order of passage—first by Neptune, then by Uranus—indicates that Marduk was coming into the Solar System not in the system's orbital direction (counterclockwise) but from the opposite direction, moving clockwise. Moving on, the oncoming planet was soon seized by the immense gravitational and magnetic forces of the giant Anshar/ Saturn, then Kishar/Jupiter. His path was bent even more inward—into the center of the Solar System, toward Tiamat (Fig. 106).

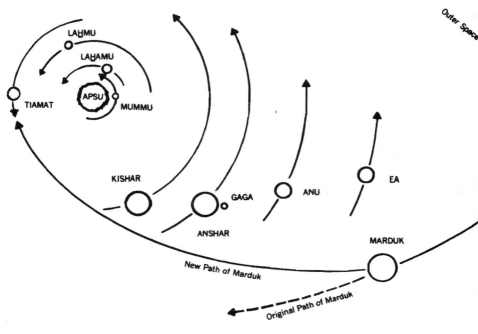

Fig. 106

The approach of Marduk soon began to disturb Tiamat and the inner planets (Mars, Venus, Mercury). "He produced streams, disturbed Tiamat; the gods were not at rest, carried as in a storm."

Though the lines of the ancient text were partially damaged here, we can still read that the nearing planet "diluted their vitals . . . pinched their eyes." Tiamat herself "paced about distraught"—her orbit, evidently, disturbed.

The gravitational pull of the large approaching planet soon began to tear away parts of Tiamat. From her midst there emerged eleven "monsters," a "growling, raging" throng of satellites who "separated themselves" from her body and "marched at the side of Tiamat." Preparing herself to face the onrushing Marduk, Tiamat "crowned them with halos," giving them the appearance of "gods" (planets).

Of particular importance to the epic and to Mesopotamian cosmogony was Tiamat's chief satellite, who was named KINGU, "the firstborn among the gods who formed her assembly."

> She exalted Kingu,
> In their midst she made him great. . . .
> The high command of the battle
> She entrusted into his hand.

Subjected to conflicting gravitational pulls, this large satellite of Tiamat began to shift toward Marduk. It was this granting to Kingu of a Tablet of Destinies—a planetary path of his own—that especially upset the outer planets. Who had granted Tiamat the right to bring forth new planets? Ea asked. He took the problem to Anshar, the giant Saturn.

> All that Tiamat had plotted, to him he repeated:
> ". . . she has set up an Assembly and is furious with
>   rage.
> She has added matchless weapons, has borne
>   monster-gods.
> Withal eleven of this kind she has brought forth;
> from among the gods who formed her Assembly,
> she has elevated Kingu, her firstborn, made him chief
>   . . .
> she has given him a Tablet of Destinies, fastened it
> on his breast."

Turning to Ea, Anshar asked him whether he could go to slay Kingu. The reply is lost due to a break in the tablets; but apparently Ea did not satisfy Anshar, for the continuing narrative has Anshar turning to Anu (Uranus) to find out whether he would "go and stand up to Tiamat." But Anu "was unable to face her and turned back."

In the agitated heavens, a confrontation builds; one god after another steps aside. Will no one do battle with the raging Tiamat?

Marduk, having passed Neptune and Uranus, is now nearing Anshar (Saturn) and his extended rings. This gives Anshar an idea: "He who is potent shall be our Avenger; he who is keen in battle: Marduk, the Hero!" Coming within reach of Saturn's rings ("he kissed the lips of Anshar"), Marduk answers:

> "If I, indeed, as your Avenger
> Am to vanquish Tiamat, save your lives—
> Convene an Assembly to proclaim my Destiny
>   supreme!"

The condition was audacious but simple: Marduk and his "destiny"— his orbit around the Sun—were to be supreme among all the celestial gods. It was then that Gaga, Anshar/Saturn's satellite—and the future Pluto—was loosened from his course:

> Anshar opened his mouth,
> To Gaga, his Counsellor, a word he
>   addressed . . .
> "Be on thy way, Gaga,
> take the stand before the gods,
> and that which I shall tell thee
> repeat thou unto them."

Passing by the other god/planets, Gaga urged them to "fix your decrees for Marduk." The decision was as anticipated: The gods were only too eager to have someone else go to settle the score for them. "Marduk is king!" they shouted, and urged him to lose no more time: "Go and cut off the life of Tiamat!"

The curtain now rises on Act IV, the celestial battle.

The gods have decreed Marduk's "destiny"; their combined gravitational pull has now determined Marduk's orbital path so that he can go but one way—toward a "battle," a collision with Tiamat.

As befits a warrior, Marduk armed himself with a variety of weapons. He filled his body with a "blazing flame"; "he constructed a bow . . . attached thereto an arrow . . . in front of him he set the lightning"; and "he then made a net to enfold Tiamat therein." These are common names for what could only have been celestial phenomena—the discharge of electrical bolts as the two planets converged, the gravitational pull (a "net") of one upon the other.

But Marduk's chief weapons were his satellites, the four "winds" with which Uranus had provided him when Marduk passed by that planet: South Wind, North Wind, East Wind, West Wind. Passing now by the giants, Saturn and Jupiter, and subjected to their tremendous gravitational pull, Marduk "brought forth" three more satellites—Evil Wind, Whirlwind, and Matchless Wind.

Using his satellites as a "storm chariot," he "sent forth the winds that he had brought forth, the seven of them." The adversaries were ready for battle.

> The Lord went forth, followed his course;
> Towards the raging Tiamat he set his face. . . .
> The Lord approached to scan the innerside of
>   Tiamat—
> The scheme of Kingu, her consort, to perceive.

But as the planets drew nearer each other, Marduk's course became erratic:

> As he looks on, his course becomes upset,
> His direction is distracted, his doings are confused.

Even Marduk's satellites began to veer off course:

> When the gods, his helpers,
> Who were marching at his side,
> Saw the valiant Kingu, blurred became their vision.

Were the combatants to miss each other after all?

But the die was cast, the courses irrevocably set on collision. "Tiamat emitted a roar" . . . "the Lord raised the flooding storm, his mighty weapon." As Marduk came ever closer, Tiamat's "fury" grew; "the roots of her legs shook back and forth." She commenced to cast "spells" against Marduk—the same kind of celestial waves Ea had earlier used against Apsu and Mummu. But Marduk kept coming at her.

> Tiamat and Marduk, the wisest of the gods,
> Advanced against one another;
> They pressed on to single combat,
> They approached for battle.

The epic now turns to the description of the celestial battle, in the aftermath of which Heaven and Earth were created.

> The Lord spread out his net to enfold her;
> The Evil Wind, the rearmost, he unleashed at her face.
> As she opened her mouth, Tiamat, to devour him—
> He drove in the Evil Wind so that she close not her
>   lips.
> The fierce storm Winds then charged her belly;
> Her body became distended; her mouth had opened
>   wide.
> He shot there through an arrow, it tore her belly;
> It cut through her insides, tore into her womb.
> Having thus subdued her, her life-breath he
>   extinguished.

Here, then, (Fig. 107) is a most original theory explaining the celestial puzzles still confronting us. An unstable Solar System, made up of the Sun and nine planets, was invaded by a large, comet-like planet from outer space. It first encountered Neptune; as it passed by Uranus, the giant Saturn, and Jupiter, its course was profoundly bent inward toward the Solar System's center, and it brought forth seven satellites. It was unalterably set on a collision course with Tiamat, the next planet in line.

But the two planets did not collide, a fact of cardinal astronomical importance: It was the satellites of Marduk that smashed into Tiamat, and not Marduk himself. They "distended" Tiamat's body, made in her a wide cleavage. Through these fissures in Tiamat, Marduk shot an "arrow," a "divine lightning," an immense bolt of electricity that jumped as a spark from the energy-charged Marduk, the planet that was "filled with brilliance." Finding its way into Tiamat's innards, it "extinguished

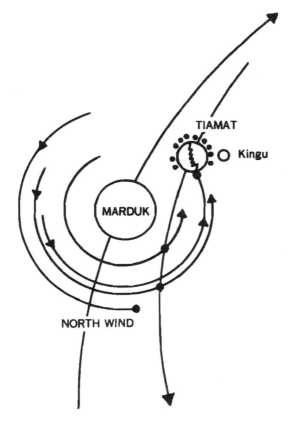

Fig. 107. THE CELESTIAL BATTLE
(A) Marduk's "winds" colliding with Tiamat and her "host" (led by Kingu).

her life-breath"—neutralized Tiamat's own electric and magnetic forces and fields, and "extinguished" them.

The first encounter between Marduk and Tiamat left her fissured and lifeless; but her final fate was still to be determined by future encounters between the two. Kingu, leader of Tiamat's satellites, was also to be dealt with separately. But the fate of the other ten, smaller satellites of Tiamat was determined at once.

> After he had slain Tiamat, the leader,
> Her band was shattered, her host broken up.
> The gods, her helpers who marched at her side,
> Trembling with fear,

> Turned their backs about so as to save and preserve
> their lives.

Can we identify this "shattered . . . broken" host that trembled and "turned their backs about"—reversed their direction?

By doing so we offer an explanation to yet another puzzle of our Solar System—the phenomenon of the comets. Tiny globes of matter, they are often referred to as the Solar System's "rebellious members," for they appear to obey none of the normal rules of the road. The orbits of the planets around the Sun are (with the exception of Pluto) almost circular; the orbits of the comets are elongated, and in most instances very much so—to the extent that some of them disappear from our view for hundreds or thousands of years. The planets (with the exception of Pluto) orbit the Sun in the same general plane; the comets' orbits lie in many diverse planes. Most significant, while all the planets known to us circle the Sun in the same counterclockwise direction, many comets move in the reverse direction.

Astronomers are unable to say what force, what event created the comets and threw them into their unusual orbits. Our answer: Marduk. Sweeping in the reverse direction, in an orbital plane of his own, he shattered, broke the host of Tiamat into smaller comets and affected them by his gravitational pull, his so-called net:

> Thrown into the net, they found themselves
> ensnared. . . .
> The whole band of demons that had marched on
> her side
> He cast into fetters, their hands he bound. . . .
> Tightly encircled, they could not escape.

After the battle was over, Marduk took away from Kingu the Tablet of Destinies (Kingu's independent orbit) and attached it to his own (Marduk's) breast: his course was bent into permanent solar orbit. From that time on, Marduk was bound always to return to the scene of the celestial battle.

Having "vanquished" Tiamat, Marduk sailed on in the heavens, out into space, around the Sun, and back to retrace his passage by the outer planets: Ea/Neptune, "whose desire Marduk achieved," Anshar/ Saturn, "whose triumph Marduk established." Then his new orbital path returned Marduk to the scene of his triumph, "to strengthen his hold on the vanquished gods," Tiamat and Kingu.

As the curtain is about to rise on Act V, it will be here—and only here, though this has not hitherto been realized—that the biblical tale of Genesis joins the Mesopotamian "Epic of Creation"; for it is only at this point that the tale of the Creation of Earth and Heaven really began.

Completing his first-ever orbit around the Sun, Marduk "then returned to Tiamat, whom he had subdued."

> The Lord paused to view her lifeless body.
> To divide the monster he then artfully planned.
> Then, as a mussel, he split her into two parts.

Marduk himself now hit the defeated planet, splitting Tiamat in two, severing her "skull," or upper part. Then another of Marduk's satellites, the one called North Wind, crashed into the separated half. The heavy blow carried this part—destined to become Earth—to an orbit where no planet had been orbiting before:

> The Lord trod upon Tiamat's hinder part;
> With his weapon the connected skull he cut
>   loose;
> He severed the channels of her blood;
> And caused the North Wind to bear it
> To places that have been unknown.

Earth had been created!

The lower part had another fate: on the second orbit, Marduk himself hit it, smashing it to pieces (Fig. 108):

> The [other] half of her he set up as a screen for the skies:
> Locking them together, as watchmen he stationed
>   them. . . .
> He bent Tiamat's tail to form the Great Band as a
>   bracelet.

The pieces of this broken half were hammered to become a "bracelet" in the heavens, acting as a screen between the inner planets and the outer planets. They were stretched out into a "great band." The asteroid belt had been created.

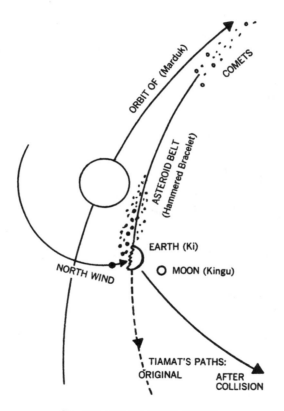

Fig. 108. THE CELESTIAL BATTLE

(B) Tiamat has been split: its shattered half is the Heaven—the Asteroid Belt; the other half, Earth, is thrust to a new orbit by Marduk's satellite "North Wind." Tiamat's chief satellite, Kingu, becomes Earth's Moon; her other satellites now make up the comets.

Astronomers and physicists recognize the existence of great differences between the inner, or "terrestrial," planets (Mercury, Venus, Earth and its Moon, and Mars) and the outer planets (Jupiter and beyond), two groups separated by the asteroid belt. We now find, in the Sumerian epic, ancient recognition of these phenomena.

Moreover, we are offered—for the first time—a coherent cosmogonic-scientific explanation of the celestial events that led to the disappearance of the "missing planet" and the resultant creation of the asteroid belt (plus the comets) and of Earth. After several of his satellites and his electric bolts split Tiamat in two, another satellite of Marduk shunted her upper half to a new orbit as our planet Earth; then Marduk, on his second orbit, smashed the lower half to pieces and stretched them in a great celestial band.

Every puzzle that we have mentioned is answered by the "Epic of Creation" as we have deciphered it. Moreover, we also have the answer to the question of why Earth's continents are concentrated on one side of it and a deep cavity (the Pacific Ocean's bed) exists on the opposite side. The constant reference to the "waters" of Tiamat is also illuminating. She was called the Watery Monster, and it stands to reason that Earth, as part of Tiamat, was equally endowed with these waters. Indeed, some modern scholars describe Earth as "Planet Ocean"—for it is the only one of the Solar System's known planets that is blessed with such life-giving waters.

New as these cosmologic theories may sound, they were accepted fact to the prophets and sages whose words fill the Old Testament. The prophet Isaiah recalled "the primeval days" when the might of the Lord "carved the Haughty One, made spin the watery monster, dried up the waters of *Tehom-Raba.*" Calling the Lord Yahweh "my primeval king," the Psalmist rendered in a few verses the cosmogony of the epic of Creation. "By thy might, the waters thou didst disperse; the leader of the watery monsters thou didst break up." Job recalled how this celestial Lord also smote "the assistants of the Haughty One"; and with impressive astronomical sophistication exalted the Lord who:

> The hammered canopy stretched out in the place of
> *Tehom,*
> The Earth suspended in the void. . . .
> His powers the waters did arrest,
> His energy the Haughty One did cleave;
> His Wind the Hammered Bracelet measured out;
> His hand the twisting dragon did extinguish.

Biblical scholars now recognize that the Hebrew *Tehom* ("watery deep") stems from Tiamat; that *Tehom-Raba* means "great Tiamat," and that the biblical understanding of primeval events is based upon the Sumerian cosmologic epics. It should also be clear that first and foremost among these parallels are the opening verses of the Book of Genesis, describing how the Wind of the Lord hovered over the waters of *Tehom,* and how the lightning of the Lord (Marduk in the Babylonian version) lit the darkness of space as it hit and split Tiamat, creating Earth and the *Rakia* (literally, "the hammered bracelet"). This celestial band (hitherto translated as "firmament") is called "the Heaven."

The Book of Genesis (1:8) explicitly states that it is this "hammered out bracelet" that the Lord had named "heaven" (*shamaim*). The Akkadian texts also called this celestial zone "the hammered bracelet" (*rakkis*), and describe how Marduk stretched out Tiamat's lower part until he brought it end to end, fastened into a permanent great circle. The Sumerian sources leave no doubt that the specific "heaven," as distinct from the general concept of heavens and space, was the asteroid belt.

Our Earth and the asteroid belt are the "Heaven and Earth" of both Mesopotamian and biblical references, created when Tiamat was dismembered by the celestial Lord.

After Marduk's North Wind had pushed Earth to its new celestial location, Earth obtained its own orbit around the Sun (resulting in our seasons) and received its axial spin (giving us day and night). The Mesopotamian texts claim that one of Marduk's tasks after he created Earth was, indeed, to have "allotted [to Earth] the days of the Sun and established the precincts of day and night." The biblical concepts are identical:

And God said:
"Let there be Lights in the hammered Heaven,
to divide between the Day and the Night;
and let them be celestial signs
and for Seasons and for Days and for Years."

Modern scholars believe that after Earth became a planet it was a hot ball of belching volcanoes, filling the skies with mists and clouds. As temperatures began to cool, the vapors turned to water, separating the face of Earth into dry land and oceans.

The fifth tablet of *Enuma Elish,* though badly mutilated, imparts exactly the same scientific information. Describing the gushing lava as Tiamat's "spittle," the Creation epic correctly places this phenomenon before the formation of the atmosphere, the oceans of Earth, and the continents. After the "cloud waters were gathered," the oceans began to form, and the "foundations" of Earth—its continents—were raised. As "the making of cold"—a cooling off—took place, rain and mist appeared. Meanwhile, the "spittle" continued to pour forth, "laying in layers," shaping Earth's topography.

Once again, the biblical parallel is clear:

And God said:
"Let the waters under the skies be gathered
    together,
unto one place, and let dry land appear."
And it was so.

Earth, with oceans, continents, and an atmosphere, was now ready for the formation of mountains, rivers, springs, valleys. Attributing all Creation to the Lord Marduk, *Enuma Elish* continued the narration:

Putting Tiamat's head [Earth] into position,
He raised the mountains thereon.
He opened springs, the torrents to draw off.

> Through her eyes he released the Tigris and
> Euphrates.
> From her teats he formed the lofty mountains,
> Drilled springs for wells, the water to carry off.

In perfect accord with modern findings, both the Book of Genesis and *Enuma Elish* and other related Mesopotamian texts place the beginning of life upon Earth in the waters, followed by the "living creatures that swarm" and "fowl that fly." Not until then did "living creatures after their kind: cattle and creeping things and beasts" appear upon Earth, culminating with the appearance of Man—the final act of Creation.

As part of the new celestial order upon Earth, Marduk "made the divine Moon appear . . . designated him to mark the night, define the days every month."

Who was this celestial god? The text calls him SHESH.KI ("celestial god who protects Earth"). There is no mention earlier in the epic of a planet by this name; yet there he is, "within *her* heavenly pressure [gravitational field]." And who is meant by "her": Tiamat or Earth?

The roles of, and references to, Tiamat and Earth appear to be interchangeable. Earth is Tiamat reincarnated. The Moon is called Earth's "protector"; that is exactly what Tiamat called Kingu, her chief satellite.

The Creation epic specifically excludes Kingu from the "host" of Tiamat that were shattered and scattered and put into reverse motion around the Sun as comets. After Marduk completed his own first orbit and returned to the scene of the battle, he decreed Kingu's separate fate:

> And Kingu, who had become chief among them,
> He made shrink;
> As god DUG.GA.E he counted him.
> He took from him the Tablet of Destinies,
> Not rightfully his.

Marduk, then, did not destroy Kingu. He punished him by taking away his independent orbit, which Tiamat had granted him as he grew in size. Shrunk to a smaller size, Kingu remained a "god"—a planetary member of our Solar System. Without an orbit he could only become a satellite again. As Tiamat's upper part was thrown into a new orbit (as the new planet Earth), we suggest, Kingu was pulled along. Our Moon, we suggest, is Kingu, Tiamat's former satellite.

Transformed into a celestial *duggae*, Kingu had been stripped of his "vital" elements—atmosphere, waters, radioactive matter; he shrank in size and became "a mass of lifeless clay." These Sumerian terms fittingly describe our lifeless Moon, its recently discovered history, and the fate that befell this satellite that started out as KIN.GU ("great emissary") and ended up as DUG.GA.E ("pot of lead").

L. W. King (*The Seven Tablets of Creation*) reported the existence of three fragments of an astronomical-mythological tablet that presented another version of Marduk's battle with Tiamat, which included verses that dealt with the manner in which Marduk dispatched Kingu. "Kingu, her spouse, with a weapon not of war he cut away . . . the Tablets of Destiny from Kingu he took in his hand." A further attempt, by B. Landesberger (in 1923, in the *Archiv für Keilschriftforschung*), to edit and fully translate the text, demonstrated the interchangeability of the names Kingu/Ensu/Moon.

Such texts not only confirm our conclusion that Tiamat's main satellite became our Moon; they also explain NASA's findings regarding a huge collision "when celestial bodies the size of large cities came crashing into the Moon." Both the NASA findings and the text discovered by L. W. King describe the Moon as the "planet that was laid waste."

Cylinder seals have been found that depict the celestial battle, showing Marduk fighting a fierce female deity. One such depiction shows Marduk shooting his lightning at Tiamat, with Kingu, clearly identified as the Moon, trying to protect Tiamat, his creator (Fig. 109).

This pictorial evidence that Earth's Moon and Kingu were the same satellite is further enhanced by the etymological fact that the name of the god SIN, in later times associated with the Moon, derived from SU.EN ("lord of wasteland").

Fig. 109

Having disposed of Tiamat and Kingu, Marduk once again "crossed the heavens and surveyed the regions." This time his attention was focused on "the dwelling of Nudimmud" (Neptune), to fix a final "destiny" for Gaga, the erstwhile satellite of Anshar/Saturn who was made an "emissary" to the other planets.

The epic informs us that as one of his final acts in the heavens, Marduk assigned this celestial god "to a hidden place," a hitherto unknown orbit facing "the deep" (outer space), and entrusted to him the "counsellorship of the Watery Deep." In line with his new position, the planet was renamed US.MI ("one who shows the way"), the outermost planet, our Pluto.

According to the Creation epic, Marduk had at one point boasted, "The ways of the celestial gods I will artfully alter . . . into two groups shall they be divided."

Indeed he did. He eliminated from the heavens the Sun's first partner-in-Creation, Tiamat. He brought Earth into being, thrusting it into a new orbit nearer the Sun. He hammered a "bracelet" in the

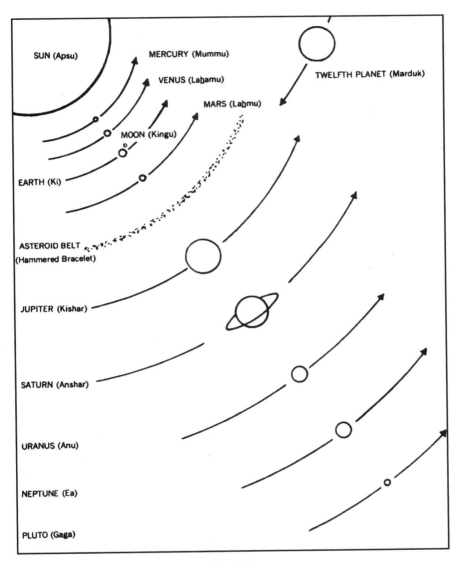

Fig. 110

heavens—the asteroid belt that does separate the group of inner planets from the group of outer planets [Fig. 110]. He turned most of Tiamat's satellites into comets; her chief satellite, Kingu, he put into orbit around Earth to become the Moon. And he shifted a satellite of Saturn, Gaga, to become the planet Pluto, imparting to it some of Marduk's own orbital characteristics (such as a different orbital plane).

The puzzles of our Solar System—the oceanic cavities upon Earth, the devastation upon the Moon, the reverse orbits of the comets, the enigmatic phenomena of Pluto—all are perfectly answered by the Mesopotamian Creation epic, as deciphered by us.

Having thus "constructed the stations" for the planets, Marduk took for himself "Station Nibiru," and "crossed the heavens and surveyed" the new Solar System. It was now made up of twelve celestial bodies, with twelve Great Gods as their counterparts (Fig. 110).

5
Is it Nibiru?

Unpublished Article, Written in 1997

A large part of the puzzle of the Anunnaki concerns their home planet, Nibiru. The orbit of Nibiru is often difficult to understand, given that it differs from the planets we are more familiar with in our solar system. And although Nibiru is unusual in comparison to these other planets, it is not unique in its elliptical orbit or retrograde direction. Recent scientific discoveries, even since the publication of *The 12th Planet* in 1976, have supported many of the conclusions that Sitchin has made about this enigmatic body, home to the ancient visitors to Earth.

WHEN THE COMET HALE-BOPP was discovered last year, I received many urgent calls from anxious fans and media representatives; their key question: "Is it Nibiru?"

No, I said, it is not Nibiru (the planet of the Anunnaki); but many aspects of Hale-Bopp do point to some association with Nibiru—first and foremost its orbital period of "between 3,000 and 4,000 years," according to astronomers—or the equivalent of the 3,600-year orbit of Nibiru established by me from Sumerian texts. Another point of similarity was the retrograde or clockwise orbit of the comet; this is contrary to the general orbital direction in the solar system—but the very same orbital direction as that of Nibiru.

I was asked the same question at the beginning of June (1997)—this time not so much from fans (who mostly were unaware of happenings) as from an increasingly alert media. "Is it Nibiru?" I was asked—this time in respect to a newly discovered celestial body bearing the uninspiring name "1996 TL66" . . . .

Although discovered back in October 1996, and although already reported in an astronomical circular in January 1997, it did not make waves until the *Los Angeles Times* splashed the news, with color diagrams and celestial photographs, on June 5, 1997 (based on an about-to-be-published study in the magazine *Nature*). ASTRONOMERS PONDER AN UNUSUAL OBJECT'S BEHAVIOR ON THE EDGE was the headline. The article by the paper's science writer highlighted the "newly discovered object, the most far-out member of the solar system yet seen by astronomers. It approaches the Sun only as far as the orbit of Pluto, then swings outward in a highly stretched orbit." Described as a "Texas-sized body orbiting the farthest reaches of our solar system," it was said to be "too big to be a comet and not quite a proper planet." (Initial data given: an orbital period of about 780 Earth-years, a maximal distance of some 12 billion miles from the Sun, and a diameter of some 300 miles).

If Nibiru is about three or four times the size of Earth, as I have estimated based on Sumerian data and as Dr. Harrington of the U.S. Naval Observatory did based on his own findings, "1996 TL66" is not Nibiru. But it does corroborate ancient astronomical knowledge and the sophisticated cosmogony that formed the scientific basis of the Sumerian Epic of Creation.

It corroborates (contrary to hitherto held notions) that the solar system can have members that far out, and with vast elliptical (rather than more or less circular) orbits. The ancient text states that as Nibiru, appearing from elsewhere, passed near Neptune, it started to acquire satellites moons. Well, that is where the newly found object seems to make its home.

Did the Sumerians know what they were writing about? To find the answer, watch the daily headlines. . . .

6
God the Extraterrestrial

Selection from
Divine Encounters (Endpaper)

One of the Hebrew words for God used in the Hebrew Bible is Eluhaynu. Its plural, Elohim, is used in the Bible as well. A major question for those who study the Hebrew Bible is this: If the Anunnaki are the Elohim of the Bible, then who is "the creator of all"? Who is Yahweh? Is the God worshipped in the Bible a specific member of the Anunnaki cohort on Earth, or a collection of many of them—as the use of Elohim (plural) instead of Eluhaynu (singular) might imply? Or is there another entity altogether that is the unseen god of the Hebrew Bible? Through a process of deduction, Sitchin examines the attributes and qualities of various descendants of the original Anunnaki on Earth to determine who the real Yahweh might be. Read the excerpt below to help you decide.

SO, WHO WAS YAHWEH?

Was He one of *them?* Was He an extraterrestrial?

The question, with its implied answer, is not so outrageous. Unless we deem Yahweh—"God" to all whose religious beliefs are founded on the Bible—to have been one of us Earthlings, then He could only be not of this Earth—which "extraterrestrial" ("outside of, not from

125

Terra") means. And the story of Man's Divine Encounters, the subject of this book, is so filled with parallels between the biblical experiences and those of encounters with the Anunnaki by other ancient peoples, that the possibility that Yahweh was one of "them" must be seriously considered.

The question and its implied answer, indeed, arise inevitably. That the biblical creation narrative with which the Book of Genesis begins draws upon the Mesopotamian *Enuma elish* is beyond dispute. That the biblical *Eden* is a rendering of the Sumerian E. DIN is almost self-evident. That the tale of the Deluge and Noah and the ark is based on the Akkadian *Atra-Hasis* texts and the earlier Sumerian Deluge tale in the *Epic of Gilgamesh,* is certain. That the plural "us" in the creation of *The Adam* segments reflects the Sumerian and Akkadian record of the discussions by the leaders of the Anunnaki that led to the genetic engineering that brought *Homo sapiens* about, should be obvious.

In the Mesopotamian versions it is Enki, the Chief Scientist, who suggests the genetic engineering to create the Earthling to serve as a Primitive Worker, and it had to be Enki whom the Bible quotes as saying "Let us make the Adam in our likeness and after our image." An Epithet of Enki was NU. DIM.MUD, "He who fashions;" the Egyptians likewise called Enki *Ptah*—"The Developer," "He who fashions things," and depicted him as fashioning Man out of clay, as a potter. "The Fashioner of the Adam," the Prophets repeatedly called Yahweh ("fashioner," not "creator"!); and comparing Yahweh to a potter fashioning Man of clay was a frequent biblical simile.

As the master biologist, Enki's emblem was that of the Entwined Serpents, representing the double-helixed DNA—the genetic code that enabled Enki to perform the genetic mixing that brought about The Adam; and then (which is the story of Adam and Eve in the Garden of Eden) to again genetically manipulate the new hybrids and enable them to procreate. One of Enki's Sumerian epithets was BUZUR; it meant both "He who solves secrets" and "He of the mines," for the knowledge of mineralogy was considered knowledge of Earth's secrets, the secrets of its dark depths.

The biblical tale of Adam and Eve in the Garden of Eden—the tale of the second genetic manipulation—assigns to the serpent the role of triggering their acquisition of "knowing" (the biblical term for sexual procreation). The Hebrew term for serpent is *Nahash;* and interestingly, the same word also means soothsayer, "He who solves secrets"—the very same second meaning of Enki's epithet. Moreover, the term stems from the same root as the Hebrew word for the mineral copper, *Nehoshet.* It was a *Nahash Nehoshet,* a copper serpent, that Moses fashioned and held up to stop an epidemic that was afflicting the Israelites during the Exodus; and our analysis leaves no alternative but to conclude that what he had made to summon divine intervention was an emblem of Enki. A passage in II Kings 18:4 reveals that this copper serpent, whom the people nicknamed *Nehushtan* (a play on the triple meaning serpent-copper-solver of secrets) had been kept in the Temple of Yahweh in Jerusalem for almost seven centuries, until the time of King Hezekiah.

Pertinent to this aspect might have been the fact that when Yahweh turned the shepherd's crook that Moses held into a magical staff, the first miracle performed with it was to turn it into a serpent. *Was Yahweh, then, one and the same as Enki?*

The combination of biology with mineralogy and with the ability to solve secrets reflected Enki's status as the god of knowledge and sciences, of the Earth's hidden metals; he was the one who set up the mining operations in southeastern Africa. All these aspects were attributes of Yahweh. "It is Yahweh who giveth wisdom, out of His mouth cometh knowledge and understanding," Proverbs asserted (2:6), and it was He who granted wisdom beyond comparison to Solomon, as Enki had given the Wise Adapa. "The gold is mine and the silver is mine," Yahweh announced (Haggai 2:8); "I shall give thee the treasures of the darkness and the hidden riches of the secret places," Yahweh promised Cyrus (Isaiah 45:3).

The clearest congruence between the Mesopotamian and biblical narratives is found in the story of the Deluge. In the Mesopotamian versions it is Enki who goes out of his way to warn his faithful follower Ziusudra/Utnapishtim of the coming catastrophe, instructs him to build the watertight ark, gives him its specifications and dimensions, and directs him to save the seed of animal life. In the Bible, all that is done by Yahweh.

The case for identifying Yahweh with Enki can be bolstered by examining the references to Enki's domains. After Earth was divided between the Enlilites and the Enki'ites (according to the Mesopotamian texts), Enki was granted dominion over Africa. Its regions included the *Apsu* (stemming from AB.ZU in Sumerian), the gold-mining region, where Enki had his principal abode (in addition to his "cult center" Eridu in Sumer). The term *Apsu*, we believe, explains the biblical term *Apsei-eretz*, usually translated "the ends of earth!"—the land at the continent's edge—southern Africa, as we understand it. In the Bible, this distant place, *Apsei-eretz*, is where "Yahweh shall judge" (I Samuel 2:10), where He shall rule when Israel is restored (Micah 5:3). Yahweh has thus been equated with Enki in his role as ruler of the Apsu.

This aspect of the similarities between Enki and Yahweh becomes more emphatic—and in one respect perhaps even embarrassingly so for the monotheistic Bible—when we reach a passage in the Book of Proverbs in which the unsurpassed greatness of Yahweh is brought out by rhetorical questions:

> Who hath ascended up to Heaven,
> and descended too?
> Who hath cupped the wind in his hands,
> and bound the waters as in a cloak?
> Who hath established the *Apsei-eretz*—
> What is his name,
> and what is his son's name—
> if thou can tell?

According to the Mesopotamian sources, when Enki divided the African continent among his sons, he granted the *Apsu* to his son Nergal. The polytheistic gloss (of asking the name of the Apsu's ruler and that of *his son*) can be explained only by an editorial inadvertent retention of a passage from the Sumerian original texts—the same gloss as had occurred in the use of "us" in "let us make the Adam" and in "let us come down" in the story of the Tower of Babel. The gloss in Proverbs (30:4) obviously substitutes "Yahweh" for Enki.

Was Yahweh, then, Enki in a biblical-Hebrew garb?

Were it so simple. . . . If we examine closely the tale of Adam and Eve in the Garden of Eden, we will find that while it is the *Nahash*—Enki's serpent guise as knower of biological secrets—who triggers the acquisition by Adam and Eve of the sexual "knowing" that enables them to have offspring, *he is not Yahweh but an antagonist of Yahweh* (as Enki was of Enlil). In the Sumerian texts it was Enlil who forced Enki to transfer some of the newly fashioned Primitive Workers (created to work in the gold mines of the *Apsu*) to the E.DIN in Mesopotamia, to engage in farming and shepherding. In the Bible, it is Yahweh who "took the Adam and placed him in the garden of Eden to tend it and to maintain it." It is Yahweh, not the serpent, who is depicted as the master of Eden who talks to Adam and Eve, discovers what they had done, and expels them. In all this, the Bible equates Yahweh not with Enki but with Enlil.

Indeed, in the very tale—the tale of the Deluge—where the identification of Yahweh with Enki appears the clearest, confusion in fact shows up. The roles are switched, and all of a sudden Yahweh plays the role not of Enki but of his rival Enlil. In the Mesopotamian original texts, it is Enlil who is unhappy with the way Mankind has turned out, who seeks its destruction by the approaching calamity, and who makes the other Anunnaki leaders swear to keep all that a secret from Mankind. In the biblical version (chapter 6 of Genesis), it is Yahweh who voices his unhappiness with Mankind and makes the decision to wipe Mankind off the face of the Earth.

In the tale's conclusion, as Ziusudra/Utnapishtim offers sacrifices on Mount Ararat, it is Enlil who is attracted by the pleasant smell of roasting meat and (with some persuasion) accepts the survival of Mankind, forgives Enki, and blesses Ziusudra and his wife. In Genesis, it is to Yahweh that Noah builds an altar and sacrifices animals on it, and it was Yahweh "who smelled the pleasant aroma."

So was Yahweh Enlil, after all?

A strong case can be made for such an identification. If there had been a "first among equals" as far as the two half brothers, sons of Anu, were concerned, the first was Enlil. Though it was Enki who was first to come to Earth, it was EN.LIL ("Lord of the Command") who took over as chief of the Anunnaki on Earth. It was a situation that corresponds to the statement in Psalms 97:9: "For thou, O Yahweh, art supreme over the whole Earth; most supreme art Thou over all the *Elohim*." The elevation of Enlil to this status is described in the *Atra-Hasis Epic* in the introductory verses, prior to the mutiny of the gold-mining Anunnaki:

> Anu, their father, was the ruler;
> Their commander was the hero Enlil.
> Their warrior was Ninurta;
> Their provider was Marduk.
>
> They all clasped hands together,
> cast lots and divided:
> Anu ascended to heaven;
> The Earth to Enlil was made subject.
> The bounded realm of the sea
> to princely Enki they had given.
> After Anu had gone up to heaven,
> Enki went down to the Apsu.

(Enki, interchangeably called in the Mesopotamian texts E.A.—"Whose home is water"—was thus the prototype of the sea god Poseidon of Greek mythology, the brother of Zeus who was head of the pantheon).

After Anu, the ruler on Nibiru, returned to Nibiru after visiting Earth, it was Enlil who summoned and presided over the council of the Great Anunnaki whenever major decisions had to be made. At various times of crucial decisions—such as to create The Adam, to divide the Earth into four regions, to institute Kingship as both buffer and liaison between the Anunnaki gods and Mankind, as well as in times of crisis between the Anunnaki themselves, when their rivalries erupted into wars and even use of nuclear weapons—"The Anunnaki who decree the fates sat exchanging their counsels." Typical was the manner in which one discussion is described in part: "Enki addressed to Enlil words of lauding: 'O one who is foremost among the brothers, Bull of Heaven, who the fate of Mankind holds.'" Except for the times when the debate got too heated and became a shouting match, the procedure was orderly, with Enlil turning to each member of the Council to let him or her have a say.

The monotheistic Bible lapses several times into describing Yahweh in like manner, chairing an assembly of lesser deities, usually called *Bnei-elim*—"sons of gods." The Book of Job begins its tale of the suffering of a righteous man by describing how the test of his faith in God was the result of a suggestion made by Satan "one day, when the sons of the *Elohim* came to present themselves before Yahweh." "The Lord stands in the assembly of the gods, among the *Elohim* He judges," we read in Psalms 82:1. "Give unto Yahweh, o sons of gods, give unto Yahweh glory and might," Psalms 29:1 stated, "bow to Yahweh, majestic in holiness." The requirement that even the "sons of the gods" bow to the Lord paralleled the Sumerian description of the status of Enlil as the Commander in Chief: "The Anunnaki humble themselves before him, the Igigi bow down willingly before him; they stand by faithfully for the instructions."

It is an image of Enlil that matches the exaltation in the Song of Miriam after the miraculous crossing of the Sea of Reeds: "Who is like thee among the gods, Yahweh? Who is like thee mighty in holiness, awesome in praises, the maker of miracles?" (Exodus 15:11).

As far as personal characters were concerned, Enki, the fashioner of Mankind, was more forebearing, less stringent with both gods and mortals. Enlil was stricter, a "law and order" type, uncompromising, unhesitant to mete out punishments when punishment was due. Perhaps it was because while Enki managed to get away with sexual promiscuities, Enlil, transgressing just once (when he date-raped a young nurse, in what turned out to be his seduction by her), was sentenced to exile (his banishment was lifted when he married her as his consort Ninlil). He viewed adversely the intermarriage between *Nefilim* and the "daughters of Man." When the evils of Mankind became overbearing, he was willing to see it perish by the Deluge. His strictness with other Anunnaki, even his own offspring, was illustrated when his son Nannar (the Moon god Sin) lamented the imminent desolation of his city Ur by the deathly nuclear cloud wafting from the Sinai. Harshly Enlil told him: "Ur was indeed granted Kingship; but an everlasting reign it was not granted."

Enlil's character had at the same time another side, a rewarding one. When the people carried out their tasks, when they were forthright and god-fearing, Enlil on his part saw to the needs of all, assured the land's and the people's well-being and prosperity. The Sumerians lovingly called him "Father Enlil" and "Shepherd of the teeming multitudes." A *Hymn to Enlil, the All-Beneficent* stated that without him "no cities would be built, no settlements founded; no stalls would be built, no sheepfolds erected; no king would be raised, no high priest born." The last statement recalled the fact that it was Enlil who had to approve the choice of kings, and by whom the line of Priesthood extended from the sacred precinct of the "cult center" Nippur.

These two characteristics of Enlil—strictness and punishment for transgressions, benevolence and protection when merited—are similar to how Yahweh has been pictured in the Bible. Yahweh can bless and Yahweh can accurse, the Book of Deuteronomy explicitly states (11:26). If the divine commandments shall be followed, the people and their offspring shall be blessed, their crops shall be plentiful, their livestock shall multiply, their enemies shall be defeated, they shall be successful in whatever trade they choose; but if they forsake Yahweh and his commandments, they, their homes and their fields shall be accursed and shall suffer afflictions, losses, deprivations, and famines (Deuteronomy 28). "Yahweh thy *Elohim* is a merciful God," Deuteronomy 4:31 stated; He is a vengeful God, the same Deuteronomy stated a chapter later (5:9). . . .

It was Yahweh who determined who shall be the priests; it was He who stated the rules for Kingship (Deuteronomy 17:16) and made clear that it will be He who chooses the king—as indeed was the case centuries after the Exodus, beginning with the selection of Saul and David. In all that, Yahweh and Enlil emulated each other.

Significant, too, for such a comparison was the importance of the numbers seven and fifty. They are not physiologically obvious numbers (we do not have seven fingers on a hand), nor does their combination fit natural phenomena (7 x 50 is 350, not the 365.25 days of a solar year). The "week" of seven days approximates the length of a lunar month (about 28.5 days) when multiplied by four, but where does the four come from? Yet the Bible introduced the count of seven, and the sanctity of the seventh day as the sacred Sabbath, from the very beginning of divine activity. The accursation of Cain was to last through seven times seven generations; Jericho was to be circled seven times so that its walls would fall down; many of the priestly rites were required to be repeated seven times, or to last seven days. Of a more lasting commandment, the New Year Festival was deliberately shifted from the first month Nisan to the seventh month Tishrei and the principal holidays were to last seven days.

The number fifty was the principal numerical feature in the construction and equipping of the Ark of the Covenant and the Tabernacle and an important element in the future Temple envisioned by Ezekiel. It was a calendrical count of days in priestly rites; Abraham persuaded the Lord to spare Sodom if fifty just men would be found there. More important, a major social and economic concept of a Jubilee Year in which slaves would be set free, real property would revert to its sellers and so on, was instituted. It was to be the fiftieth year: "Ye shall hallow the fiftieth year and proclaim freedom throughout the land," was the commandment in Leviticus chapter 25.

Both numbers, seven and fifty, were associated in Mesopotamia with Enlil. He was "the god who is seven" because, as the highest-ranking Anunnaki leader on Earth, he was in command of the planet, which was the seventh planet. And in the numerical hierarchy of the Anunnaki, in which Anu held the highest numeral 60, Enlil (as his intended successor on Nibiru) held the numerical rank of fifty (Enki's numerical rank was forty). Significantly, when Marduk took over the supremacy on Earth circa 2000 B.C., one of the measures taken to signify his ascendancy was to grant him fifty names, signifying his assumption of the Rank of Fifty.

The similarities between Yahweh and Enlil extend to other aspects. Though he might have been depicted on cylinder seals (which is not certain, since the representation might have been of his son Ninurta), he was by and large an unseen god, ensconced in the innermost chambers of his ziggurat or altogether away from Sumer. In a telltale passage in the *Hymn to Enlil, the All-Beneficent* it is thus said of him:

> When in his awesomeness he decrees the fates,
> no god dares look at him;
> Only to his exalted emissary, Nusku,
> the command, the word that is in his heart,
> does he make known.

No man can see me and live, Yahweh told Moses in a similar vein; and His words and commandments were known through Emissaries and Prophets.

While all these reasons for equating Yahweh with Enlil are fresh in the reader's mind, let us hasten to offer the contrary evidence that points to other, different identifications.

One of the most powerful biblical epithets for Yahweh is *El Shaddai*. Of an uncertain etymology, it assumed an aura of mystery and by medieval times became a code word for kabbalistic mysticism. Early Greek and Latin translators of the Hebrew Bible rendered *Shaddai* as "omnipotent," leading to the rendering of *El Shaddai* in the King James translation as "God Almighty" when the epithet appears in the tales of the Patriarchs (e.g. "And Yahweh appeared unto Abram and said to him: 'I am *El Shaddai*; walk before me and be thou perfect,'" in Genesis 17:1), or in Ezekiel, in Psalms, or several times in other books of the Bible.

Advances in the study of Akkadian in recent years suggest that the Hebrew word is related to *shaddu,* which means "mountain" in Akkadian; so that *El Shaddai* simply means "God of mountains." That this is a correct understanding of the biblical term is indicated by an incident reported in I Kings chapter 20. The Arameans, who were defeated in an attempt to invade Israel (Samaria), recouped their losses and a year later planned a second attack. To win this time, the Aramaean king's generals suggested that a ruse be used to lure the Israelites out of their mountain strongholds to a battlefield in the coastal plains. "Their god is a god of mountains," the generals told the king, "and that is why they prevailed over us; but if we shall fight them in a plain, we shall be the stronger ones."

Now, there is no way that Enlil could have been called, or reputed to be, a "god of mountains," for there are no mountains in the great plain that was (and still is) Mesopotamia. In the Enlilite domains the land that was called "Mountainland" was Asia Minor to the north, beginning with the Taurus ("Bull") mountains; and that was the region of Adad, Enlil's youngest son. His Sumerian name was ISH.KUR (and his "cult animal" was the bull), which meant "He of the mountain-land." The Sumerian ISH was rendered *shaddu* in Akkadian; so that *Il Shaddu* became the biblical *El Shaddai*.

Scholars speak of Adad, whom the Hittites called Teshub as a "storm god," always depicted with a lightning, thundering, and windblowing, and thus the god of rains. The Bible credited Yahweh with similar attributes. "When Yahweh uttereth His voice," Jeremiah said (10:13), "there is a rumbling of waters in the skies and storms come from the ends of the earth; He maketh lightnings with the rain, and blows a wind from its sources." The Psalms (135:7), the Book of Job, and other Prophets reaffirmed Yahweh's role as giver or withholder of rains, a role initially expounded to the Children of Israel during the Exodus.

While these attributes tarnish the similarities between Yahweh and Enlil, they should not carry us away to assume that, if so, Yahweh was the mirror image of Adad. The Bible recognized the existence of Hadad (as his name was spelled in Hebrew) as one of the "other gods" of other nations, not of Israel, and mentions various kings and princes (in the Aramean Damascus and other neighboring capitals) who were called Ben-Hadad ("Son of Adad"). In Palmyra (the biblical Tadmor), capital of eastern Syria, Adad's epithet was *Ba'al Shamin*, "Lord of Heaven," causing the Prophets to count him as just one of the Ba'al gods of neighboring nations who were an abomination in the eyes of Yahweh. There is no way, therefore, that Yahweh could have been one and the same as Adad.

The comparability between Yahweh and Enlil is further diminished by another important attribute of Yahweh, that of a warrior. "Yahweh goes forth like a warrior, like a hero He whips up His rage; He shall roar and cry out and over His enemies He shall prevail," Isaiah (42:13) stated, echoing the verse in the Song of Miriam that stated, "A Warrior is Yahweh" (Numbers chapter 15). Continuously, the Bible refers to and describes Yahweh as the "Lord of hosts," "Yahweh, the Lord of hosts, a warring army commands," Isaiah (13:4) declared. And Numbers 21:14 refers to a *Book of the Wars of Yahweh* in which the divine wars were recorded.

There is nothing in the Mesopotamian records that would suggest such an image for Enlil. The warrior *par excellence* was his son, Ninurta, who fought and defeated Zu, engaged in the Pyramid Wars with the Enki'ites, and fought and imprisoned Marduk in the Great Pyramid. His frequent epithets were "the warrior" and "the hero" and hymns to him hailed him as "Ninurta, Foremost Son, possessor of divine powers . . . Hero who in his hand the divine brilliant weapon carries." His feats as a warrior were described in an epic text whose Sumerian title was *Lugal-e Ud Melam-bi* that scholars have called *The Book of The Feats and Exploits of Ninurta.* Was it, one wonders, the enigmatic *Book of the Wars of Yahweh* of which the Bible spoke?

In other words, *could Yahweh have been Ninurta?*

As Foremost Son and heir apparent of Enlil, Ninurta too bore the numerical rank of fifty, and could thus qualify no less than Enlil to have been the Lord who decreed the fifty-year Jubilee and other fifty-related aspects mentioned in the Bible. He possessed a notorious Divine Black Bird that he used both for combat and on humanitarian missions; it could have been the *Kabod* flying vehicle that Yahweh possessed. He was active in the Zagros Mountains to the east of Mesopotamia, the lands of Elam, and was revered there as Ninshushinak, "Lord of Shushan city" (the Elamite capital). At one time he performed great dyking works in the Zagros mountains; at another, he diked and diverted mountain rain channels in the Sinai peninsula to make its mountainous part cultivable for his mother Ninharsag; in a way he, too, was "god of mountains." His association with the Sinai peninsula and the channeling of its rain-waters, which come in winter bursts only, into an irrigation system is still recalled to this day: the largest *Wadi* (a river that fills up in winter and dries up in summer) in the peninsula is still called *Wadi El-Arish,* the wadi of the *Urash*—the Ploughman—a nickname of Ninurta from way back. An association with the Sinai peninsula, through his water-works and his mother's residence there, also offers links to a Yahweh identification.

Another interesting aspect of Ninurta that invokes a similarity to the Biblical Lord comes to light in an inscription by the Assyrian king Ashurbanipal, who at one time invaded Elam. In it the king called him, "The mysterious god who lingers in a secret place where no one can see what his divine being is about." An unseen god!

But Ninurta, as far as the earlier Sumerians were concerned, was not a god in hiding, and graphic depictions of him, as we have shown, were not even rare. Then, in conflict with a Yahweh-Ninurta identification, we come across a major ancient text, dealing with a major and unforgettable event, whose specifics seem to tell us that Ninurta was not Yahweh.

One of the most decisive actions attributed in the Bible to Yahweh, with lasting effects and indelible memories, was the upheavaling of Sodom and Gomorrah. The event, as we have shown in great detail in *The Wars of Gods and Men,* was described and recalled in Mesopotamian texts, making possible a comparison of the deities involved.

In the biblical version Sodom (where Abram's nephew and his family lived) and Gomorrah, cities in the verdant plain south of the Sea of Salt, were sinful. Yahweh "comes down" and, accompanied by two Angels, visits Abram and his wife Sarai in their encampment near Hebron. After Yahweh predicts that the aged couple would have a son, the two Angels depart for Sodom to verify the extent of the cities' "sinning." Yahweh then reveals to Abram that if the sins would be confirmed, the cities and their residents would be destroyed. Abram pleads with Yahweh to spare Sodom if fifty just men be found there, and Yahweh agrees (the number was bargained by Abram down to ten) and departs. The Angels, having verified the cities' evil, warn Lot to take his family and escape. He asks for time to reach the mountains, and they agree to delay the destruction. Finally, the cities' doom begins as "Yahweh rained upon Sodom and Gomorrah sulfurous fire, coming from Yahweh from the skies; and He upheavaled those cities and the whole plain and all the inhabitants thereof, and all that which grew upon the ground . . . And Abraham went early in the morning to the place where he had stood before Yahweh, and gazed in the direction of Sodom and Gomorrah, toward the land of the Plain, and he beheld vapor arising from the earth as the smoke of a furnace" (Genesis chapter 19).

The same event is well documented in Mesopotamian annals as the culmination of Marduk's struggle to attain supremacy on Earth. Living in exile, Marduk gave his son Nabu the assignment of converting people in western Asia to become followers of Marduk. After a series of skirmishes, Nabu's forces were strong enough to invade Mesopotamia and enable Marduk to return to Babylon, where he declared his intention to make it the Gateway of the Gods (what its name, *Bab-Ili,* implied). Alarmed, the Council of the Anunnaki met in emergency sessions chaired by Enlil. Ninurta, and an alienated son of Enki called Nergal (from the south African domain), recommended drastic action to stop Marduk. Enki vehemently objected. Ishtar pointed out that while they were debating, Marduk was seizing city after city. "Sheriffs" were sent to seize Nabu, but he escaped and was hiding among his followers in one of the "sinning cities." Finally, Ninurta and Nergal were authorized to retrieve from a hiding place awesome nuclear weapons, and to use them to destroy the Spaceport in the Sinai (lest it fall into Mardukian hands) as well as the area where Nabu was hiding.

The unfolding drama, the heated discussions, the accusations, and the final drastic action—the use of nuclear weapons in 2024 B.C.—are described in great detail in a text that scholars call the *Erra Epic.*

In this document Nergal is referred to as Erra ("Howler") and Ninurta is called Ishum ("Scorcher"). Once they were given the go-ahead they retrieved "the awesome seven weapons, without parallel" and went to the Spaceport near the "Mount Most Supreme." The destruction of the Spaceport was carried out by Ninurta/Ishum: "He raised his hand; the Mount was smashed; the plain by the Mount Most Supreme he then obliterated; in its forests not a tree-stem was left standing."

Now it was the turn of the sinning cities to be upheavaled, and the task was carried out by Nergal/Erra. He went there by following the King's Highway that connected the Sinai and the Red Sea with Mesopotamia:

> Then, emulating Ishum,
> Erra the King's Highway followed.
> The cities he finished off,
> to desolation he overturned them.

The use of nuclear weapons there broke open the sand barrier that still partly exists in the shape of a tongue (called *El Lissan*), and the waters of the Salt Sea poured south, inundating the low-lying plain. The ancient text records that Erra/Nergal "dug through the sea, its wholeness he divided." And the nuclear weapons turned the Salt Sea to the body of water now called the Dead Sea: "That which lives in it he made wither," and what used to be a thriving and verdant plain, "as with fire he scorched the animals, burned its grains to become as dust."

As was the clear-cut case of the divine actors in the Deluge tale, so we find in this one concerning the upheavaling of Sodom, Gomorrah, and the other cities of that plain astride the Sinai peninsula, whom does and whom does not Yahweh match when the biblical and Sumerian texts are compared. The Mesopotamian text clearly associates Nergal and not Ninurta as the one who had upheavaled the sinning cities. Since the Bible asserts that it was not the two Angels who had gone to verify the situation, but Yahweh himself who had rained destruction on the cities, *Yahweh could not have been Ninurta.*

(The reference in Genesis chapter 10 to *Nimrod* as the one credited with starting Kingship in Mesopotamia, which we have discussed earlier, is interpreted by some as a reference not to a human king but to a god, and thus to Ninurta to whom the task of setting up the first Kingships was assigned. If so, the biblical statement that Nimrod "was a mighty hunter before Yahweh" also nullifies the possibility that Ninurta/Nimrod could have been Yahweh.)

But Nergal too was not Yahweh. He is mentioned by name as the deity of the Cutheans who were among the foreigners brought over by the Assyrians to replace the Israelites who were exiled. He is listed among the "other gods" that the newcomers worshiped and for whom they set up idols. He could not have been "Yahweh" and Yahweh's abomination at one and the same time.

If Enlil and two of his sons, Adad and Ninurta, are not finalists in the lineup to identify Yahweh, what about Enlil's third son, Nannar/Sin (the "Moon god")?

His "cult center" (as scholars call it) in Sumer was Ur, the very city from which the migration of Terah and his family began. From Ur, where Terah performed priestly services, they went to Barran on the Upper Euphrates—a city that was a duplicate (even if on a smaller scale) of Ur as a cult center of Nannar. The migration at that particular time was connected, we believe, with religious and royal changes that might have affected the worship of Nannar. Was he then the deity who had instructed Abram the Sumerian to pick up and leave?

Having brought peace and prosperity to Sumer when Ur was its capital, he was venerated in Ur's great ziggurat (whose remains rise awesomely to this day) with his beloved wife NIN.GAL ("Great Lady"). At the time of the new moon, the hymns sung to this divine couple expressed the people's gratitude to them; and the dark of the moon was considered a time of "the mystery of the great gods, a time of Nannar's oracle," when he would send "Zaqar, the god of dreams during the night" to give commands as well as to forgive sins. He was described in the hymns as "decider of destinies in Heaven and on Earth, leader of living creatures . . . who causes truth and justice to be."

It all sounds not unlike some of the praises of Yahweh sung by the Psalmist. . . .

The Akkadian/Semitic name for Nannar was Sin, and there can be no doubt that it was in honor of Nannar as Sin that the part of the Sinai peninsula called in the Bible the "Wilderness of Sin" and, for that matter, the whole peninsula, were so named. It was in that part of the world that Yahweh appeared to Moses for the first time, where the "Mount of the gods" was located, where the greatest Theophany ever had taken place. Furthermore, the principal habitat in the Sinai's central plain, in the vicinity of what we believe is the true Mount Sinai, is still called *Nakhl* in Arabic after the goddess Ningal whose Semitic name was pronounced *Nikal*.

Was it all indicative of a Yahweh = Nannar/Sin identification?

The discovery several decades ago of extensive Canaanite literature ("myths" to scholars) dealing with their pantheon revealed that while a god they called *Ba'al* (the generic word for "Lord" used as a personal name) was running things, he was in fact not entirely independent of his father El (a generic term meaning "god" used as a personal name). In these texts *El* is depicted as a retired god, living with his spouse Asherah away from the populated areas, at a quiet place where "the two waters meet"—a place that we have identified in *The Stairway To Heaven* as the southern tip of the Sinai peninsula, where the two gulfs extending from the Red Sea meet. This fact and other considerations have led us to the conclusion that the Canaanite El was the retired Nannar/Sin; included in the reasons upon which we had expounded is the fact that a "cult center" to Nannar/Sin has existed at a vital crossroads in the ancient Near East and even nowadays, the city known to us as Jericho but whose biblical/Semitic name is *Yeriho,* meaning "City of the Moon God"; and the adoption by tribes to the south thereof of *Allah*—"El" in Arabic—as the God of Islam represented by the Moon's crescent.

Described in the Canaanite texts as a retired deity, El as Nannar/Sin would indeed have been forced into retirement: Sumerian texts dealing with the effects of the nuclear cloud as it wafted eastward and reached Sumer and its capital Ur, reveal that Nannar/Sin—refusing to leave his beloved city—was afflicted by the deathly cloud and was partly paralyzed.

The image of Yahweh, especially in the period of the Exodus and the settlement of Canaan, i.e. after—not prior to—the demise of Ur, does not sound right for a retired, afflicted, and tired deity as Nannar/Sin had become by then. The Bible paints a picture of an active deity, insistent and persistent, fully in command, defying the gods of Egypt, inflicting plagues, dispatching Angels, roaming the skies; omnipresent, performing wonders, a magical healer, a Divine Architect. We find none of that in the descriptions of Nannar/Sin.

Both his veneration and fear of him stemmed from his association with his celestial counterpart, the Moon; and this celestial aspect serves as a decisive argument against identifying him with Yahweh: In the biblical divine order, it was Yahweh who ordered the Sun and the Moon to serve as luminaries; "the Sun and the Moon praise Yahweh," the Psalmist (148:3) declared. And on Earth, the crumbling of the walls of Jericho before the trumpeters of Yahweh symbolized the supremacy of Yahweh over the Moon god Sin.

There was also the matter of Ba'al, the Canaanite deity whose worship was a constant thorn in the side of Yahweh's faithful. The discovered texts reveal that Ba'al was a son of El. His abode in the mountains of Lebanon is still known as *Baalbek,* "The valley of Ba'al"—the place that was the first destination of Gilgamesh in his search for immortality. The biblical name for it was *Beit-Shemesh*— the "House/abode of Shamash;" and Shamash, we may recall, was a son of Nannar/Sin. The Canaanite "myths" devote much clay tablet space to the shenanigans between Ba'al and his sister *Anat;* the Bible lists in the area of *Beit-Shemesh* a place called *Beit Anat;* and we are as good as certain that the Semitic name Anat was a rendering of *Anunitu* ("Anu's beloved")—a nickname of Inanna/Ishtar, the twin sister of Utu/Shamash.

All that suggests that in the Canaanite trio El-Ba'al-Anat we see the Mesopotamian triad of Nannar/Sin-Utu/Shamash-Inanna/Ishtar— the gods associated with the Moon, the Sun, and Venus. *And none of them could have been Yahweh,* for the Bible is replete with admonitions against the worship of these celestial bodies and their emblems.

If neither Enlil nor any one of his sons (or even grandchildren) fully qualify as Yahweh, the search must turn elsewhere, to the sons of Enki, where some of the qualifications also point.

The instructions given to Moses during the sojourn at Mount Sinai were, to a great extent, of a medical nature. Five whole chapters in Leviticus and many passages in Numbers are devoted to medical procedures, diagnosis, and treatment. "Heal me, O Yahweh, and I shall be healed," Jeremiah (17:14) cried out: "My soul blesses Yahweh . . . who heals all my ailments," the Psalmist sang (103:1–3). Because of his piety, King Hezekiah was not only cured on Yahweh's say-so of a fatal disease, but was also granted by Yahweh fifteen more years to live (II Kings chapter 19). Yahweh could not only heal and extend life, he could also (through his Angels and Prophets) revive the dead; an extreme example was provided by Ezekiel's vision of the scattered dry bones that came back alive, their dead resurrected by Yahweh's will.

The biological-medical knowledge underlying such capabilities was possessed by Enki, and he passed such knowledge to two of his sons: Marduk (known as Ra in Egypt), and Thoth (whom the Egyptians called Tehuti and the Sumerians NIN.GISH.ZIDDA—"Lord of the Tree of Life"). As for Marduk, many Babylonian texts refer to his healing abilities; but—as his own complaint to his father reveals—he was given knowledge of healing but not that of reviving the dead. On the other hand, Thoth did possess such knowledge, employing it on one occasion to revive Horus, the son of the god Osiris and his sister-wife Isis. According to the hieroglyphic text dealing with this incident, Horus was bitten by a poisonous scorpion and died. As his mother appealed to the "god of magical things," Thoth, for help, he came down to Earth from the heavens in a sky boat and restored the boy back to life.

When it came to the construction and equipping of the Tabernacle in the Sinai wilderness and later on of the Temple in Jerusalem, Yahweh displayed an impressive knowledge of architecture, sacred alignments, decorative details, use of materials, and construction procedures—even to the point of showing the Earthlings involved scale models of what He had designed or wanted. Marduk has not been credited with such an all-embracing knowledge; but Thoth/Ningishzidda was. In Egypt he was deemed the keeper of the secrets of pyramid building, and as Ningishzidda he was invited to Lagash to help orientate, design, and choose materials for the temple that was built for Ninurta.

Another point of major congruence between Yahweh and Thoth was the matter of the calendar. It is to Thoth that the first Egyptian calendar was attributed, and when he was expelled from Egypt by Ra/Marduk and went (according to our findings) to Mesoamerica, where he was called "The Winged Serpent" (Quetzalcoatl), he devised the Aztec and Mayan calendars there. As the biblical books of Exodus, Leviticus, and Numbers make clear, Yahweh not only shifted the New Year to the "seventh month," but also instituted the week, the Sabbath, and a series of holidays.

Healer; reviver of the dead who came down in a sky boat; a Divine Architect; a great astronomer; and designer of calendars. The attributes common to Thoth and Yahweh seem overwhelming.

So was Thoth Yahweh?

Though known in Sumer, he was not considered there one of the Great Gods, and thus not fitting at all the epithet "the God Most High" that both Abraham and Melchizedek, priest of Jerusalem, used at their encounter. Above all, he was a *god of Egypt*, and (unless excluded by the argument that he was Yahweh), he was one of those upon whom Yahweh set out to make judgments. Renowned in ancient Egypt, there could be no Pharaoh ignorant of this deity. Yet, when Moses and Aaron came before Pharaoh and told him, "So sayeth Yahweh, the God of Israel: Let My people go that they may worship Me in the desert," Pharaoh said: "Who is this Yahweh that I should obey his words? I know not Yahweh, and the Israelites I shall not let go."

If Yahweh were Thoth, not only would the Pharaoh not answer thus, but the task of Moses and Aaron would have been made easy and attainable were they just to say, Why, "Yahweh" is just another name for Thoth . . . And Moses, having been raised in the Egyptian court, would have had no difficulty knowing that—if that were so.

If Thoth was not Yahweh, the process of elimination alone appears to leave one more candidate: Marduk.

That he was a "god most high" is well established; the Firstborn of Enki who believed that his father was unjustly deprived of the supremacy on Earth—a supremacy to which he, Marduk, rather than Enlil's son Ninurta, was the rightful successor. His attributes included a great many—almost all—the attributes of Yahweh. He possessed a *Shem*, a skychamber, as Yahweh did; when the Babylonian king Nebuchadnezzar

II rebuilt the sacred precinct of Babylon, he built there an especially strengthened enclosure for the "chariot of Marduk, the Supreme Traveler between Heaven and Earth."

When Marduk finally attained the supremacy on Earth, he did not discredit the other gods. On the contrary, he invited them all to reside in individual pavilions within the sacred precinct of Babylon. There was only one catch: their specific powers and attributes were to pass to him—just as the "Fifty Names" (i.e. rank) of Enlil had to. A Babylonian text, in its legible portion, listed thus the functions of other great gods that were transferred to Marduk:

Ninurta	=	Marduk of the hoe
Nergal	=	Marduk of the attack
Zababa	=	Marduk of the combat
Enlil	=	Marduk of lordship and counsel
Nabu	=	Marduk of numbers and counting
Sin	=	Marduk the illuminator of the night
Shamash	=	Marduk of justice
Adad	=	Marduk of rains

This was not the monotheism of the Prophets and the Psalms; it was what scholars term henotheism—a religion wherein the supreme power passes from one of several deities to another in succession. Even so, Marduk did not reign supreme for long; soon after the institution of Marduk as national god by the Babylonians, it was matched by their Assyrian rivals by the institution of *Ashur* as "lord of all the gods."

Apart from the arguments that we have mentioned in the cases of Thoth that negate an identification with any major Egyptian deity (and Marduk was the great Egyptian god Ra after all), the Bible itself specifically rules out any equating of Yahweh with Marduk. Not only is Yahweh, in sections dealing with Babylon, portrayed as greater, mightier, and supreme over the gods of the Babylonians—it explicitly foretells their demise by naming them. Both Isaiah (46:1) and Jeremiah (50:2) foresaw Marduk (also known as *Bel* by his Babylonian epithet) and his son Nabu fallen and collapsed before Yahweh on the Day of Judgment.

Those prophetic words depict the two Babylonian gods as antagonists and enemies of Yahweh; *Marduk (and for that matter, Nabu) could not have been Yahweh.*

(As far as Ashur is concerned, the God Lists and other evidence suggest that he was a resurgent Enlil renamed by the Assyrians "The All Seeing," and as such, he could not have been Yahweh.)

As we find so many similarities, and on the other hand crucial differences and contradicting aspects, in our search for a matching "Yahweh" in the ancient Near Eastern pantheons, we can continue only by doing what Yahweh had told Abraham: Lift thine eyes toward the heavens. . . .

The Babylonian king Hammurabi recorded thus the legitimization of Marduk's supremacy on Earth:

> Lofty Anu,
> Lord of the Anunnaki,
> and Enlil,
> Lord of Heaven and Earth
> who determines the destinies of the land,
> Determined for Marduk, the firstborn of Enki,
> the Enlil-functions over all mankind
> and made him great among the Igigi.

As this makes clear, even Marduk as he assumed supremacy on Earth recognized that it was Anu, and not he, who was "Lord of the Anunnaki." Was he the "God Most High" by whom Abraham and Melchizedek greeted each other?

The cuneiform sign for Anu (AN in Sumerian) was a star; it had the multiple meanings of "god, divine," "heaven," and this god's personal name. Anu, as we know from the Mesopotamian texts, stayed in "heaven"; and numerous biblical verses also described Yahweh as the One Who Is in Heaven. It was "Yahweh, the God of Heaven," who commanded him to go to Canaan, Abraham stated (Genesis 24:7). "I am a Hebrew and it is Yahweh, the God of Heaven that I venerate," the Prophet Jonah said (1:9). "Yahweh, the God of Heaven commanded me to build for Him a House in Jerusalem, in Judaea," Cyrus stated in his edict regarding the rebuilding of the Temple in Jerusalem (Ezra 1:2). When Solomon completed the construction of the (first) Temple in Jerusalem, he prayed to Yahweh to hear him from the heavens to bless the Temple as His House, although, Solomon admitted, it was hardly possible that "Yahweh *Elohim*" would come to dwell on Earth, in this House, "when the heaven and the heaven-of-heavens cannot contain Thee" (I Kings 8:27); and the Psalms repeatedly stated, "From the heaven did Yahweh look down upon the Children of Adam" (14:2); "From Heaven did Yahweh behold the Earth" (102:20); and "In Heaven did Yahweh establish His throne" (103:19).

Though Anu did visit Earth several times, he was residing on Nibiru; and as the god whose abode was in Heaven, he was truly an unseen god: among the countless depictions of deities on cylinder seals, statues and statuettes, carvings, wall paintings, amulets—his image does not appear even once!

Since Yahweh, too, was unseen and unrepresented pictorially, residing in "Heaven," the inevitable question that arises is, *Where was the abode of Yahweh?* With so many parallels between Yahweh and Anu, did Yahweh, too, have a "Nibiru" to dwell on?

The question, and its relevance to Yahweh's invisibility, does not originate with us. It was sarcastically posed by a heretic to a Jewish savant, Rabbi Gamliel, almost two thousand years ago; and the answer that was given is truly amazing!

The report of the conversation, as rendered into English by S. M. Lehrman in *The World of the Midrash,* goes thus:

> When Rabbi Gamliel was asked by a heretic to cite the exact location of God, seeing that the world is so vast and there are seven oceans, his reply was simply, "This I cannot tell you."
>
> Whereupon the other tauntingly retorted: "And this you call Wisdom, praying to a God, daily, whose whereabouts you do not know?"
>
> The Rabbi smiled: "You ask me to put my finger on the exact spot of His Presence, albeit that *tradition avers that the distance between*

heaven and earth would take a journey of 3,500 years to cover. So, may I ask you the exact whereabouts of something which is always with you, and without which you cannot live a moment?"

The pagan was intrigued. "What is this?" he eagerly queried.

The Rabbi replied: "The soul which God had planted within you; pray tell me where exactly is it?"

It was a chastened man that shook his head negatively.

It was now the Rabbi's turn to be amazed and amused. "If you do not know where your own soul is located, how can you expect to know the precise habitation of One who fills the whole world with His glory?"

Let us note carefully what Rabbi Gamliel's answer was: according to Jewish tradition, he said, the exact spot in the heavens where God has a dwelling is so distant that it would require a journey of 3,500 years. . . .

How much closer can one get to the 3,600 years that it takes Nibiru to complete one orbit around the Sun?

Although there are no specific texts dealing with or describing Anu's abode on Nibiru, some idea thereof can be gained indirectly from such texts as the tale of Adapa, occasional references in various texts, and even from Assyrian depictions. It was a place—let us think of it as a royal palace—that was entered through imposing gates, flanked by towers. A pair of gods (Ningishzidda and Dumuzi are mentioned in one instance) stood guard at the gates. Inside, Anu was seated on a throne; when Enlil and Enki were on Nibiru, or when Anu had visited Earth, they flanked the throne, holding up celestial emblems.

(The *Pyramid Texts* of ancient Egypt, describing the Afterlife ascent of the Pharaoh to the celestial abode, carried aloft by an "Ascender," announced for the departing king: "The double gates of heaven are opened for thee, the double gates of the sky are opened for thee" and envisioned four scepter-holding gods announcing his arrival on the "Imperishable Star.")

In the Bible, too, Yahweh was described as seated on a throne, flanked by Angels. While Ezekiel described seeing the Lord's image, shimmering like electrum, seated on a throne inside a Flying Vehicle, "the throne of Yahweh is in Heaven," the Psalms (11:4) asserted; and the Prophets described seeing Yahweh seated on a throne in the Heavens. The Prophet Michaiah ("Who is like Yahweh?"), a contemporary of Elijah, told the king of Judaea who had sought a divine oracle (I Kings chapter 22):

> I saw Yahweh sitting on his throne,
> and the host of heaven were standing by Him,
> on His right and on His left.

The Prophet Isaiah recorded (chapter 6) a vision seen by him "in the year in which king Uzziah died" in which he saw God seated on His throne, attended by fiery Angels:

> I beheld my Lord seated on a high and lofty throne,
> and the train of His robe filled the great hall.
> Seraphs stood in attendance on Him,
> each one of them having six wings:
> with twain each covered his face,
> with twain each covered his legs,
> and with twain each one would fly.
> And one would call out to the other:
> Holy, holy, holy is the Lord of Hosts!

Biblical references to Yahweh's throne went further: they actually stated its location, in a place called *Olam*. "Thy throne is established forever, from *Olam* art Thou," the Psalms (93:2) declared; "Thou, Yahweh, are enthroned in *Olam,* enduring through the ages," states the Book of Lamentations (5:19).

Now, this is not the way these verses, and others like them, have been usually translated. In the King James Version, for example, the quoted verse from Psalms is translated "Thy throne is established of old, thou art from *everlasting,*" and the verse in Lamentations is rendered "Thou, O Lord, remainest *for ever;* thy throne from generation to generation." Modern translations likewise render *Olam* as "everlasting" and "forever" (*The New American Bible*) or as "eternity" and "for ever" (*The New English Bible*), revealing an indecision whether to treat the term as an adjective or as a noun. Recognizing, however, that *Olam* is clearly a noun, the most recent translation by the Jewish Publication Society adopted "eternity," an abstract noun, as a solution.

The Hebrew Bible, strict in the precision of its terminology, has other terms for stating the state of "lasting forever." One is *Netzah*, as in Psalm 89:47 that asked, "How long, Yahweh, wilt Thou hide Thyself— *forever?*" Another term that means more precisely "perpetuity" is *Ad*, which is also usually translated "for ever," as in "his seed I will make endure for ever" in Psalm 89:30. There was no need for a third term to express the same thing. *Olam*, often accompanied by the adjective *Ad* to denote its everlasting nature, was itself not an adjective but a noun derived from the root that means "disappearing, mysteriously hidden." The numerous biblical verses in which *Olam* appears indicate that it was deemed a physical place, not an abstraction. "Thou art from *Olam*," the Psalmist declared—God is from a place which is a hidden place (and therefore God has been unseen).

It was a place that was conceived as physically existing: Deuteronomy (33:15) and the Prophet Habakkuk (3:6) spoke of the "hills of *Olam*." Isaiah (33:14) referred to the "heat sources of *Olam*." Jeremiah (6:16) mentioned the "pathways of *Olam*" and (18:5) "the lanes of *Olam*," and called Yahweh "king of *Olam*" (10:10) as did Psalms 10:16. The Psalms, in statements reminiscent of the references to the gates of Anu's abode (in Sumerian texts) and to the Gates of Heaven (in ancient Egyptian texts), also spoke of the "Gates of *Olam*" that should open and welcome the Lord Yahweh as He arrives there upon His Kabod, His Celestial Boat (24:7–10):

> Lift up your heads, O gates of *Olam*
> so that the King of *Kabod* may come in!
> Who is the King of *Kabod*?
> Yahweh, strong and valiant, a mighty warrior!

*

Lift up your heads, O gates of Olam,
and the King of *Kabod* shall come in!
Who is the King of *Kabod*?
Yahweh lord of hosts is the King of *Kabod*.

"Yahweh is the God of *Olam*," declared Isaiah (40:28), echoing the biblical record in Genesis (21:33) of Abraham's "calling in the name of Yahweh, the God of *Olam*." No wonder, then, that the Covenant symbolized by circumcision, "the celestial sign," was called by the Lord when he had imposed it on Abraham and his descendants "the Covenant of *Olam*:"

And my Covenant shall be in your flesh,
the Covenant of *Olam*.

(GENESIS 17:13)

In post-biblical rabbinic discussions, and so in modern Hebrew, *Olam* is the term that stands for "world." Indeed, the answer that Rabbi Gamliel gave to the question regarding the Divine Abode was based on rabbinic assertions that it is separated from Earth by seven heavens, in each of which there is a different world; and that the journey from one to the other requires five hundred years, so that the complete journey through seven heavens from the world called Earth to the world that is the Divine Abode lasts 3,500 years. This, as we have pointed out, comes as close to the 3,600 (Earth) years' orbit of Nibiru as one could expect; and while Earth to someone arriving from space would have been the seventh planet, Nibiru, to someone on Earth would indeed be seven celestial spaces away when it disappears to its apogee.

Such a disappearing—the root meaning of *Olam*—creates of course the "year" of Nibiru—an awesomely long time in human terms. The Prophets similarly, in numerous passages, spoke of the "Years of Olam" as a measure of a very long time. A clear sense of periodicity, as would result from the periodic appearance and disappearance of a planet, was conveyed by the frequent use of "from Olam to Olam" as a definite (though extremely long) measure of time: "I had given you this land from Olam to Olam," the Lord was quoted as saying by Jeremiah (7:7 and 25:5). And a possible clincher for identifying *Olam* with Nibiru was the statement in Genesis 6:4 that the Nefilim, the young Anunnaki who had come to Earth from Nibiru, were the "people of the Shem" (the people of the rocketships), "those who were from Olam."

With the obvious familiarity of the Bible's editors, Prophets, and Psalmists with Mesopotamian "myths" and astronomy, it would have been peculiar not to find knowledge of the important planet Nibiru in the Bible. *It is our suggestion that yes, the Bible was keenly aware of Nibiru—and called it* Olam, *the "disappearing planet."*

Does all that mean that therefore Anu was Yahweh? Not necessarily. . . .

Though the Bible depicted Yahweh as reigning in His celestial abode, as Anu did, it also considered Him "king" over the Earth and all upon it—whereas Anu clearly gave the command on Earth to Enlil. Anu did visit Earth, but extant texts describe the occasions mostly as ceremonial state and inspection visits; there is nothing in them comparable to the active involvement of Yahweh in the affairs of nations and individuals. Moreover, the Bible recognized a god, other than Yahweh, a "god of other nations" called *An;* his worship is noted in the listing (II Kings 17:31) of gods of the foreigners whom the Assyrians had resettled in Samaria, where he is referred to as *An-melekh* ("Anu the king"). A personal name Anani, honoring Anu, and a place called Anatot, are also listed in the Bible. And the Bible had nothing for Yahweh that paralleled the genealogy of Anu (parents, spouse, children), his lifestyle (scores of concubines), or his fondness for his granddaughter Inanna (whose worship as the "Queen of Heaven"—Venus—was deemed an abomination in the eyes of Yahweh).

And so, in spite of the similarities, there are also too many essential differences between Anu and Yahweh for the two to have been one and the same.

Moreover, in the biblical view Yahweh was more than "king, lord" of *Olam,* as Anu was king on Nibiru. He was more than once hailed as *El Olam,* the God of *Olam* (Genesis 21:33) and *El Elohim,* the God of the *Elohim* (Joshua 22:22, Psalms 50:1 and Psalms 136:2).

The biblical suggestion that the Elohim—the "gods," the Anunnaki—had a God, seems totally incredible at first, but quite logical on reflection.

At the very conclusion of our first book in The Earth Chronicles series (*The 12th Planet*), having told the story of the planet Nibiru and how the Anunnaki (the biblical Nefilim) who had come to Earth from it "created" Mankind, we posed the following question:

> And if the Nefilim were the "gods" who "created" Man on Earth,
> did evolution alone, on the Twelfth Planet, create the Nefilim?

Technologically advanced, capable hundreds of thousands of years before us to travel in space, arriving at a cosmological explanation for the creation of the Solar System and, as we begin to do, to contemplate and understand the universe—the Anunnaki must have pondered their origins, and arrived at what we call Religion—their religion, *their concept of God.*

Who created the Nefilim, the Anunnaki, on their planet? The Bible itself provides the answer. Yahweh, it states, was not just "a great God, a great king over all of the *Elohim*" (Psalms 95:3); He was there, on Nibiru, before they had come to be on it: "Before the *Elohim* upon *Olam* He sat," Psalm 61:8 explained. Just as the Anunnaki had been on Earth before The Adam, so was Yahweh on Nibiru/Olam before the Anunnaki. The creator preceded the created.

We have already explained that the seeming immortality of the Anunnaki "gods" was merely their extreme longevity, resulting from the fact that one Nibiru-year equaled 3,600 Earth-years; and that in fact they were born, grew old, and could (and did) die. A time measure applicable to *Olam* ("days of *Olam*" and "years of *Olam*") was recognized by the Prophets and Psalmist; what is more impressive is their realization that the various *Elohim* (the Sumerian DIN.GIR, the Akkadian *Ilu*) were in fact not immortal—but Yahweh, God, was. Thus, Psalm 82 envisions God passing judgment on the *Elohim* and reminding them that they—the *Elohim*!—are also mortal: "God stands in the divine assembly, among the *Elohim* He judges," and tells them thus:

I have said, ye are *Elohim,*
all of you sons of the Most High;
But ye shall die as men do,
like any prince ye shall fall.

We believe that such statements, suggesting that the Lord Yahweh created not only the Heaven and the Earth but also the *Elohim,* the Anunnaki "gods," have a bearing on a puzzle that has baffled generations of biblical scholars. It is the question why the Bible's very first verse that deals with the very Beginning, does not begin with the first letter of the alphabet, but rather with the second one. The significance and symbolism of beginning the Beginning with the proper beginning must have been obvious to the Bible's compilers; yet, this is what they chose to transmit to us:

Breshit hara Elohim
et Ha'Shamaim v'et Ha'Aretz

which is commonly translated, "In the beginning God created the Heaven and the Earth."

Since the Hebrew letters have numerical values, the first letter, *Aleph* (from which the Greek *alpha* comes) has the numerical value "one, the first"—the beginning. Why then, scholars and theologians have wondered, does the Creation start with the second letter, *Beth,* whose value is "two, second"?

While the reason remains unknown, the result of starting the first verse in the first book of the Bible with an *Aleph* would be astounding, for it would make the sentence read thus:

Ab-reshit hara Elohim,
et Ha'Shamaim v'et Ha'Aretz

The Father-of-Beginning created the *Elohim,*
the Heavens, and the Earth.

By this slight change, by just starting the beginning with the letter that begins it all, an omnipotent, omnipresent Creator of All emerges from the primeval chaos: *Ab-Reshit*, "the Father of Beginning." The best modern scientific minds have come up with the Big Bang theory of the beginning of the universe—but have yet to explain who caused the Big Bang to happen. Were Genesis to begin as it should have, the Bible—which offers a precise tale of Evolution and adheres to the most sensible cosmogony—would have also given us the answer: the Creator who was there to create it all.

And all at once Science and Religion, Physics and Metaphysics, converge into one single answer that conforms to the credo of Jewish monotheism: "I am Yahweh, there is none beside me!" It is a credo that carried the Prophets, and us with them, from the arena of gods to the God who embraces the universe.

One can only speculate why the Bible's editors, who scholars believe canonized the *Torah* (the first five books of the Bible) during the Babylonian exile, omitted the *Aleph*. Was it in order to avoid offending their Babylonian exilers (because a claim that Yahweh had created the Anunnaki-gods would have not excluded Marduk)? But what is, we believe, not to be doubted is that at one time the first word in the first verse in the Bible did begin with the first letter of the alphabet. This certainty is based on the statements in the Book of Revelation ("The Apocalypse of St. John" in the New Testament), in which God announces thus:

> I am Alpha and Omega,
> the Beginning and the End,
> the First and the Last.

The statement, repeated three times (1:8, 21:6, 22:13), applies the first letter of the alphabet (by its Greek name) to the Beginning, to the divine First, and the last letter of the (Greek) alphabet to the End, to God being the Last of all as He has been the First of All.

That this had been the case at the beginning of Genesis is confirmed, we believe, by the certainty that the statements in Revelation harken back to the Hebrew scriptures from which the parallel verses in Isaiah (41:6, 42:8, 44:6) were taken, the verses in which Yahweh proclaims His absoluteness and uniqueness:

> I, Yahweh, was the First
> And the Last I will also be!
>
> I am the First
> and I am the Last;
> There are no *Elohim* without Me!
>
> I am He,
> I am the First,
> I am the Last as well.

It is these statements that help identify the biblical God by the answer that He himself gave when asked: Who, O God, are you? It was when He called Moses out of the Burning Bush, identifying Himself only as "the God of thy father, the God of Abraham, the God of Isaac and the God of Jacob." Having been given his mission, Moses pointed out that when he would come to the Children of Israel and say, "the God of your forefathers has sent me to you, and they will say to me: What is His name?—what shall I tell them?"

> And God said to Moses:
> *Ehyeh-Asher-Ehyeh*—
> this is what thou shalt say
> unto the Children of Israel:
> *Ehyeh* sent me.
> And God said further to Moses:
> Thus shalt say unto the Children of Israel:
> *Yahweh,* the God of your fathers,
> the God of Abraham, the God of Isaac,
> and the God of Jacob,
> hath sent me unto you;

This is my name unto *Olam,*
this is my appellation unto all generations.
(EXODUS 3:13–15)

The statement, *Ehyeh-Asher-Ehyeh,* has been the subject of discussion, analysis, and interpretation by generations of theologians, biblical scholars, and linguists. The King James Version translates it "I am that I am . . . *I am* hath sent me to you." Other more modern translations adopt "I am, that is who I am . . . *I am* has sent you." The most recent translation by the Jewish Publication Society prefers to leave the Hebrew intact, providing the footnote, "meaning of the Hebrew uncertain."

The key to understanding the answer given during this Divine Encounter are the grammatical tenses employed here. *Ehyeh-Asher-Ehyeh* is not given in the present but in the future tense. In simple parlance it states: "Whoever I shall be, I shall be." And the Divine Name that is revealed to a mortal for the first time (in the conversation Moses is told that the sacred name, the Tetragrammaton YHWH, had not been revealed even to Abraham) combines the three tenses from the root meaning "To Be"—the One who was, who is, and who shall be. It is an answer and a name that befit the biblical concept of Yahweh as eternally existing—One who was, who is, and who shall continue to be.

A frequent form of stating this everlasting nature of the biblical God is the expression "Thou art from *Olam* to *Olam.*" It is usually translated, "Thou art everlasting"; this conveys undoubtedly the sense of the statement, but not its precise meaning. Literally taken it suggests that the existence and reign of Yahweh extended from one *Olam* to another—that He was "king, lord" not only of the one *Olam* that was the equivalent of the Mesopotamian Nibiru—but of other Olams, of other worlds!

No less than eleven times, the Bible refers to Yahweh's abode, domain, and "kingdom" using the term *Olamim,* the plural of Olam—a domain, an abode, a kingdom that encompasses many worlds. It is an expansion of Yahweh's Lordship beyond the notion of a "national god" to that of a Judge of all the nations; beyond the Earth and beyond Nibiru, to the "Heavens of Heaven" (Deuteronomy 10:14, I Kings 8:27,

II Chronicles 2:5 and 6: 18) that encompass not only the Solar System but even the distant stars (Deuteronomy 4: 19, Ecclesiastes 12:2).

THIS IS THE IMAGE OF A COSMIC VOYAGER.

All else—the celestial planetary "gods," Nibiru that remade our Solar System and remakes the Earth on its near passages, the Anunnaki "Elohim," Mankind, nations, kings—all are His manifestations and His instruments, carrying out a divine and universal everlasting plan. In a way we are all His Angels, and when the time comes for Earthlings to travel in space and emulate the Anunnaki, on some other world, we too shall only be carrying out a destined future.

It is an image of a universal Lord that is best summed up in the hymnal prayer *Adon Olam* that is recited as a majestic song in Jewish synagogue services on festivals, on the Sabbath, and on each and every day of the year:

> Lord of the universe, who has reigned
> Ere all that exists had yet been created.
> When by His will all things were wrought,
> "Sovereign" was His name was then pronounced.
>
> And when, in time, all things shall cease,
> He shall still reign in majesty.
> He was, He is, He shall remain,
> He shall continue gloriously.
>
> Incomparable, unique He is,
> No other can His Oneness share.
> Without beginning, without end.
> Dominion's might is His to bear.

7

The
Cosmic Connection—DNA

Selection from
The Cosmic Code *(Chapter 6)*

The Anunnaki came to Earth seeking gold for their planet, Nibiru, given that they had destroyed its atmosphere and gold was needed to restore it. Knowing that Earth was rich in gold, they first extracted gold from the Persian Gulf, and when that proved too limited a supply, they began mining in Africa and were successful until the miners went on to revolt against the hard labor. This prompted the Anunnaki to realize that they were capable of creating a new hybrid worker for the mines, and thus the first Adam was created. Applying their knowledge of advanced genetics, the Anunnaki experimented with the formation of the perfect being, one who would be ideally suited to their purposes. However, there was much trial and error along the way. Sometimes a being would be created with three heads, for instance, or two faces. Representations of these ancient mutants exist in Mesopotamian art left to us from these earlier times.

Eventually, Enki and Ninharsag (the children of Anu) were able to successfully create "The Adam," who was formed utilizing the DNA of the hominids on Earth and the DNA of the

Anunnaki female who would bear the child. Today, science has caught up with some of the ancient accounts. Gilgamesh, as depicted in an ancient Mesopotamian text, had claimed to be two-thirds divine. By modern standards this was deemed to be genetically impossible until the 1980s, when it was found that another type of DNA, transmitted only from the mother, was discovered. This DNA, known as mitochondrial DNA, would allot an extra portion of the mother's collective DNA to her offspring. In Gilgamesh's case, and assuming that his mother was a goddess, he would, in fact, be two-thirds divine, as he claimed.

This attests to the fact that, while modern knowledge of DNA is advancing, we are not anywhere near the sophisticated level of genetic engineering described in these ancient stories.

EVEN BEFORE TELEVISION, courtroom dramas have titillated many and trials made history. We have come a long way from the biblical rule, "by two witnesses shall the verdict be." From eyewitnesses, court evidence has moved to documentary evidence, to forensic evidence, and—what seems at the moment as the epitome—to DNA evidence.

Having discovered that all life is determined by the tiny bits of nucleic acids that spell out heredity and individuality on chains called chromosomes, modern science has attained the capability of reading those entwined DNA letters to distinguish their unique, individually spelled "words." Using DNA readings to prove guilt or innocence has become the highlight of courtroom dramas.

An unmatched feat of twentieth-century sophistication? No, a feat of 100th-century sophistication *in the past*—a court drama from 10,000 B.C.

The ancient celebrated case took place in Egypt, at a time when gods and not yet men reigned over the land; and it concerned not men but the gods themselves. It concerned the adversaries Seth and Horus and had its roots in the rivalry between the half brothers Seth and Osiris. Seth, it will be recalled, resorted to foul play to get rid of Osiris and take over his domains. The first time he tricked Osiris into a chest that Seth quickly sealed and sank in the Mediterranean Sea; but Isis found the chest and, with the help of Thoth, revived Osiris. The next time the frustrated Seth seized and cut up Osiris into fourteen pieces. Isis located the dispersed pieces and put them together, and mummified Osiris to start the Afterlife legend. She missed, however, the god's phallus, which she could not find, for Seth had disposed of it so that Osiris would have no heir.

Determined to have one so that he would avenge his father, Isis appealed to Thoth, the Keeper of Divine Secrets, to help her. Extracting the "essence" of Osiris from the dead god's available parts, Thoth helped Isis impregnate herself and give birth to a son, Horus.

The "essence" (not "seed"!), we now know, was what we nowadays call DNA—the genetic nucleic acids that form chains on the chromosomes, chains that are arranged in base pairs in a double helix. At conception, when the male sperm enters the female egg, the entwined double helixes separate, and one strand from the male combines with one strand from the female to form a new double-helixed DNA for their offspring. It is thus essential not only to bring together the two double-helixed DNAs, but also to attain a separation—an unwinding—of the double strands, and then a recombining of only one strand from each source into the new entwined double-helixed DNA.

Pictorial depictions from ancient Egypt indicate that Thoth—the son of Ptah/Enki—was well aware of these biological-genetic processes and employed them in his genetic feats. In Abydos, a wall painting (Fig. 40), in which the Pharaoh Seti I acted out the role of Osiris, showed Thoth giving Life (the *Ankh* symbol) back to the dead god while obtaining from him the two distinct strands of DNA. In a depiction from the *Book of the Dead* dealing with the subsequent birth of Horus, we see (Fig. 41) how the two Birth Goddesses assisting Thoth hold *one strand each* of DNA, the DNA's double helix having been separated so that only one strand recombines with that of Isis (shown holding the newborn Horus).

Isis raised the boy in secret. When he came of age, his mother decided that it was time to claim for him his father's inheritance. So one day, to Seth's utter surprise, Horus appeared before the Council of

Figure 40

Figure 41

the Great Gods and announced that he was the son and heir of Osiris. It was an incredible claim, yet one that could not be dismissed out of hand. Was the young god really the son of the dead Osiris?

As recorded in a text known as the *Chester Beatty Papyrus N*, the appearance of Horus astounded the assembled gods, and of course Seth more than any other. As the council began to deliberate the sudden claim, Seth had a conciliatory suggestion: Let the deliberations be recessed, so as to give him a chance to get acquainted with Horus and see if the matter could be settled amicably. He invited Horus to "come, let us pass a happy day in my house," and Horus agreed. But Seth, who had once tricked Osiris to his death, had new treachery in mind:

> When it was eventide,
> the bed was spread for them,
> and the twain lay thereon.
> And in the night
> Seth caused his member to become stiff,
> and he made it go between the loins of Horus.

When the deliberations were resumed, Seth made an astounding announcement. Whether or not Horus is the son of Osiris, he said, matters no more. For now his, Seth's, seed is in Horus, and that makes Horus a successor of Seth rather than a front-runner for the succession!

Then Horus made an even more surprising announcement. On the contrary, he said, it is not I who have been disqualified—it is Seth! And he went on to tell that he was not really asleep when Seth poured his semen. It did not enter my body, he said, because "I caught the seed between my hands." In the morning he took the semen to show it to his mother, Isis, and the report gave her an idea. She made Horus erect his member and ejaculate his semen into a cup; then she spread the semen of Horus on lettuce in Seth's garden—a favorite breakfast food of Seth. Unknowingly, he ended up ingesting the semen of Horus. So, Horus said, it is my semen that is in Seth, and now he can succeed me but not precede me on the divine throne. . . .

Totally baffled, the Council of the Gods turned to Thoth to resolve the issue. Using his powers of genetic knowledge, he checked the semen that Isis had kept in a pot, and found it to indeed be that of Seth. He examined Horus and found no traces of Seth's DNA in him.

ed Seth, and found that he had indeed ingested the

forensic expert in a modern court, but evidently armed abilities which we are yet to attain, he submitted the results to the Council of the Gods. They voted unanimously to grant the dominion over Egypt to Horus.

(Seth's refusal to yield the dominion led to what we have termed the First Pyramid War, in which Horus enlisted, for the first time, humans in a war between the gods. We have detailed those events in *The Wars of Gods and Men*.)

Recent discoveries in genetics throw light on a persistent and seemingly odd custom of the gods, and at the same time highlight their biogenetic sophistication.

The importance of the wife-sister in the succession rules of the gods of Mesopotamia and Egypt, evident from all that we have reported thus far, was echoed also in the Greek myths regarding their gods. The Greeks named the first divine couple, emerging out of Chaos, *Gaea* ("Earth") and *Uranus* ("Sky" or "Heaven"). Of them twelve *Titans* were brought forth, six males and six females. Their intermarriages and varied offspring laid the groundwork for later struggles for supremacy. Of the earliest struggles the one who emerged on top was *Cronus,* the youngest male Titan, whose spouse was his sister *Rhea;* their children were the three sons *Hades, Poseidon,* and *Zeus,* and the three daughters *Hestia, Demeter,* and *Hera.* Though Zeus fought his way up to the supremacy, he had to share dominion with his brothers. The three divided the domains among them—some versions say by drawing lots— very much as Anu, Enlil, and Enki had: Zeus was the heavenly god (yet residing on Earth, on Mount Olympus); Hades was accorded the Lower World; and Poseidon the seas.

The three brothers and three sisters, offspring of Cronus and Rhea, constituted the first half of the Olympian Circle of twelve. The other six were offspring of Zeus, born when Zeus consorted with a variety of goddesses. Of one of them, Leto, he had his Firstborn Son, the great Greek and Roman god *Apollo.* When it was time, however, to obtain a male heir in accordance with the succession rules of the gods, Zeus turned to his own sisters. Hestia, the oldest, was by all accounts a recluse, too old or too sick to be the object of matrimony and childbearing. Zeus thus sought a son by his middle sister, Demeter; but instead of a son she bore him a daughter, Persephone. This paved the way for Zeus to marry Hera, the youngest sister; and she did bear to Zeus a son, *Ares,* and two daughters (Ilithyia and Hebe). When the Greeks and Romans, who lost the knowledge of the planets beyond Saturn, named the known planets, they assigned one—Mars—to Ares; though not the Firstborn Son, he was Zeus's Foremost Son. Apollo, as great a god as he was, had no planet named after him by the Greeks and Romans.

All this reinforces the importance of the wife-sister in the annals of the gods. In matters of succession, the issue arose again and again: Who will the successor to the throne be—the Firstborn Son or the Foremost Son, if the latter was born by a half sister and the former not? That issue appears to have dominated and dictated the course of events on Earth from the moment Enlil joined Enki on this planet, and the rivalry was continued by their sons (Ninurta and Marduk, respectively). In Egyptian tales of the gods, a conflict for similar reasons reared its head between Ra's descendants, Seth and Osiris.

The rivalry, which from time to time flared into actual warfare (Horus in the end fought Seth in single combat in the skies of the Sinai peninsula), by all accounts did not begin on Earth. There were similar conflicts of succession on Nibiru, and Anu did not come by his rulership without fights and battles.

Like the custom that a widow left without a son could demand the husband's brother to "know" her as a surrogate husband and give her a son, so did the Anunnaki's rules of succession, giving priority to a son by a half sister, find their way into the customs of Abraham and his descendants. In his case, his first son was Ishmael, born by the handmaiden Hagar. But when, at an incredible old age and after divine intervention, Sarah bore Isaac—it was Isaac who was the Legitimate Heir. Why? Because Sarah was Abraham's half sister. "She is my sister, the daughter of my father but not of my mother," Abraham explained (Genesis 20:12).

The marrying of a half sister as a wife was prevalent among the Pharaohs of Egypt, as a means both to legitimize the king's reign and the succession. The custom was even found among the Inca kings of Peru, so much so that the occurrence of calamities during a certain king's reign was attributed to his marrying a woman who was not his half sister. The Inca custom had its roots in the Legends of Beginnings of the Andean peoples, whereby the god Viracocha created four brothers and four sisters who intermarried and were guided to various lands. One such brother-sister couple, which was given a golden wand with which to find the Navel of the Earth in South America, began kingship in Cuzco (the erstwhile Inca capital). That was why Inca kings—providing they had been born of a succession of brother-sister royal couples—could claim direct lineage to the Creator God Viracocha.

(Viracocha, according to Andean legends, was a great God of Heaven who had come to Earth in antiquity and chose the Andean mountains as his arena. In *The Lost Realms* we have identified him as the Mesopotamian god Adad = the Hittite god Teshub, and pointed to many other similarities, besides the brother-sister customs, between the Andean cultures and those of the ancient Near East.)

The persistence of the brother-sister intermarriage and the seemingly totally out of proportion significance attached to it, among gods and mortals alike, is puzzling. The custom on the face of it appears to be more than a localized "let's keep the throne in the family" attitude, and at worst the courting of genetic degradation. Why, then, the lengths to which the Anunnaki (example: Enki's repeated efforts to have a son by Ninmah) went to attain a son by such a union? What was so special about the genes of a half sister—the daughter, let us keep in mind, of the male's *mother* but definitely not of the father?

As we search for the answer, it will help to note other biblical practices affecting the mother/father issues. It is customary to refer to the period of Abraham, Isaac, Jacob, and Joseph as the Patriarchal Age, and when asked most people would say that the history related in the Old Testament has been presented from a male-oriented viewpoint. Yet the fact is that it was the *mothers,* not the fathers, who controlled the act that, in the ancients' view, gave the subject of the tale its status of "being"—the *naming* of the child. Indeed, not only a person but a place, a city, a land, were not deemed to have come into being until they were given a name.

This notion, in fact, goes back to the beginning of time, for the very opening lines of the *Epic of Creation,* wishing to impress on the listener that the story begins before the Solar System had been fully fashioned, declare that the story of Tiamat and the other planets begins

> *Enuma elish la nabu shamamu*
> When in the heights heaven had not been named
> *Shapiltu ammatum shuma la zakrat*
> And below, firm ground (Earth) had not been called

And in the important matter of naming a son, it was either the gods themselves or the mother whose privilege it was. We thus find that when the *Elohim* created *Homo sapiens,* it was they who named the new being "Adam" (Genesis 5:2). But when Man was given the ability to procreate on his own, it was Eve—not Adam—who had the right and privilege of naming their first male child Cain (Genesis 4:1) as well as Seth who replaced the slain Abel (Genesis 4:25).

At the start of the "Patriarchal (!) Age" we find that the privilege of naming the two sons of Abraham was taken over by divine beings. His firstborn by Hagar, his wife's hand-maiden, was called Ishma'el by an Angel of Yahweh (Genesis 16:11); and the Legitimate Heir Isaac (*Itzhak,* "Who causes laughter") was so named by one of the three divine beings who visited Abraham before the destruction of Sodom and Gomorrah (because when Sarah had heard God saying that she would have a son, she laughed; Genesis 17:19; 18:12). No specific information is provided in the Bible regarding the two sons of Isaac by Rebecca, Esau and Jacob (it is simply stated that this is how they were called). But then it is clearly stated that it was Leah who named Jacob's sons by her and by her hand-maiden, as did Rachel (Genesis chapters 29 and 30). Centuries later, after the Israelites had settled in Canaan, it was Samson's mother who so named him (Judges 13:24); so did the mother of the Man of God, Samuel (1 Samuel 1:20).

Figure 42

The Sumerian texts do not provide this kind of information. We do not know, for example, who named Gilgamesh—his mother the goddess or his father the High Priest. But the tale of Gilgamesh provides an important clue to the solution of the puzzle at hand: the importance of the mother in determining the son's hierarchical standing.

His search for attaining the longevity of the gods, it will be recalled, led him first to the Landing Place in the Cedar Mountains; but he and his companion Enkidu were prevented from entering by its robotic guardian and the Bull of Heaven. Gilgamesh then journeyed to the spaceport in the Sinai peninsula. The access to it was guarded by awesome Rocketmen who trained on him "the dreaded spotlight that sweeps the mountains" whose "glance was death" (Fig. 42); but Gilgamesh was not affected; whereupon one Rocketman shouted to his comrade:

> He who comes,
> of the flesh of the gods
> is his body!

Permitted to approach, Gilgamesh confirmed the guard's conclusion: Indeed he was immune to the death rays because his body was of the "flesh of the gods." He was, he explained, not just a *demi*god—he was "*two-thirds* divine," because it was not his father but his *mother* who was a goddess, one of the female Anunnaki.

Here, we believe, is the key to the puzzle of the succession rules and other emphasis on the mother. It is through her that an extra "qualifying dose" was given to the hero or the heir (be it Anunnaki or patriarchal).

This seemed to make no sense even after the discovery, in 1953, of the double-helix structure of DNA and the understanding how the two strands unwind and separate so that only one strand from the female egg and one strand from the male sperm recombine, making the offspring a fifty-fifty image of its parents. Indeed, this understanding, while explaining the demigod claims, defied the inexplicable claim of Gilgamesh to be two-thirds divine.

It was not until the 1980s that the ancient claims began to make sense. This came with the discovery that in addition to the DNA stored in the cells of both males and females in the double-helix structures on the chromosome stems, forming the cell's nucleus, there was another kind of DNA that floats in the cell outside the nucleus. Given the designation Mitochondrial DNA (mtDNA), it was found to be transmitted *only from the mother* as is, i.e. without splitting and recombining with any DNA from the male.

In other words, if the mother of Gilgamesh was a goddess, then he had indeed inherited both her half of the regular DNA *plus* her mtDNA, making him, as he had claimed, two-thirds divine.

It was this discovery of the existence and transmittal as is of mtDNA that has enabled scientists, from 1986 on, to trace the mtDNA in modern humans to an "Eve" who had lived in Africa some 250,000 years ago.

At first scientists believed that the sole function of mtDNA was to act as the cell's power plant, providing the energy required for the cell's myriad chemical and biological reactions. But then it was ascertained that the mtDNA was made of "mitochondrions" containing 37 genes arranged in a closed circle, like a bracelet; and that such a genetic "bracelet" contains over 16,000 base pairs of the genetic alphabet (by comparison, each of the chromosomes making up the cell's core that are inherited half from each parent contains upward of 100,000 genes and an aggregate of more than three billion base pairs).

It took another decade to realize that impairments in the makeup or functions of mtDNA can cause debilitating disorders in the human body, especially of the nervous system, of heart and skeletal muscles, and of the kidneys. In the 1990s researchers found that defects ("mutations") in mtDNA also disrupt the production of 13 important body proteins, resulting in various severe ailments. A list published in 1997 in *Scientific American* starts with Alzheimer's disease and goes on to include a variety of vision, hearing, blood, muscle, bone marrow, heart, kidney, and brain malfunctions.

These genetic ailments join a much longer list of bodily malfunctions and dysfunctions that defects in the nuclear DNA can cause. As scientists unravel and understand the "genome"—the complete genetic code—of humans (a feat recently achieved for a single lowly bacterium), the function that each gene performs (and as the other side of the coin, the ailments if it is absent or malfunctions) is steadily becoming known. By not producing a certain protein or enzyme or other key bodily compound, the gene regulating that has been found to cause breast cancer, or hinder bone formation, deafness, loss of eyesight, heart disorders, the excessive gain of weight or the opposite thereof, and so on and on.

What is interesting in this regard is that we come across a list of similar genetic defects as we read the Sumerian texts about the creation of the Primitive Worker by Enki with the assistance of Ninmah. The attempt to recombine the strands of hominid DNA with strands of Anunnaki DNA to create the new hybrid being was a process of trial and error, and the beings initially brought about sometimes lacked organs or limbs—or had too many of them. The Babylonian priest Berossus, who in the third century B.C. compiled for the Greeks the history and knowledge of the earlier Sumerians, described the failed results of Man's creators by reporting that some of the trial-and-error beings had two heads on one body. Such "monsters" have indeed been

Figures 43a and 43b

depicted by the Sumerians (Fig. 43a), as well as another anomaly—a being with one head but two faces called Usmu (Fig. 43b). Specifically mentioned in the texts was a being who could not hold its urine, and a variety of malfunctions including eye and eyesight diseases, trembling hands, an improper liver, a failing heart, and "sicknesses of old age." The text called *Enki and Ninmah: The Creation of Mankind,* besides listing more dysfunctions (rigid hands, paralyzed feet, dripping semen) also depicted Enki as a caring god who, rather than destroying such deformed beings, found some useful life for them. Thus, when one outcome was a man with faulty eyesight, Enki taught him an art that did not require seeing—the art of singing and the playing of a lyre.

To all those, the text states, Enki decreed this or that Fate. He then challenged Ninmah to try the genetic engineering on her own. The results were terrible: the beings she brought about had the mouth in the wrong place, a sick head, sore eyes, aching neck, shaky ribs, malfunctioning lungs, a heart ailment, inability to move the bowels, hands that were too short to reach the mouth, and so on and on. But as the trial and error continued, Ninmah was able to correct the various defects. Indeed, she reached a point that she became so knowledgeable of the

Anunnaki/hominid genomes that she boasted that she could make the
new being as perfect or imperfect as she wished:

How good or bad is man's body?
As my heart prompts me,
I can make its fate good or bad.

We, too, have now reached the stage where we can insert or replace
a certain gene whose role we have uncovered, and try to prevent or cure
a specific disease or shortcoming. Indeed, a new industry, the biotech-
nology industry, has sprung up, with a seemingly limitless potential in
medicine (and the stock market). We have even learned to perform what
is called transgenic engineering—the transfer of genes between different
species, a feat that is achievable because *all* the genetic material on this
planet, from the lowest bacterium to the most complex being (Man),
of all living organisms that roam or fly or swim or grow, is made up of
the same genetic ABC—the same nucleic acids that formed the "seed"
brought into our Solar System by Nibiru.
   Our genes are, in fact, our cosmic connection.

Modern advances in genetics move along two parallel yet intercon-
nected routes. One is to ascertain the human genome, the total genetic
makeup of the human being; this involves the reading of a code that
although written with just four letters (A-G-C-T, short for the initials
of the names given to the four nucleic acids that make up all DNA)
is made up of countless combinations of those letters that then form
"words" that combine into "sentences" and "paragraphs" and finally a
complete "book of life." The other research route is to determine the
function of each gene; that is an even more daunting task, facilitated by
the fact that if that very same gene ("genetic word") can be found in a
simpler creature (such as a lowly bacterium, or a laboratory mouse) and
its function could be experimentally determined, it is virtually certain
that the same gene in humans would have the same functions (or its
absence the same malfunctions). The discovery of genes related to obe-
sity, for example, has been achieved that way.

The ultimate goal of this search for the cause, and thus the cure, of human ailments and deficiencies is twofold: to find the genes that control the body's physiology and those that control the brain's neurological functions. To find the genes that control the process of aging, the cell's internal clock of the span of life—the genes of longevity—and the genes that control memory, reasoning, intelligence. Experiments on laboratory mice on the one hand and on human twins on the other hand, and extensive researches in between, indicate the existence of genes and groups of genes that account for both. How tedious and elusive these research targets are can be illustrated by the conclusion of a search for an "intelligence gene" by comparing twins: the researchers concluded that there might be as many as 10,000 "gene sites" or "genetic words" responsible for intelligence and cognitive diseases, each playing a tiny part by itself.

In view of such complexities, one wishes that modern scientists would avail themselves of a road map provided by—yes!—the Sumerians. The remarkable advances in astronomy keep corroborating the Sumerian cosmogony and the scientific data provided in the *Epic of Creation:* the existence of other solar systems, highly elliptic orbital paths, retrograde orbits, catastrophism, water on the outer planets— as well as explanations for why Uranus lies on its side, the origin of the Asteroid Belt and of the Moon, the Earth's cavity on one side and the continents on the other side. All is explained by the scientifically sophisticated tale of Nibiru and the Celestial Battle.

Why not then take seriously, as a scientific road map, the other part of the Sumerian creation tales—that of the creation of The Adam?

The Sumerian texts inform us, first of all, that the "seed of life"— the genetic alphabet—was imparted to Earth by Nibiru during the Celestial Battle, some four billion years ago. If the evolutionary processes on Nibiru began a mere one percent before they were launched on Earth, evolution there had begun forty million years before it started on Earth. It is thus quite plausible that the advanced superhumans, Anunnaki, were capable of space travel half a million years ago. It is also plausible that when they came here, they found on Earth the parallel intelligent beings still at the hominid stage.

But coming from the same "seed," transgenic manipulation was possible, as Enki had discovered and then suggested. "The being we need already exists!" he explained. "All we need to do is put our [genetic] mark on it."

One must presume that by then the Anunnaki were aware of the complete genome of the Nibiruans, and capable of determining no less of the hominids' genome as we are by now of ours. What traits, specifically, did Enki and Ninmah choose to transfer from the Anunnaki to the hominids? Both Sumerian texts and biblical verses indicate that while the first humans possessed some (but not all) of the longevity of the Anunnaki, the creator couple deliberately withheld from The Adam the genes of immortality (i.e., the immense longevity of the Anunnaki that paralleled Nibiru's orbital period). What defects, on the other hand, remained hidden in the depths of the recombined genome of The Adam?

We strongly believe that were qualified scientists to study in detail the data recorded in the Sumerian texts, valuable biogenetic and medical information could be obtained. An amazing case in point is the deficiency known as Williams Syndrome. Afflicting roughly one in 20,000 births, its victims have a very low IQ verging on retardation; but at the same time they excel in some artistic field. Recent research has discovered that the syndrome resulting in such "idiot savants" (as they are sometimes described) is caused by a minute gap in Chromosome 7, depriving the person of some fifteen genes. One of the frequent impairments is the inability of the brain to recognize what the eyes see—*impaired eyesight;* one of the most common talents is *musical.* **But that is exactly the instance recorded in the Sumerian text of the man with impaired eyesight whom Enki taught to sing and play music!**

Because The Adam could not, at first, procreate (requiring the Anunnaki to engage in cloning), we must conclude that at that stage the hybrid being possessed only the basic twenty-two chromosomes. The types of ailments, deficiencies (and cures) that modem biomedicine should expect to find on those chromosomes are the types and range listed in the Enki and Ninmah texts.

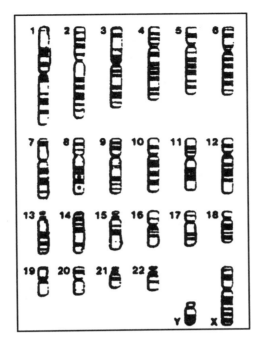

Figure 44

The next genetic manipulation (echoed in the Bible in the tale of Adam and Eve in the Garden of Eden) was the granting of the ability to procreate—the addition of the X (female) and Y (male) chromosomes to the basic 22 (Fig. 44). Contrary to long-held beliefs that these two chromosomes have no other function besides determining the offspring's sex, recent research has revealed that the chromosomes play wider and more diverse roles. For some reason this astonished the scientists in particular regarding the Y (male) chromosome. Studies published at the end of 1977 under scientific headings as "Functional Coherence of the Human Y Chromosome" received bold headlines in the press such as "Male Chromosome Is Not a Genetic Wasteland After All" (the *New York Times,* October 28, 1997). (These discoveries confirmed, as an unexpected bonus, that "Adam," too, like Eve, had come out of southeastern Africa).

Where did Enki—the *Nachash*—obtain the X and Y chromosomes? And what about the source of the mtDNA? Hints scattered in the Sumerian texts suggest that Ninki, Enki's spouse, played some crucial role in the final stage of human creation. It was she, Enki decided, who would give the humans the final touch, one more genetic heritage:

> The newborn's fate,
> thou shalt pronounce;
> Ninki would fix upon it
> the image of the gods.

The words echo the biblical statement that "in their *image* and after their *likeness* did the *Elohim* create The Adam." And if indeed it was Ninki, Enki's spouse and mother of Marduk, who was the source of the mtDNA of "Eve," the importance attached to the sister-wife lineage begins to make sense; for it constituted one more link to Man's cosmic origins.

Sumerian texts assert that while the gods kept "Eternal Life" to themselves, they did give Mankind "*Wisdom*," an extra dose of intelligence genes. That additional genetic contribution, we believe, is the subject of a text that scholars call *The Legend of Adapa*.

Clearly identified in the text as a "Son of Eridu," Ea/Enki's "cult center" in the Edin, he was also called in the text "the son of Ea"—an offspring, as far as other pieces of data suggest, of Ea/Enki himself by a woman other than his spouse. By dint of this lineage, as well as by deliberate action, Adapa was recalled for generations as the Wisest of Men, and was nicknamed the Sage of Eridu:

> In those days, in those years,
> Ea created the Sage of Eridu
> as a model of men.
> Wide understanding he perfected for him,
> disclosing the designs of the Earth.
> To him he had given Widsom;
> Eternal Life he had not given him.

This clash between Fate and Destiny takes us to the moment when *Homo sapiens-sapiens* appeared; Adapa, too, being the son of a god, asked for immortality. That, as we know from the *Epic of Gilgamesh,* could be obtained by ascending heavenward to the abode of the Anunnaki; and that was what Ea/Enki told Adapa. Undaunted, Adapa asked for and received Enki's "road map" for reaching the place: "He made Adapa take the way to heaven, and to heaven he ascended." Enki provided him with correct instructions of how to gain admittance to the throne room of Anu; but also gave him completely wrong instructions on how to behave when he would be offered the Bread of Life and the Water of Life. If you accept them and partake of them, Enki warned Adapa, surely you shall die! And, so misled by his own father, Adapa refused the food and the waters of the gods and ended up subject to his mortal's Destiny.

But Adapa did accept a garment that was brought to him and wrapped himself in it, and did take the oil that was offered to him, and anointed himself with it. Therefore, Anu declared, Adapa would be *initiated into the secret knowledge of the gods.* He showed him the celestial expanse, "from the horizon of heaven to heaven's zenith." He would be allowed to return to Eridu safe and sound, and there would be initiated by the goddess Ninkarrak into the secrets of "the ills that were allotted to Mankind, the diseases that were wrought upon the bodies of mortals," and taught by her how to heal such ailments.

It would be relevant here to recall the biblical assurances by Yahweh to the Israelites in the wilderness in Sinai. Wandering three days without any water, they reached a watering hole whose water was unpotable. So God pointed out to Moses a certain tree and told him to throw it into the water, and the water became potable. And Yahweh said to the Israelites: If you shall give ear to my commandments, I shall not impose on thee the illnesses of Egypt; "I Yahweh shall be thine healer" (Exodus 15:26). The promise by Yahweh to act as the healer of his chosen people is repeated in Exodus 23:25, where a specific reference is made to enabling a woman who is barren to bear children. (That particular promise was kept in regard to Sarah and other female heroines of the biblical narrative.)

Since we are dealing here with a divine entity, it is safe to assume that we are dealing here also with *genetic healing.* The incident with the

Nefilim, who had found on the eve of the Deluge that the "Daughters of The Adam" were compatible, and sufficiently so to be able to have children together, also involves genetics.

Was such knowledge of genetics, for healing purposes, imparted to Adapa or other demigods or initiates? And if so—how? How could the complex genetic code be taught to Earthlings in those "primitive" times?

For the answer, we believe, we have to search in letters and in numbers.

8
The Pyramid Wars

Selection from
The Wars of Gods and Men *(Chapter 8)*

Much of the infighting between the Anunnaki had to do with the struggle between the brothers Enki and Enlil, who were the sons of Anu. Although Enki was the firstborn son, Enlil was the primary son by virtue of being born to a half sister/wife; Enki was the son of a concubine. According to the succession rules that are echoed in biblical tales and the dictates of human kingship succession, the offspring of a half sister is next in line to inherit, then followed by offspring of the official spouse. This mandate created conflict for the Anunnaki leadership and in the relationships that existed between the brothers, Enki and Enlil, and their descendants. Due to the fact that Enki and Enlil were powerful leaders of their people, their sibling rivalry extended beyond their personal relationships. Alliances were formed and the Enlilites vs. the Enki-ites fought several battles. Sitchin calls these the Pyramid Wars.

According to Sitchin, the Great Pyramids had a large role to play in the activities of the Anunnaki, especially regarding communication and space travel. Not only were the pyramids post-diluvian landmarks that indicated the incoming flight path for spacecraft landing on Earth, they also contained equipment to assist in communication and to defend the pyramids from rival

Anunnaki who wanted to control them. Modern-day archaeologists and Egyptologists found the Great Pyramids empty, but the ancient tales indicate that this was not always the case.

"IN THE YEAR 363 His Majesty Ra, the holy one, the Falcon of the Horizon, the Immortal who forever lives, was in the land of Khenn. He was accompanied by his warriors, for the enemies had conspired against their lord. . . . Horus, the Winged Measurer, came to the boat of Ra. He said to his forefather: 'O Falcon of the Horizon, I have seen the enemy conspire against thy Lordship, to take the Luminous Crown unto themselves.' . . . Then Ra, the holy one, the Falcon of the Horizon, said unto Horus, the Winged Measurer: 'Lofty issue of Ra, my begotten: Go quickly, knock down the enemy whom you have seen.'"

Thus began the tale inscribed on the temple walls in the ancient Egyptian city of Edfu. It is the tale, we believe, of what could only be called the First Pyramid War—a war that had its roots in the never-ending struggle for control over Earth and its space facilities and in the shenanigans of the Great Anunnaki, especially Enki/Ptah and his son Ra/Marduk.

According to Manetho, Ptah turned over the dominion over Egypt after a reign of 9,000 years; but the reign of Ra was cut short after 1,000 years—by the Deluge, we have concluded. Then there followed a reign of 700 years by Shu, who helped Ra "control the skies over Earth," and the 500-year reign of Geb ("Who Piles Up the Earth"). It was at that time, circa 10,000 B.C., that the space facilities—the Spaceport in the Sinai and the Giza pyramids—were built.

Although the Sinai peninsula, where the Spaceport was established, and the Giza pyramids were supposed to remain neutral under the aegis of Ninharsag, it is doubtful whether the builders of these facilities—Enki and his descendants—had really any intention of relinquishing control over these installations. A Sumerian text, which begins with an idyllic description, has been named by scholars a "Paradise Myth." Its ancient name was *Enki and Ninharsag*, and it is, in fact, a record of the politically motivated lovemaking between the two, a tale of a deal between Enki and his half sister Ninharsag pertaining to the control of Egypt and the Sinai peninsula—of the pyramids and the Spaceport.

The tale's time is after Earth was apportioned between the Anunnaki, with Tilmun (the Sinai peninsula) granted to Ninharsag and Egypt to Enki's clan. It was then, the Sumerian tale relates, that Enki crossed the marshy lakes that separated Egypt and the Sinai peninsula and came unto the lonely Ninharsag for an orgy of lovemaking:

> To the one who is alone.
> To the Lady of Life, mistress of the land.
> Enki came unto the wise Lady of Life.
> He causes his phallus to water the dikes;
> He causes his phallus to submerge the reeds . . .
> He poured his semen into the great lady of the
>   Anunnaki,
> poured the semen in the womb of Ninharsag;
> She took the semen into the womb, the semen of Enki.

Enki's real intention was to obtain a son by his half sister; but the offspring was a daughter. Enki then made love to the daughter as soon as she became "young and fair," and then to his granddaughter. As a result of these sexual activities, a total of eight gods—six female and two male—were born. Angered by the incest, Ninharsag used her medical skills to sicken Enki. The Anunnaki who were with him pleaded for his life, but Ninharsag was determined: "Until he is dead, I shall not look upon him with the 'Eye of Life'!"

Satisfied that Enki had indeed been finally stopped, Ninurta—who went to Tilmun for inspection—returned to Mesopotamia to report the developments at a meeting attended by Enlil, Nanna/Sin, Utu/Shamash and Inanna/Ishtar. Unsatisfied, Enlil ordered Ninurta to return to Tilmun and bring back Ninharsag with him. But in the interim, Ninharsag had pity on her brother and changed her mind. "Ninharsag seated Enki by her vulva and asked: 'My brother, what hurts thee?'" After she cured his body part by part, Enki proposed that the two of them as masters of Egypt and the Sinai assign tasks, spouses, and territories to the eight young gods:

> Let Abu be the master of the plants;
> Let Nintulla be the lord of Magan;
> Let Ninsutu marry Ninazu;
> Let Ninkashi be she who sates the thirsts;
> Let Nazi marry Nindara;
> Let Azimua marry Ningishzida;
> Let Nintu be the queen of the months;
> Let Enshag be the lord of Tilmun!

Egyptian theological texts from Memphis likewise held that "there came into being" eight gods from the heart, tongue, teeth, lips, and other parts of the body of Ptah. In this text, too, as in the Mesopotamian one, Ptah followed up the bringing forth of these gods by assigning abodes and territories to them: "After he had formed the gods, he made cities, established districts, put the gods in their sacred abodes; he built their shrines and established their offerings." All that he did "to make rejoice the heart of the Mistress of Life."

If, as it appears, these tales had a basis in fact, then the rivalries that such confused parentages brought about could only be aggravated by the sexual shenanigans attributed to Ra as well. The most significant among these was the assertion that Osiris was truly the son of Ra and not of Geb, conceived when Ra had come by stealth unto his own granddaughter. This, as we have earlier related, lay at the core of the Osiris-Seth conflict.

Why had Seth, to whom Upper Egypt had been allotted by Geb, coveted Lower Egypt, which was granted to Osiris? Egyptologists have offered explanations in terms of geography, the land's fertility, etc. But as we have shown, there was one more factor—one that, from the gods' point of view, was more important than how many crops a region could grow: the Great Pyramid and its companions at Giza; whoever controlled them shared in the control of the space activities, of the comings and goings of the gods, of the vital supply link to and from the Twelfth Planet.

For a while Seth succeeded in his ambition, having outwitted Osiris. But "in the year 363" following the disappearance of Osiris, the young Horus became the avenger of his father and launched a war against Seth—the First Pyramid War. It was, as we have seen, also the first war in which the gods involved men in their struggles.

Supported by other Enki-gods reigning in Africa, the avenger Horus began the hostilities in Upper Egypt. Aided by the Winged Disk that Thoth had fashioned for him, Horus persistently advanced northward, toward the pyramids. A major battle took place in the "water district," the chain of lakes that separates Egypt from the Sinai peninsula, and a good many of Seth's followers were slain. After peacemaking efforts by other gods had failed, Seth and Horus engaged in personal combat in and over the Sinai peninsula. In the course of one battle, Seth hid in "secret tunnels" somewhere in the peninsula; in another battle, he lost his testicles. So the Council of the Gods gave the whole of Egypt "as heritage . . . to Horus."

And what had become of Seth, one of the eight gods descended from Ptah?

He was banished from Egypt and took up abode in Asiatic lands to the east, including a place that enabled him "to speak out from the sky." Was he the god called Enshag in the Sumerian tale of Enki and Ninharsag, the one to whom Tilmun (the Sinai peninsula) was allotted by the two lovemakers? If so, then he was the Egyptian (Hamitic) god who had extended his domain over the land of Shem later known as Canaan.

It was in this outcome of the First Pyramid War that there lies an understanding of biblical tales. Therein also lay the causes of the Second Pyramid War.

In addition to the Spaceport and the guidance facilities, there was also a need after the Deluge for a new Mission Control Center, to replace the one that had existed before in Nippur. We have shown (in *The Stairway to Heaven*) that the need to equidistance this center from the other space-related facilities dictated its locating on Mount Moriah ("The Mount of Directing"), the site of the future city of Jerusalem.

That site, by both Mesopotamian and biblical accounts, was located in the lands of Shem—a dominion of the Enlilites. Yet it ended up under an illegal occupation by the line of Enki, the Hamitic gods, and by the descendants of the Hamitic Canaan.

The Old Testament refers to the land of which Jerusalem in time became the capital as Canaan, after the fourth and youngest son of Ham. It also singled out Canaan for special rebuke and consigned his descendants to be subservient to the descendants of Shem. The improbable excuse for this treatment was that Ham—not his son Canaan—had inadvertently seen the naked genitals of his father Noah; therefore, the Lord had put a curse upon Canaan: "Cursed be Canaan; a servant of servants shall he be unto his brethren . . . Blessed be Yahweh the god of Shem; may Canaan be a servant unto them."

The tale in the Book of Genesis leaves many aspects unexplained. Why was Canaan accursed if it was his father who had accidentally transgressed? Why was his punishment to be a slave of Shem and to the god of Shem? And how were the gods involved in the crime and its punishment? As one reads the supplemental information in the ex-biblical *Book of Jubilees,* it becomes clear that the real offense was the illegal occupation of Shem's territory.

After mankind was dispersed and its various clans allotted their lands, the *Book of Jubilees* relates, "Ham and his sons went to the land which he was to occupy, [the land] which he acquired as his portion in the country of the south." But then, journeying from where Noah had been saved to his allotted land in Africa, "Canaan saw the land of Lebanon [all the way down] to the river of Egypt, that it was very good." And so he changed his mind: "He went not into the land of his inheritance to the west of the sea [west of the Red Sea]; he dwelt [instead] in the land of Lebanon, eastward and westward of the Jordan."

His father and his brothers tried to dissuade Canaan from such an illegal act: "And Ham his father, and Cush and Mizra'im his brothers, said unto him: "Thou hast settled in a land which is not thine, and which did not fall to us by lot; do not do so; for if thou dost do so, thou and thy sons will be fallen in the land and be accursed through sedition; for by sedition ye have settled, and by sedition will thy children fall, and thou shall be rooted out forever. Dwell not in the dwelling of Shem; for to Shem and his sons did it come by their lot."

Were he to illegally occupy the territory assigned to Shem, they pointed out, "Cursed art thou and cursed shalt thou be beyond the sons of Noah, by the curse which we bound ourselves by an oath in the presence of the Holy Judge and in the presence of Noah our father. . . ."

"But Canaan did not hearken unto them, and dwelt in the land of Lebanon from Hamath to the entering of Egypt, he and his sons until this day. For this reason is that land named Canaan."

Behind the biblical and pseudoepigraphical tale of a territorial usurpation by a descendant of Ham must lie a tale of a similar usurpation by a descendant of the God of Egypt. We must bear in mind that at the time the allotment of lands and territories was not among the peoples but among the gods; the gods, not the people, were the landlords. A people could only settle a territory allotted to their god and could occupy another's territory only if their god had extended his or her dominion to that territory, by agreement or by force. The illegal seizure of the area between the Spaceport in the Sinai and the Landing Place in Baalbek by a descendant of Ham could have occurred only if that area had been usurped by a descendant of the Hamitic deities, by a younger god of Egypt.

And that, as we have shown, was indeed the result of the First Pyramid War.

Seth's trespass into Canaan meant that all the space-related sites—Giza, the Sinai peninsula, Jerusalem—came under the control of the Enki gods. It was a development in which the Enlilites could not acquiesce. And so, soon thereafter—300 years later, we believe—they deliberately launched a war to dislodge the illegal occupiers from the vital space facilities. This Second Pyramid War is described in several texts, some found in the original Sumerian, others in Akkadian and Assyrian renderings. Scholars refer to these texts as the "Myths of Kur"—"myths" of the Mountain Lands; they are, in fact, poetically rendered chronicles of the war to control the space-related peaks—Mount Moriah; the Harsag (Mount St. Katherine) in the Sinai; and the artificial mount, the Ekur (the Great Pyramid) in Egypt.

It is clear from the texts that the Enlilite forces were led and commanded by Ninurta, "Enlil's foremost warrior," and that the first encounters were in the Sinai peninsula. The Hamitic gods were beaten there; but they retreated to continue the war from the mountain lands of Africa. Ninurta rose to the challenge, and in the second phase of the war carried the battle to the strongholds of his foes; that phase entailed vicious and ferocious battles. Then, in its final phase, the war was fought at the Great Pyramid, the last and impregnable stronghold of Ninurta's opponents; there the Hamitic gods were besieged until they ran out of food and water.

This war, which we call the Second Pyramid War, was commemorated extensively in Sumerian records—both written chronicles and pictorial depictions.

Hymns to Ninurta contain numerous references to his feats and heroic deeds in this war; a great part of the psalm "Like Anu Art Thou Made" is devoted to a record of the struggle and the final victory. But the principal and most direct chronicle of the war is the epic text *Lugal-e Ud Melam-bi,* best collated and edited by Samuel Geller in *Altorientalische Texte und Untersuchungen.* Like all Mesopotamian texts, it is so titled after its opening line:

> King, the glory of thy day is lordly;
> Ninurta, Foremost, possessor of the Divine Powers,
> who into the throes of the Mountainlands stepped forth.
> Like a flood which cannot be stopped,
> the Enemyland as with a girdle you tightly bound.
> Foremost one, who in battle vehemently enters;
> Hero, who in his hand the Divine Brilliant Weapon carries;
> Lord: the Mountainland you subdued as your creature.
> Ninurta, royal son, whose father to him had given might;
> Hero: in fear of thee, the city has surrendered . . .
> O mighty one—
> the Great Serpent, the heroic god,
> you tore away from all the mountains.

Thus extolling Ninurta, his feats, and his Brilliant Weapon, the poem also describes the location of the conflict ("the Mountainlands") and his principal enemy: "The Great Serpent," leader of the Egyptian deities. The Sumerian poem identifies this adversary several times as *Azag* and once refers to him as *Ashar,* both well-known epithets for Marduk, thereby establishing the two principal sons of Enlil and Enki—Ninurta and Marduk—as the leaders of the opposing camps in the Second Pyramid War.

The second tablet (one of thirteen on which the long poem was inscribed) describes the first battle. Ninurta's upper hand is ascribed to both his godly weapons and a new airship that he built for himself after his original one had been destroyed in an accident. It was called IM.DU.GUD, usually translated "Divine Storm Bird" but which literally means "That Which Like Heroic Storm Runs"; we know from various texts that its wingspan was about seventy-five feet.

Archaic drawings depicted it as a mechanically constructed "bird," with two wing surfaces supported by cross beams (Fig. 47a); an undercarriage reveals a series of round openings, perhaps air intakes for jetlike engines. This aircraft, from millennia ago, bears a remarkable resemblance not only to the early biplanes of the modern air age, but also an incredible likeness to the sketch made in 1497 by Leonardo da Vinci, depicting his concept of a man-powered flying machine (Fig. 47b).

The Imdugud was the inspiration for Ninurta's emblem—a heroic lion-headed bird resting on two lions (Fig. 48) or sometimes on two bulls. It was in this "crafted ship"—a manufactured vehicle—"that which in war destroys the princely abodes," that Ninurta soared into the skies during the battles of the Second Pyramid War. He soared so high that his companions lost sight of him. Then, the texts relate, "in his Winged Bird, against the walled abode" he swooped down. "As his Bird neared the ground, the summit [of the enemy's stronghold] he smashed."

Chased out of his strongholds, the Enemy began to retreat. While Ninurta kept up the frontal attack, Adad roamed the countryside behind the enemy lines, destroying the adversary's food supplies: "In the Abzu, Adad the fish caused to be washed away . . . the cattle he

a

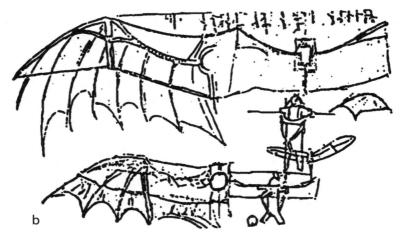

b

Fig. 47

Fig. 48

dispersed." When the Enemy kept retreating into the mountains, the two gods "like an onrushing flood the mountains ravaged."

As the battles extended in time and scope, the two leading gods called on the others to join them. "My lord, to the battle which is becoming extensive, why don't you go?" they asked a god whose name is missing in a damaged verse. The question was clearly also addressed to Ishtar, for she is mentioned by name: "In the clash of weapons, in the feats of heroship, Ishtar her arm did not hold back." As the two gods saw her, they shouted encouragingly to her: "Advance hither without stopping! Put your foot down firmly on the Earth! In the mountains, we await thee!"

"The weapon which is lordly brilliant, the goddess brought forth . . . a horn [to direct it] she made for it." As she used it against the enemy in a feat "that to distant days" shall be remembered, "the skies were like red-hued wool in color." The explosive beam "tore apart [the enemy], made him with his hand clutch his heart."

The continued tale, on tablets v–viii, is too damaged to be properly read. The partial verses suggest that after the intensified attack with Ishtar's assistance, there arose a great cry and lamentation in the Enemyland. "Fear of Ninurta's Brilliance encompassed the land," and its residents had to use substitutes instead of wheat and barley "to grind and mill as flour."

Under this onslaught the Enemy forces kept retreating south. It was then that the war assumed its ferocious and vicious character, when Ninurta led the Enlilite gods in an attack on the heartland of Nergal's African domain and his temple-city, Meslam. They scorched the earth and made the rivers run red with the blood of the innocent bystanders—the men, women, and children of the Abzu.

The verses describing this aspect of the war are damaged on the tablets of the main text; its details are, however, available from various other fragmented tablets that deal with the "overwhelming of the land" by Ninurta, "a feat whereby he earned the title "Vanquisher of Meslam." In these battles the attackers resorted to chemical warfare. We read that Ninurta rained on the city poison-bearing missiles, which "he catapulted into it; the poison, by itself, destroyed the city."

Those who survived the attack on the city escaped to the surrounding mountains. But Ninurta "with the Weapon That Smites threw fire upon the mountains; the godly Weapon of the Gods, whose Tooth is bitter, smote down the people." Here, too, some kind of chemical warfare is indicated:

> The Weapon Which Tears Apart
> robbed the senses:
> The Tooth skinned them off.
> Tearing-apart he stretched upon the land;
> The canals he filled with blood,
> in the Enemyland for dogs like milk to lick.

Overwhelmed by the merciless onslaught. Azag called on his followers to show no resistance: "The arisen Enemy to his wife and child called; against the lord Ninurta he raised not his ami. The weapons of Kur with soil were covered" (i.e., hidden away); "Azag them did not raise."

Ninurta took the lack of resistance as a sign of victory. A text reported by F. Hrozny ("Mythen von dem Gotte Ninib") relates how, after Ninurta killed the opponents occupying the land of the Harsag (Sinai) and went on "like a Bird" to attack the gods who "behind their walls retreated" in Kur, he defeated them in the mountains. He then burst out in a song of victory:

> My fearsome Brilliance like Anu's is mighty;
> Against it, who can rise?
> I am lord of the high mountains.
> of the mountains which to the horizon raise their peaks.
> In the mountains, I am the master.

But the claim of victory was premature. By his nonresistance tactics, Azag had escaped defeat. The capital city was indeed destroyed, but not so the leaders of the Enemy. Soberly, the text *Lugal-e* observed: "The scorpion of Kur Ninurta did not annihilate." Instead, the Enemy gods retreated into the Great Pyramid, where "the Wise Craftsman"—Enki? Thoth?—raised up a protective wall "which the Brilliance could not match," a shield through which the death rays could not penetrate.

Our knowledge of this final and most dramatic phase of the Second Pyramid War is augmented by texts from "the other side." Just as Ninurta's followers composed hymns to him, so did the followers of Nergal. Some of the latter, which have also been discovered by archaeologists, were put together in *Gebete und Hymnen an Nergal* by J. Bollenrücher.

Recalling the heroic feats of Nergal in this war, the texts relate how, as the other gods found themselves hemmed in within the Giza complex, Nergal—"Lofty Dragon Beloved of Ekur"—"at night stole out" and, carrying awesome weapons and accompanied by his lieutenants, broke through the encirclement to reach the Great Pyramid (the Ekur). Reaching it at night, he entered through "the locked doors which by themselves can open." A roar of welcome greeted him as he entered:

> Divine Nergal,
> Lord who by night stole out,
> had come to the battle!
> He cracks his whip, his weapons clank . . .
> He who is welcome, his might is immense:
> Like a dream at the doorstep he appeared.
> Divine Nergal, the One Who Is Welcome:
> Fight the enemy of Ekur,
> lay hold on the Wild One from Nippur!

But the high hopes of the besieged gods were soon dashed. We learn more of the last phases of this Pyramid War from yet another text, first pieced together by George A. Barton (*Miscellaneous Babylonian Texts*) from fragments of an inscribed clay cylinder found in the ruins of Enlil's temple in Nippur.

As Nergal joined the defenders of the Great Pyramid ("the

Formidable House Which Is Raised Up Like a Heap"), he strengthened its defenses through the various ray-emitting crystals (mineral "stones") positioned within the pyramid:

> The Water-Stone,
> the Apex-Stone,
> the . . . -Stone, the . . .
> . . . the lord Nergal
> increased its strength.
> The door for protection he . . .
> To heaven its Eye he raised,
> Dug deep that which gives life . . .
> . . . in the House
> he fed them food.

With the pyramid's defenses thus enhanced, Ninurta resorted to another tactic. He called upon Utu/Shamash to cut off the pyramid's water supply by tampering with the "watery stream" that ran near its foundations. The text here is too mutilated to enable a reading of the details; but the tactic apparently achieved its purpose.

Huddled in their last stronghold, cut off from food and water, the besieged gods did their best to ward off their attackers. Until then, in spite of the ferocity of the battles, no major god had fallen a casualty to the fighting. But now one of the younger gods—Horus, we believe—trying to sneak out of the Great Pyramid disguised as a ram, was struck by Ninurta's Brilliant Weapon and lost the sight of his eyes. An Olden God then cried out to Ninharsag—reputed for her medical wonders—to save the young god's life:

> At that time the Killing Brightness came;
> The House's platform withstood the lord.
> Unto Ninharsag there was an outcry:
> ". . . The weapon . . . my offspring
> with death is accursed. . . ."

Other Sumerian texts call this young god "offspring who did not know his father," an epithet befitting Horus, who was born after his father's death. In Egyptian lore the *Legend of the Ram* reports the injuries to the eyes of Horus when a god "blew fire" at him.

It was then, responding to the "outcry," that Ninharsag decided to intervene to stop the fighting.

The ninth tablet of the *Lugal-e* text begins with the statement of Ninharsag, her address to the Enlilite commander, her own son Ninurta, "the son of Enlil . . . the Legitimate Heir whom the sister-wife had brought forth." In telltale verses she announced her decision to cross the battle lines and bring an end to the hostilities:

> To the House Where Cord-Measuring begins.
> Where Asar his eyes to Anu raised,
> I shall go.
> The cord I will cut off,
> for the sake of the warring gods.

Her destination was the "House Where Cord-Measuring begins," the Great Pyramid!

Ninurta was at first astounded by her decision to "enter alone the Enemyland"; but since her mind was made up, he provided her with "clothes which should make her unafraid" (of the radiation left by the beams?). As she neared the pyramid, she addressed Enki: "She shouts to him . . . she beseeches him." The exchanges are lost by the breaks in the tablet; but Enki agreed to surrender the pyramid to her:

> The House that is like a heap,
> that which I have as a pile raised up—
> its mistress you may be.

There was, however, a condition: The surrender was subject to a final resolution of the conflict until "the destiny-determining time" shall come. Promising to relay Enki's conditions, Ninharsag went to address Enlil.

The events that followed are recorded in part in *the Lugal-e* epic and in other fragmentary texts. But they are most dramatically described in a text titled *I Sing the Song of the Mother of the Gods*. Surviving in great length because it was copied and recopied throughout the ancient Near East, the text was first reported by P. Dhorme in his study *La Souveraine des Dieux*. It is a poetic text in praise of *Ninmah* (the "Great Lady") and her role as *Mammi* ("Mother of the Gods") on both sides of the battle lines.

Opening with a call upon "the comrades in arms and the combatants" to listen, the poem briefly describes the warfare and its participants, as well as its nearly global extent. On the one side were "the firstborn of Ninmah" (Ninurta) and Adad, soon joined by Sin and later on by Inanna/Ishtar. On the opposing side are listed Nergal, a god referred to as "Mighty, Lofty One"—Ra/Marduk—and the "God of the two Great Houses" (the two great pyramids of Giza) who had tried to escape camouflaged in a ram's skin: Horus.

Asserting that she was acting with the approval of Anu, Ninharsag took the surrender offer of Enki to Enlil. She met him in the presence of Adad (while Ninurta remained at the battlefield). "O hear my prayers!" she begged the two gods as she explained her ideas. Adad was at first adamant:

> Presenting himself there, to the Mother,
> Adad thus said:
> "We are expecting victory.
> The enemy forces are beaten.
> The trembling of the land he could not withstand."

If she wants to bring about a cessation of hostilities, Adad said, let her call discussions on the basis that the Enlilites are about to win:

> "Get up and go—talk to the enemy.
> Let him attend the discussions
> so that the attack be withdrawn."

Enlil, in less forceful language, supported the suggestion:

> Enlil opened his mouth;
> In the assembly of the gods he said:
> "Whereas Anu at the mountain the gods assembled,
> warfare to discourage, peace to bring,
> and has dispatched the Mother of the Gods
> to entreat with me—
> Let the Mother of the Gods be an emissary."

Turning to his sister, he said in a conciliatory vein:

> "Go, appease my brother!
> Raise unto him a hand for Life;
> From his barred doorway, let him come out!"

Doing as suggested, Ninharsag "his brother went to fetch, put her prayers before the god." She informed him that his safety, and that of his sons, was assured: "by the stars she gave a sign."

As Enki hesitated she said to him tenderly: "Come, let me lead you out." And as he did, he gave her his hand. . . .

She conducted him and the other defenders of the Great Pyramid to the Harsag, her abode. Ninurta and his warriors watched the Enkites depart.

And the great and impregnable structure stood unoccupied, silent.

Nowadays the visitor to the Great Pyramid finds its passages and chambers bare and empty, its complex inner construction apparently purposeless, its niches and nooks meaningless.

It has been so ever since the first men had entered the pyramid. But it was not so when Ninurta had entered it—circa 8670 B.C. according to our calculations. "Unto the radiant place," yielded by its defenders, Ninurta had entered, the Sumerian text relates. And what he had done after he had entered changed not only the Great Pyramid from within and without but also the course of human affairs.

When, for the first time ever, Ninurta went into the "House Which Is Like a Mountain," he must have wondered what he would find inside. Conceived by Enki/Ptah, planned by Ra/Marduk, built by Geb, equipped by Thoth, defended by Nergal, what mysteries of space guidance, what secrets of impregnable defense did it hold?

In the smooth and seemingly solid north face of the pyramid, a swivel stone swung open to reveal the entranceway, protected by the massive diagonal stone blocks, just as the text lauding Ninharsag had described. A straight Descending Passage led to the lower service chambers where Ninurta could see a shaft dug by the defenders in search for subterranean water. But his interest focused on the upper passages and chambers; there, the magical "stones" were arrayed—minerals and crystals, some earthly, some heavenly, some the likes of which he had never seen. From them there were emitted the beamed pulsations for the guidance of the astronauts and the radiations for the defense of the structure.

Escorted by the Chief Mineralmaster, Ninurta inspected the array of "stones" and instruments. As he stopped by each one of them, he determined its destiny—to be smashed up and destroyed, to be taken away for display, or to be installed as instruments elsewhere. We know of these "destinies," and of the order in which Ninurta had stopped by the stones, from the text inscribed on tablets 10–13 of the epic poem *Lugal-e*. It is by following and correctly interpreting this text that the mystery of the purpose and function of many features of the pyramid's inner structure can be finally understood.

Going up the Ascending Passage, Ninurta reached its junction with the imposing Grand Gallery and a Horizontal Passage. Ninurta followed the Horizontal Passage first, reaching a large chamber with a corbeled roof. Called the "vulva" in the Ninharsag poem, this chamber's axis lay exactly on the east-west center line of the pyramid. Its emission ("an outpouring which is like a lion whom no one dares attack") came from a stone fitted into a niche that was hollowed out in the east wall (Fig. 49). It was the SHAM ("Destiny") Stone. Emitting a red radiance which Ninurta "saw in the darkness," it was the pulsating heart of the pyramid. But it was anathema to Ninurta, for during the battle, when

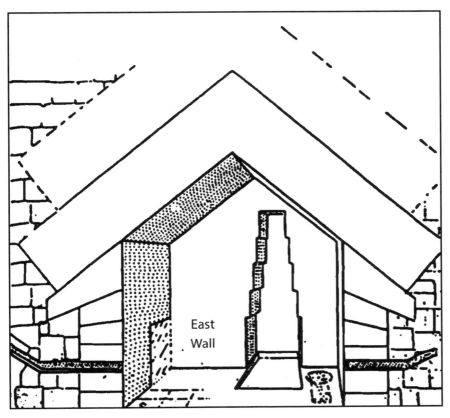

East
Wall

Fig. 49

he was aloft, this stone's "strong power" was used "to grab to kill me, with a tracking which kills to seize me." He ordered it "pulled out . . . be taken apart . . . and to obliteration be destroyed."

Returning to the junction of the passages, Ninurta looked around him in the Grand Gallery. As ingenious and complex as the whole pyramid was, this gallery was breathtaking and a most unusual sight. Compared to the low and narrow passages, it rose high (some twenty-eight feet) in seven overlapping stages, its walls closing in ever more at each stage. The ceiling was also built in slanting sections, each one angled into the massive walls so as not to exert any pressure on the segment below it. Whereas in the narrow passages only "a dim green light glowed," the Gallery glittered in multicolored lights—"its vault is like a rainbow, the darkness ends there." The many-hued glows were emitted by twenty-seven pairs of diverse crystal stones that were evenly spaced along the whole length of each side of the Gallery (Fig. 50a). These glowing stones were placed in cavities that were precisely cut into the ramps that ran the length of the Gallery on both sides of its floor. Firmly held in place by an elaborate niche in the wall (Fig. 50b), each crystal stone emitted a different radiance, giving the place its rainbow effect. For the moment Ninurta passed by them on his way up; his priority was the uppermost Grand Chamber and its pulsating stone.

Atop the Grand Gallery, Ninurta reached a great step, which led through a low passage to an Antechamber of unique design. There three portcullises—"the bolt, the bar and the lock" of the Sumerian poem—elaborately fitted into grooves in the walls and floor, hermetically sealed off the uppermost Great Chamber: "to foe it is not opened; only to Them Who Live, for them it is opened." But now, by pulling some cords, the portcullises were raised, and Ninurta passed through.

He was now in the pyramid's most restricted ("sacred") chamber, from which the guiding "Net" (radar?) was "spread out" to "survey Heaven and Earth." The delicate mechanism was housed in a hollowed-out stone chest; placed precisely on the north-south axis of the pyramid, it responded to vibrations with bell-like resonance. The heart of the guidance unit was the GUG ("Direction Determining") Stone; its emissions, amplified by five hollow compartments constructed above the chamber, were beamed out and up through two sloping channels leading to the north and south faces of the pyramid. Ninurta ordered this stone destroyed: "Then, by the fate-determining Ninurta, on that day was the Gug stone from its hollow taken out and smashed."

To make sure no one would ever attempt to restore the "Direction Determining" functions of the pyramid, Ninurta also ordered the three portcullises removed. First to be tackled were the SU ("Vertical") Stone and the KA.SHUR.RA ("Awesome, Pure Which Opens") Stone. Then "the hero stepped up to the SAG.KAL Stone" ("Sturdy Stone Which Is In Front"). "He called out his full strength,"

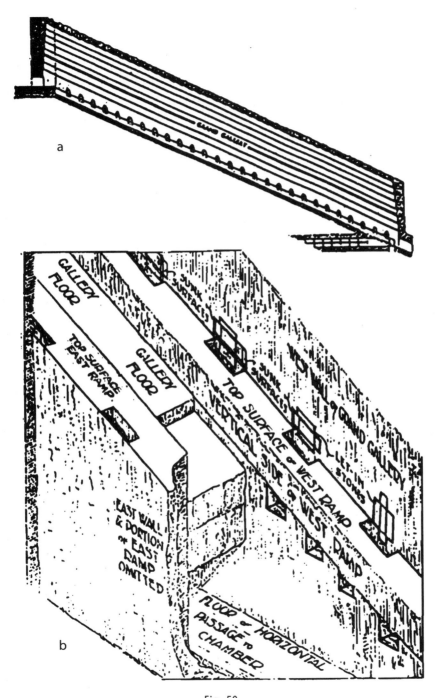

a

b

Fig. 50

shook it out of its grooves, cut the cords that were holding it, and "to the ground set its course."

Now came the turn of the mineral stones and crystals positioned atop the ramps in the Grand Gallery. As he walked down Ninurta stopped by each one of them to declare its fate. Were it not for breaks in the clay tablets on which the text was written, we would have had the names of all twenty-seven of them; as it is, only twenty-two names are legible. Several of them Ninurta ordered to be crushed or pulverized; others, which could be used in the new Mission Control Center, were ordered given to Shamash; and the rest were carried off to Mesopotamia, to be displayed in Ninurta's temple, in Nippur, and elsewhere as constant evidence of the great victory of the Enlilites over the Enki-gods.

All this, Ninurta announced, he was doing not only for his sake but for future generations, too: "Let the fear of thee"—the Great Pyramid—"be removed from my descendants; let their peace be ordained."

Finally there was the Apex Stone of the Pyramid, the UL ("High As The Sky") Stone: "Let the mother's offspring see it no more," he ordered. And, as the stone was sent crashing down, "let everyone distance himself," he shouted. The "Stones," which were "anathema" to Ninurta, were no more.

The deed having been done, Ninurta's comrades urged him to leave the battleground and return home. AN DIM DIM.MA, "Like Anu Art Thou Made," they told him in praise; "The Radiant House where the cord-measuring begins, the House in the land which thou hast come to know—rejoice in having entered it." Now, return to thy home, where thy wife and son await thee: "In the city which thou lovest, in the abode of Nippur, may thy heart be at rest . . . may thy heart become appeased."

The Second Pyramid War was over: but its ferocity and feats, and Ninurta's final victory at the pyramids of Giza, were remembered long thereafter in epic and song—and in a remarkable drawing on a cylinder seal, showing Ninurta's Divine Bird within a victory wreath, soaring in triumph above the two great pyramids (Fig. 51).

Fig. 51

And the Great Pyramid itself, bare and void and without its apex stone, has been left standing as a mute witness to the defeat of its defenders.

9

The Elusive Mount

Unpublished Article, Written Circa 1978

The contents of this chapter are derived from an article Zecharia Sitchin wrote that later became chapter 11 in *The Stairway to Heaven* (published in 1980). (In it there are some slight modifications, which I'll leave to the reader to compare for themselves.) Sitchin felt that a mount in the Sinai peninsula was a pre-diluvian spaceport for the Anunnaki, thus its significance to our story. Scholars have long debated the location of the real Mount Sinai, and many explorers over the years have set out to find it once and for all. Various contenders that have been put forth as candidates include Mount Mussa and Mount Serbal. Others suggest that Mount Sinai wasn't located in the southern Sinai at all. Even the great Napoleon Bonaparte got in on the search. Sitchin felt that finding Mount Sinai would be of interest not just for showing the historical validity of the biblical narrative but also in fitting this in with the information about the Anunnaki and their activities while on Earth. In this chapter, Sitchin recounts the many adventurers who set out to solve the riddle and he herein details their exploits. In so doing, he provides their respective rationale for believing that they had discovered the true location of this historically and culturally significant place.

A JEWISH LEGEND, recorded in the Talmud and going back thousands of years, relates that when the news of the death of the mighty leader of the Israelites had spread throughout the lands, the king of the Aramaeans sought the burial place. As his men ascended Mount Nebo, they could see the grave down in the valley, but as they came down to take a closer look, they found nothing there. Instead, they saw the grave atop the mount. After more searching, they gave up. Indeed did Moses die, they reported to the king; but no one knows the whereabouts of the burial place.

Similar legends pertained to the burial place of Aaron. They relate that when Aaron failed to return with Moses and Elazar from Mount Hor, the people could not believe that he had died there. They were not convinced until the Lord ordered his angels to bring Aaron's body out of a secret cave, and hold it up for the people to see. Then the angels hid the body again.

There was a purpose to the graves' anonymity, Jewish traditions held: to prevent worship of these human leaders. Though Moses was later referred to as "The Man of the Gods," he was not *divine* but *only a mortal,* and there was to be no "personality cult." Similarly, there was to be no more worship at Mount Sinai. The Theopany and the making of the Covenant were unique, one-time events, and the people were gathered unto the Mount only for that purpose. As in the case of the burial places of Moses and Aaron, so was pilgrimage to the Mount discouraged.

The Exodus from Egypt has been commemorated each year for the past thirty-three centuries by the celebration of Passover. The historical and religious records of the Hebrews are replete with references to the Exodus, the wanderings in the Wilderness, the Covenant at Sinai. The people have been constantly reminded, throughout the ancient centuries, of the Theophany and the miracles. Yet there is no record in the Old Testament of anyone even trying to pay a return visit to the Holy Mount, with one exception.

The exception to the rule was the prophet Elijah—the miracle maker who later on ascended to heaven in a fiery chariot. The time (some four hundred years after the presumed date of the Exodus) was the reign of King Ahab and Queen Jezebel. She introduced into Israel the worship of the Phoenician god Ba'al, and Elijah faced all the priests of Ba'al on Mount Carmel in a final contest of divine miracles. When the might of Yahweh prevailed, the crowd killed all the priests of Ba'al; whereupon Elijah had to flee for his life from a vengeful Jezebel. He escaped to the holy mount, but enroute became exhausted and lost his way. An angel of the Lord revived him, and led him to the mount.

Nowadays, one does not need a heavenly angel to be guided to Mount Sinai. After Israel occupied the Sinai peninsula in 1967, the domestic airline Arkia began regular flights to a naturally flat and hardsoiled airstrip, which in time was developed into "Mount Sinai Airfield." About an hour's drive away from there, the visitor is taken by bus to the vicinity of Mount Sinai.

There is no actual road, just tire marks made by previous buses. The way winds its course southward. The amazingly flat and hard, but dust-covered plateau, is surrounded on all sides by mountain peaks that compete with each other in size and shape. After a while, the mountains begin to converge and the course becomes more rocky, narrow, and steep. Then a short ascent; and from atop one of the uncountable mountains a valley can be seen down below, with an oasis of date palms in the distance; it is the oasis of Firan. Then another stop, and through a gap in the mountain chain that begins to block the sky in the distance, there are sharp peaks to be seen: it is there that the traditional Mount Sinai is.

Except for the oasis of Firan, the mountains are completely barren. It is not, however, a moonlike landscape. The whole panorama of peaks rising above peaks is bursting with color—browns, yellows, greys— standing out in agelong serenity against a blue sky. The visibility is limitless. Strewn rocks, some red, some greenish, indicate the presence of iron and copper minerals.

When the towering range is reached, there is not a flat spot to be seen. The mountains are solid granite, rising skyward like rows of a giant's teeth. The bus creaks along a rocky path cleared among boulders that have rolled off the mountainsides. A sharp descent begins, and the visitor wonders where the plunge is leading. And then an unexpected valley appears—the "cavity" of the "giant's mouth" surrounded by his awesome granite "teeth." The sight is unbelievable: Down there lies cathedral square of a medieval European town, surrounded by the town's wall!

It is the Monastery of Santa Katarina (or Katherine). Its few Greek Orthodox monks tend a nearby garden, guard the monastery's relics and library, and act as hosts (including overnight stays) for the pilgrims and sightseers who have been coming here for centuries.

The monastery, however, does not mark the site of Mount Sinai; it marks, instead, the presumed site of the Burning Bush that Moses had seen. Nor is it called after the hallowed mount, but bears the name of another nearby peak—Mount St. Katarina. The monastery's tradition explains that its history goes back to the beginning of Christianity, when early converts in Egypt (then under Roman rule) escaped into the Sinai peninsula to avoid persecution. After Constantine granted Christianity recognition in the year 313, the Byzantine rulers encouraged the hermits to form monastic communities.

In the year 330 the Empress Helena, acting on a petition by a group of monks that selected the small oasis as their abode, made possible the erection of a church and a tower at the spot that the monks described as the site of the Burning Bush. Three centuries later the Emperor Justinian—with state interests in mind—ordered the erection of a larger church and built a strong wall around the place, turning the monastery into a fortress; entrance, for a long time, was by a basket raised on a pulley.

Then a miracle happened. Among the last martyrs of Christianity to have been tortured and executed by the Romans was Katherine of Alexandria. On her execution, her body vanished; according to legend, angels had carried it to the highest peak in the peninsula of Sinai. Four centuries later, the burial place was revealed to the monks in a dream. They brought the body down and put it in a golden casket, which was placed in the church built by Justinian. The casket can be viewed there to this very day. Centuries later, the Crusaders spread word of the monastery and Katherine's miracle. The monastery and the mount on which the body was found were named after this saint. Many pilgrims ascend Mount St. Katarina (or Katherine) with the same reverence they have when ascending Mount Sinai. Situated some distance to the southwest of the monastery, Mount St. Katarina can be ascended by a path hewn out centuries ago by a pious monk who was named Mussa ("Moses" in Arabic).

The peak associated with the Exodus is the one called Jebel Mussa, the "Mountain of Moses." Like Mount St. Katarina, it cannot be seen from the monastery, for other high peaks surrounding the valley hide the two hallowed mounts from sight. The holy mount is, in fact, a massif two miles long and one mile wide. Its northern peak, called *Ras Sufsafeh* ("The Willow Head") can be seen south of the monastery. But it is the southern peak that bears the name *Jebel Mussa* and with which the Theophany and the Lawgiving are associated; it is that southernmost peak, lying some two hours' walk away, that is the traditional Mount Sinai.

The climb to that peak is long and difficult, involving an ascent of some 2,500 feet. One path is by way of some 4,000 steps laid out by the monks along the western slopes of the massif. An easier way that takes several hours longer begins in the valley between the massif and a mountain appropriately named after Jethro, the father-in-law of Moses, and rises gradually along the eastern slopes until it connects with the last 750 steps of the first path. It was at that intersection, according to the monks' tradition, that Elijah encountered the Lord.

A Christian chapel and a Moslem shrine, both small and crudely built, mark the spot where the Tablets of the Law were given to Moses. A cave nearby is revered as the "cleft in the rock" wherein the Lord placed Moses as He passed by him, as related in Exodus 33:22. A well along the descent route is identified as the well from which Moses watered the flock of his father-in-law. Every possible event relating to the Holy Mount is thus assigned by the monks' traditions a definite spot on the peak of Jebel Mussa and its surroundings.

From the peak of Jebel Mussa, one can see some of the other peaks of which this mount is a member. The Sinai peninsula is shaped like an inverted triangle, its wide base in the north along the Mediterranean coast, its tip where the Red Sea divides into the Gulf of Suez and Gulf of Eilat. Beginning with low sand dunes in the north, through a flat central core surrounded by mountains as by a pincer, the elevation of the peninsula begins to rise appreciably as one goes south. The southern third of the peninsula is taken up by rugged, mostly granite mountains that rise steeply from the gulfs' shores. The elevation changes quickly from 1,500 feet to double and treble heights. Among the highest mountains that average 4,500 feet, there lies the even loftier range of which Jebel Mussa is a member.

But Jebel Mussa, hallowed as Mount Sinai, is the shortest of them all. Indeed, in support of the legend of St. Katarina, the monks have put up a sign in the main building which proclaims:

ALTITUDE	5012 FT
MOSES MOUNT	7560 FT
STA. KATHERINE MOUNT	8576 FT

As one is convinced that Mount St. Katarina is indeed the higher one, and thus rightly chosen by the angels to hide the saint's body thereon, one is also disappointed that—contrary to long-held beliefs— God had brought the children of Israel to this forbidding area, to impress upon them his might and his laws not from the tallest, but from the shortest mount around.

Has God missed the right mountain?

In 1809, the Swiss scholar Johann Ludwig Burckhardt arrived in the Near East on behalf of the British Association for Promoting the Discovery of the Interior Parts of Africa. Studying Arabic and Moslem customs, he put a turban on his head, dressed as an Arab, and changed his name to Ibrahim Ibn Abd Allah—Abraham the Son of Allah's Servant. He was thus able to travel in parts hitherto forbidden to the infidels, discovering ancient Egyptian temples at Abu Simbel and the Nabatean rock city of Petra in Tranjordan.

On April 15, 1816, he set out on camelback from the town of Suez, at the head of the Gulf of Suez. His goal was to retrace the Route of the Exodus, and thereby establish the true identity of Mount Sinai. Following the presumed route taken by the Israelites, he travelled south along the western coast of the peninsula, where the mountains begin some ten to twenty miles away from the coast. The coastal strip, running from Suez to the tip of the peninsula (and then partly up the eastern coastline) is desert land, cut here and there by *wadis*—dry, shallow river courses that drain off the waters from the nearby mountains after the brief rains, but that are otherwise dry and passable throughout most other days of the year.

As he went south, he noted the geography, topography, distances. He compared conditions and place names with the descriptions and names of the stations mentioned in the Old Testament. Through such wadis in the zone where the sandstone plateau ends and the high granite mountains begin, he turned east and inland, then south, reaching the Monastary of Santa Katarina from the north, as today's traveler does. He toured the area, ascending Mounts Mussa and Katarina. His way back was via the large wadi Firan and its oasis—the largest in Sinai. Where wadi Firan leaves the mountains and reaches the coastal strip, Burckhardt went up a magnificent mountain rising some 6,800 feet—Mount Serbal.

He found out that the main monastic center, through most of the centuries, had been Firan and not Katarina. At Serbal he found shrines and pilgrims' inscriptions. He shook the scholarly and biblical world by concluding, in his *Travels in Syria and the Holy Land,* that the true Mount Sinai was not Mount Mussa, but Mount Serbal.

Inspired by Burckhardt's writings, the French Count Leon de Laborde toured the Sinai in 1826 and 1828; his main contributions to the knowledge of the area were his fine maps and drawings. He was followed in 1839 by the Scottish artist David Roberts, whose magnificent drawings, wherein he embellished accuracy with some imaginative flair, aroused great interest in an era before photography.

The next major journey to Sinai was undertaken by the American Edward Robinson, together with Eli Smith. Like Burckhardt, they left Suez city on camelback, armed with his book and de Laborde's maps. It took them thirteen early spring days to reach the Monastery of Santa Katarina. There, Robinson gave the monks' legends a thoroughgoing examination. He found out that at Firan there indeed was a superior monastic community, sometimes led by full bishops, to which Katarina and several other monastic communities in southern Sinai were subordinate—thus tradition must have placed greater emphasis on Firan. In the tales and documents, he discovered that Mounts Mussa and Katarina were of no Christian consequence in the early Christian centuries, and that Katarina's supremacy had developed only in the seventeenth century, as other monastic communities (including Firan) fell prey to invaders and marauders. (Katarina had been fortified by Justinian, and thus escaped this fate.) Checking local Arab traditions, he found that the biblical names "Sinai" and "Horeb" were totally unknown to the Bedouins, the local nomads; it was the monks who began to apply these names to certain mountains.

Was Burckhardt then right? Well, Robinson found a problem with Mount Serbal. Affirming or correcting some of Burckhardt's station identification, Robinson's own innovation was the suggestion that Rephidim—where the battle with the Amalekites had taken place—was located in a wadi (wadi el-Sheikh) northeast of Serbal. The route was assumed to have taken the Israelites first to wadi Firan, past Serbal, then through wadi el-Sheikh towards Katarina. But how could this newly identified Rephidim be *past* Serbal, if the battle had taken place *before* the Israelites had reached Mount Sinai?

As much as Robinson shared the doubts regarding Mount Mussa, his identification of Rephidim (in *Biblical Researches in Palestine, Mount Sinai and Arabia Petraea*) knocked out Serbal on a technicality.

The possibility that the long-held tradition identifying Mount Sinai with Mount Mussa was incorrect, was a challenge that the great Egyptologist and founder of scientific archaeology, Karl Richard Lepsius, could not resist. In his *Letters from Egypt; Ethiopia and Sinai* (1847) he at once voiced doubts regarding Mount Mussa, even before publishing his full scientific reports. "The remoteness of that district," he wrote, "and its distance from frequented roads of communication, though from its position in the lofty range offering sufficient subsistence for the trifling necessities of the single, scattered monks, rendered it peculiarly applicable for individual hermits; but for the same reason inapplicable for a large people, ruling the land for a certain period of time and exhausting all its resources." He felt certain that the hundreds of thousands of Israelites could not have subsisted in the desolate area of Mount Mussa for almost a full year.

Under the title *Discoveries in Egypt, Ethiopia and the Peninsula of Sinai in the Years 1842–1845* (translated from the original German), Lepsius published the full texts of his reports to the King of Prussia, under whose patronage he had traveled.

In a letter written "at the Convent of Sinai" on Easter Monday, 1845, Lepsius prepared the monarch for the bad news regarding Mount Mussa. The next very long letter was written after Lepsius explored extensively Mount Serbal and its environs.

Discounting the monastic traditions regarding Mount Mussa, Lepsius found its lesser height, inaccessibility, desolation, and location to weigh decisively against its acceptance as Mount Sinai. Throughout the mountainous area, he found only one place—wadi Firan—that could sustain the Israelite multitudes, and their cattle, for a whole year. Moreover, only possession of this unique fertile valley could have justified the Amalekite attack at Rephidim. Rephidim, as the biblical narrative made clear, was at the edge of Horeb, the Dryness, almost at Sinai. Where near Mount Mussa was there a vast fertile place offering food and water—subsistence worth fighting for? Moses first came to the mount in search of grazing for his flock. This he could find at Firan but not at the desolate Mount Mussa.

But if not Mount Mussa, why Mount Serbal? Besides its "correct" location at wadi Firan, Lepsius found some concrete evidence. Describing the mount in glowing terms, he reported finding on its top "a deep mountain hollow, around which the five summits of Serbal unite in a half circle and form a towering crown. In the middle of this hollow, called wadi Siqelji, lies the ruins of an old convent."

The place, then, was revered from olden times, enshrined by traditions of its own. And was not the hollow "crowned" by five summits the throne-like place wherein the Glory of the Lord had landed, in full view of the Israelites for whom there was ample room in the valley on the west, facing the peaks of Serbal?

But how could Serbal be the Holy Mount, if Rephidim lay beyond it? Not so, said Lepsius. As an archaeologist, he reported extensively upon Egyptian ruins at a place called Serabit-el-Khadim. In a wadi nearby, appropriately called wadi *Mukatib* (the wadi of Writings), there were found numerous hieroglyphic and other, later inscriptions. It was the area where the pharaohs had mined for turquoise and copper, and others too before and after them. Lepsius suggested that it was there that the main ancient route was from Egypt into the mountains. Lepsius suggested that the Israelites followed that route; that the pharaonic ore-port now called Abu-Zelimeh was the Israelite station of Elim; and that they turned inland there, rather than farther on south as has been previously suggested. Following such a route, the Israelites reached Firan/Rephidim from the north—before reaching Serbal, which lay farther to the southwest.

When the conclusions of the prestigious Lepsius were published, they shook tradition in two ways: he emphatically denied the identification of Mount Sinai with Mount Mussa, voting for Serbal; and he challenged the route that had been previously taken for granted.

The debate that followed raged for almost a quarter of a century and produced discourses by other researchers, such as Charles Foster (*The Historical Geography of Arabia; Israel in the Wilderness*) and William H. Bartlett (*Forty Days in the Desert on the Track of the Israelites*). They added suggestions, confirmations, and doubts. In 1868 the British government joined the Palestine Exploration Fund in sending a full-scale expedition to Sinai. Its mission, in addition to extensive geodesic and mapping work, was to establish once and for all the route of the Exodus and the location of Mount Sinai. The group was led by Captains Charles W. Wilson and Henry Spencer Palmer of the Royal Engineers; it included Prof. Edward Henry Palmer, a noted Orientalist and Arabist. The expedition's official report (*Ordnance Survey of the Peninsula of Sinai*) was enlarged upon by the two Palmers, in separate works.

Previous researchers went to the Sinai for brief tours mostly in springtime. The Wilson-Palmer expedition departed from Suez on November 11th, 1868, and returned to Egypt on April 24th, 1869—

staying in the peninsula from the beginning of winter until the following spring. Thus, one of its first discoveries was that the mountainous south gets very cold in winter (with day-night temperature changes of up to 50 degrees Fahrenheit) and that it snows there, making passage difficult, if not impossible. Furthermore, the higher peaks, such as Mussa and Katarina remain snow-covered for many months. In spite of lingering doubts, the group vetoed Serbal and voted for Mount Mussa as Mount Sinai.

In his own writings (*Sinai: Ancient History from the Monuments*), Captain Palmer summarized his findings against the background of Egyptian history, and described the evidence of very early habitations in Sinai: dwellings of unhewn stone built like beehives, sepulchral stone circles, and many inscriptions in what he called a "Sinaitic Script." Professor E. H. Palmer (*The Desert of the Exodus*) attempted to pinpoint the Israelite stations, before and after Mount Sinai, by employing his knowledge of Arabic lore and language. Although he realized as his travels progressed that some place names were simply made up for him by his Bedouin informants, he saw—in the names and tales—survivors from oral traditions rooted in the time of the Exodus itself. Yet, when they did not suit him, he brushed tradition aside and discounted a name as a distortion.

He accepted the view that the shallow waters of the head of the Gulf of Suez, or an ancient extension thereof, were the place of the Passage of the Red Sea: a strong east wind at ebb time can drive away the shallow waters even today. The fact that a place on the Sinai side of the Gulf's head is called *Ayun Mussa* ("The Spring of Moses") served to him as irrefutable evidence that it was thereabouts that the Israelites emerged after the Passage. More so since Arab lore supported this conclusion. It was true, he conceded, that a similar tradition placed the Passage much farther south at a place called "Pharaoh's Hot Waters," but that other tradition he dismissed because "the Arabs, with their usual inconsistency, adopt two sites for the miracle."

Palmer's route of the Exodus basically agreed with Lepsius. But he disavowed the Serbal contention and would not entertain any Mount Sinai other than Mount Mussa. Its very name—Mount Moses—"and tradition would go far towards excluding the other mountains of the Peninsula which have been proposed as the scene of the Law-giving." Also, it was near Mount Mussa and not near Serbal that a Mount Aribeh was situated—obviously the biblical Mount Horeb, because "the name Horeb, having no meaning to the Arab ear, has long since perished; but it reappears in Mount Aribeh." Moreover, near Mount Mussa there was a peak named in Arabic "Hill of the Golden Calf." That, he believed, was conclusive evidence.

Palmer acknowledged a problem: there was no valley wide enough in front of Mount Mussa where the Israelites could encamp and from which they could see the Theophany.

His response was that while this held true for the southern summit, the one actually called Mount Mussa, the northern summit—Ras Sufsafeh—faces "the spacious plain of Er-Rahah where no less than two million Israelites could encamp."

He thus came up with the unorthodox suggestion, that the place of the Law Giving was not Mount Mussa but the peak called Ras Sufsafeh, the two being admittedly at the opposite ends of the two-mile long massif. "As there is no other spot but the plain of Er-Rahah upon which the Children of Israel could have all assembled as spectators, and as from this plain the summit of Mount Mussa is invisible, we are compelled to reject the latter as the site of the proclamation of the Law."

What about tradition, and all the places atop the Mount Mussa peak revered as the sites of the various Exodus details? "It may be argued," Palmer wrote, "that tradition points to the summit itself"— "the Mussa peak—as the spot on which the Law was delivered, and that no legendary interest whatever attaches to the Ras Sufsafeh or to the plain at the northern end of the mountain;" but—"having found our mountain, we are not compelled servilely to follow tradition any further, but may exercise our common sense in determining the rest."

The views of Professor Palmer were soon criticized, supported, or modified by other scholars. Before long, there were four peaks in the same area that were offered as the true Mount Sinai—the highest of all, Katarina; Mussa; Sufsafeh; and Mount Monejah, across the valley east of Mount Mussa. And, aloof but majestic, there was also Serbal—a candidate with many followers. So now there were five southern peaks, as well as several different routes, to choose from.

But were these the only candidates?

Back in April 1860, the Journal of Sacred Literature published a revolutionary suggestion (by an anonymous contributor) that the Holy Mount was not in the southern Sinai at all, but should be looked for in the vast plateau called *Badiyeht el-Tih*—"The Wilderness of the Wandering," the sandstone escarpment that lies north of the high granite mountains; a vast mountain named *Jebel el-Ojmeh* was indicated. So, in 1873, a geographer and linguist named Charles T. Beke (who explored and mapped the origins of the Nile) set out "in search of the true Mount Sinai."

His research established that Mount Mussa was so named after the fourth-century monk Mussa who was famed for his piety and miracles, and not after the biblical Moses; and that the claims for Mount Mussa were begun only circa 550 A.D. He also pointed out that the Jewish historian Josephus Flavius (who recorded his people's history for the Romans after the fall of Jerusalem in 70 A.D.) described Mount Sinai as the highest in its area, which ruled out both Mussa and Serbal. And Beke also asked, how could the Israelites have gone south at all, past the Egyptian garrisons in the mining area?

Searching for new clues, he raised the question: *What* was Mount Sinai? He suggested that it was a volcano, perhaps a dormant one that erupted at the time of the Exodus. But there are no known volcanoes in the Sinai peninsula. He also asked: Where was Midian, which appeared to be not too far from the Holy Mount? The title of his major work bespoke his conclusions: *Discoveries of Sinai in Arabia and of Midian*. Mount Sinai, he wrote, was beyond the Sinai peninsula, northeast of Aqaba.

Charles Beke will not be remembered as the man who finally found the true Mount Sinai. A main problem with his theory was the very large distance from his indicated point to Egypt, whereas Moses had kept asking for permission to worship at the Holy Mount "a distance of three days' march in the desert." To tackle this problem, Beke placed the Israelites not in Egypt at all but in the Sinai peninsula. Though thi no one accepted, his researches cleared the deck for fresh thinking regarding the route of the Exodus and the possible location of Mount Sinai elsewhere than in the southern granite area.

Beke's critics, and he himself, saw the distance problem in terms of a Southern Passage, namely the Crossing of the Red Sea through or at the head of the Gulf of Suez. If Mount Sinai, as he suggested, was north of the head of the Gulf of Aqaba, the Israelites had to travel down the west coast of the Sinai peninsula and up its east coast—a difficult journey of hundreds of miles—in the stated three days. This was obviously impossible.

A Southern Crossing, through or near the head of the Gulf of Suez, was indeed a deep-rooted (and plausible) tradition, buttressed by several legends. Thus it was told in ancient Greek writings that when Alexander the Great was in Egypt (332–331 B.C.), he was told that the Israelites had crossed the Red Sea at the head of the Gulf of Suez; there the shallow waters could be blown away by strong winds. Confidently, he attempted to emulate the Passage—with little success, it seems.

The next great conqueror known to have attempted the feat was Napoleon in 1799. His engineers established that where the head of the Gulf of Suez sends a "tongue" inland, south of where Suez City is located, there exists an underwater ridge, some 600 feet wide, which extends from coast to coast. Daredevil natives cross there at ebb time, with the waters up to their shoulders. And if a strong east wind blows, the seabed is almost cleared of all water.

Napoleon's engineers worked out for their emperor the right place and time for emulating the children of Israel. But an unexpected change in the wind's direction brought a sudden onrush of waters, covering the ridge with more than seven feet of water within minutes. The great Napoleon escaped with his life in the nick of time.

These experiences only served to convince nineteenth-century scholars that it was indeed at that northern end of the Gulf of Suez that the miraculous Passage had taken place: a wind could create a dry path, and a change in wind could indeed sink the Egyptians soon thereafter. On the opposite, Sinai side of the gulf, there was a place named *Jebel Murr* ("The Bitter Mountain") and near it *Bir Murr* ("The Bitter Well"), invitingly fitting as Marah, the place of bitter waters, encountered after the Crossing. Further south lay *Ayun Mussa*—"The Spring of Moses"; now was not the next station, Elim, remembered for its beautiful springs and numerous date palms? A Passage south of Suez City—from west to east—thus seemed to fit well into the southern route theory, no matter where the turn inland had taken place further on.

The construction of the Suez Canal (1859–1869) and the geological, topographical, climatic, and marine data obtained thereby, inadvertently shook these long-held theories by showing that there were not one, but four possible crossing points.

Linking the Mediterranean Sea in the north with the Gulf of Suez in the south, the canal follows a natural rift that in an earlier geological age may have joined the two seas. That watery link has shrunk under the influence of climate, earthquakes, and other geological forces; it is represented today by marshy lagoons in the north, the smaller lakes Ballah and Timsah, and the larger Great Bitter Lake and Little Bitter Lake. These lakes may have been more extensive at the time of the Exodus; the head of the Gulf of Suez may have also been extended farther inland.

The engineers of the Suez Canal, under Ferdinand Marie de Lesseps, made public in 1867 the following diagram (Fig. A) of a north-south section of the Isthmus showing the four high-ground ridges along the line. It was suggested that if the water barrier was almost continuous, these ridges served as the four crossing points in antiquity (Fig. B):

A) Between the marshy lagoons of Menzaleh and Lake Ballah
B) Between Lake Ballah and Lake Timsah
C) Between Lake Timsah and the Bitter Lakes
D) Between the Bitter Lakes and the Gulf of Suez

The heart of Egypt, where the historical Upper and Lower Egypt met, is the point where the Nile River, having snaked its way along

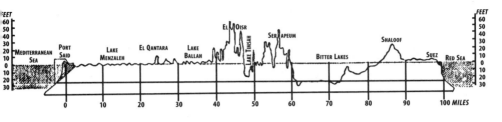

Fig. A

Fig. B

4,000 miles from deep in Africa, suddenly fans out to form the Nile Delta. There, in antiquity, was the religious-political-commercial hub of Memphis-Heliopolis; there, in modern times, is Cairo. From that hub, three principal routes led to the many lands of Asia; today's roads and railroads still follow these ancient crossing points.

The twin southernmost routes run parallel, having connected Heliopolis and Memphis with crossing points "C" and "D." Once across, there lies a stretch of desert; then the traveler reaches a mountain ridge that rises sharply to some 1,500 feet. Two passes are available to the traveler; both have been the scenes of decisive Israeli-Egyptian battles between 1956 and 1973. They are the *Giddi Pass* and the *Mitla Pass*. (When the two combatants agreed to separate their forces, it was only on condition that electronic monitoring posts, manned by Americans, be set up at these two strategic passes.) Beyond the passes, there are routes that lead northeast, east, and southeast.

At the crossing points above the Gulf's head, another route begins to run southward, down the western coast of the Sinai peninsula. The early notions regarding the Israelites in Egypt were that they slaved in the construction of the pyramids of Giza, near Memphis. It was thus only logical that they would take the nearest escape route, through crossing point "D." But since the pharaoh changed his mind and they could not pass through a regular (and well-guarded) crossing point, they ended up crossing through the waters of the head of the Gulf of Suez. Then taking the southward route they marched toward Mount Sinai—be it Mussa, Katarina, or Serbal.

But as archaeological discoveries began to fill in the historical picture and provide an accurate chronology, it was established that the great pyramids were built some fifteen centuries before the Exodus—more than a thousand years before the Hebrews even came to Egypt. The Israelites, more and more scholars agreed as the nineteenth century entered into its last quarter, must have toiled in the construction of a new capital, which the Pharaoh Rameses II had built circa 1260 B.C. It was named *Tanis* and it was located in the northeastern part of the Delta.

The possibility that the Israelite abode—the land of Goshen—was in the northeast rather near the center of Egypt, combined with the engineering data, started a spate of new crossing theories. A lingering problem with the theory of a crossing through the waters of the head of the Red Sea was the Hebrew term *Yam Suff,* which literally means "Sea (or Lake) of Reeds." Since this description does not fit the Red Sea, the chain of shallow and marshy lakes seemed much more suitable.

De Lesseps, the Suez Canal's master builder, voiced the opinion that the watery chain was crossed south of Lake Timsah, at Point "C." Others, like Olivier Ritt (*Histoire de l'isthme de Suez*), concluded from the same data regarding past topography that the crossing was at "D," through the then-extended chain of lakes rather than through the Gulf's present head. Both, however, conceived of the continued route only in terms of a turn southward, toward a Mount Sinai in the peninsula's south.

Then, in 1874, the Egyptologist Heinrich Karl Brugsch put forth a revolutionary theory as he addressed the International Congress of Orientalists. Presenting strong arguments identifying the Israelite abode and the landmarks connected with their enslavement and Exodus (*Pithom, Succoth, Migdol,* etc.) at the very northeastern edge of Egypt, he suggested that they had taken the closest crossing point and route at hand: the northernmost "A." The waters they had crossed were neither the Red Sea at all, nor the lakes extending above it, he said; it was the body of shallow waters, marshes, and shoals on the Mediterranean coast known as the Serbonic Sea, or (in Arabic) the Sealet of Bardawil.

Among his impressive identifications was that of *Ba'al Zaphon* in front of which the Israelites waited to cross the waters. He pointed out the connection between this place name and the Phoenician god *Ba'al Zaphon,* a protector of seafarers; and he showed that the arching shoal that separated the Serbonic Sealet from the Mediterranean had a promontory named Zeus Cassius in antiquity—which was the Greek name for Ba'al Zaphon. It was conclusive proof, he suggested, that the Israelites had crossed there, and that the "Sea of Reeds" was the Serbonic Sea.

As it turned out, such a theory of a Northern Passage was nearly a century old when Brugsch launched it, having been suggested in *Hamelsveld's Biblical Geography* back in 1796, and by various researchers thereafter. But Brugsch, as even his adversaries conceded, presented the theory with "a really brilliant and dazzling array of claimed corroboratory evidence from the Egyptian monuments." His paper was published the following year under the title *L'Exode et les Monuments Egyptiens*.

Brugsch realized that a main objection to a northern route to Canaan—"The Way of the Sea"—would be the fact that it was fortified and garrisoned all along. This is known from Egyptian texts and from a pictorial representation of the coastal route ("A"), its fortifications and wells by Seti I on a temple wall in Karnak. In anticipation of such an objection, Brugsch had the Israelites make a dash from the Serbonic Sea all the way south to Ayun Mussa, where they joined the traditional Southern Route.

In 1883, Edouard H. Naville (*The Store City of Pithom and the Route of the Exodus*) identified a site west of Lake Timsah as Pithom; Tanis, the new capital city of Rameses II, was identified as Raamses, the other city of slave labor. The mounting evidence, ably presented by such scholars as Georg Ebers (*Durch Gosen zum Sinai*), indicated that the Israelite Goshen stretched from Lake Timsah westward along Wadi Tumilat—a valley through which the sweet waters of the Nile were carried towards the line of marshy lakes, and which served as the northeastern route from Egypt's hub. Goshen was thus not in the extreme northeast of Egypt, but in the center of its eastern frontier.

The critics of Brugsch—as numerous as his supporters—who saw fault with the "dash from north to south" rationalization, now were convinced that he was wrong in placing Goshen too far north. H. Clay Trumbull (*Kadesh Barnea*) further argued that *Succoth* was not a city but a camping area west of Lake Timsah where caravans gathered before leaving Egypt. *Migdol,* he showed, was not one specific place but one of several fortified towers (which is what *Migdol* means in Hebrew) that guarded the eastern approaches to Egypt. Summing up the vast literature on the subject that had been published by then (1895), he offered a compromise: the Israelites did go northward, toward crossing point "A"; but before they reached it, they were ordered by the Lord to turn back (Exodus 14:1–4) and went south, to crossing point "D." Pursued by pharaoh, they ended up crossing miraculously through the waters of the Gulf's head.

In 1897 Samuel C. Bartlett (*The Veracity of the Hexateuch*) sought to close the century with a final word; the crossing was at Suez; the route was southward; Mount Sinai was Mount Mussa.

But the final word was still far off; for no one had by then faced up to the simple question: If the Israelites resided astride route B and just off crossing point B—why have they not taken this nearest exit to freedom?

The Book of Exodus vividly describes not only the readiness of the Israelites to leave on short notice, but also the anxiety of the Egyptians to see them go at once. It was midnight when the Lord smote all the firstborn of Egypt, "and (Pharaoh) called for Moses and Aaron in the night, and said: rise up and get you out from among my people . . . And the Egyptians were urging the people to make haste, to send them away out of the land," for the Egyptians feared that all of them, and not only the firstborn, were about to be smitten.

Why then select a crossing point that required a march of several days within the boundaries of Egypt, rather than leave Egypt at once, as both the Israelites and the Egyptians desired?

10
When Gods, Not Men, Roamed the New World

Unpublished Article, Written in 1992

In the 1990 book *The Lost Realms,* Sitchin discusses his findings in the Americas. This unpublished article further elaborates his thinking on this fascinating subject of early visitors to the New World.

What was puzzling to the early Spanish Conquistadores when they first set foot in the New World was how much the culture in South America resembled their own. The culture that they encountered was a relatively developed high culture, replete with complete systems of governance, the arts, and religion. The Spanish were even more surprised to realize that not only did the natives worship one god in a monotheistic fashion but that they were also familiar with the symbol of the cross.

Thus Sitchin poses the question: "Was it possible that the impossible did happen—that somehow, sometime in the past, people from the Old World had come to these lands, bringing with them the religious beliefs, the social structures, and the civilizations of the Old World—but from a time too long ago to be remembered in the Old World, from an era that preceded Christianity, millennia upon millennia ago?" Further exploration on Sitchin's part revealed strong cultural similarities between the Aztecs, Maya, and Incas. Even more astoundingly, it appeared that the Indians of Peru had knowledge of the Hebrew Bible and practiced some of the rituals of the Old Testament!

Further study involves the early peoples of Mesoamerica: the Olmecs, who, it has been established, were of "Negroid" stock, originally from Africa, who had come to South America in search of gold to be mined. Early depictions of these Olmecs show them with bearded strangers, including the god Quetzalcoatl. Sitchin goes on to posit that this revered god Quetzalcoatl was in fact the Egyptian god Thoth who had come to South America to search for gold under the aegis of the Anunnaki, as did his counterpart Viracocha.

IN THIS YEAR 1992, as we mark the 500th anniversary of the discovery of America by Columbus, we are also marking—without knowing it—an *earlier* arrival in the New World.

Indeed, the arrival of new people (the Spaniards) in the New World in 1492 only repeated the saga of the no less dramatic arrival there of people from elsewhere millennia earlier—and, as fate would have it—the replaying of the saga of the arrival of people *from another planet* on planet Earth.

The clues have been there, all the time; but they were either misinterpreted, ignored—or disbelieved. The truth was always there, in the legends of the native "Indians"; but their tales, whether oral or written in hieroglyphs, were treated as myth, as mythology.

And thus it had taken all these centuries to rediscover the true story of the Americas, by going back to the time when the gods were actually on Earth, and when the migrations and endeavors of Man were in the service of the gods.

THE PUZZLING SIMILARITIES

A basic assumption that persisted throughout the five centuries since the discovery of America in 1492 has been that there was total ignorance of the New World by the Old World and vice versa, and thus the conclusion that the two were never in contact. This fallacious assumption that has blocked the way to the truth about pre-Columbian civilizations in the Americas was only temporarily suspended when the Conquistadores realized the implications of what they had found.

When the Spaniard Conquistadores and other Europeans moved from one conquered land to another in the Americas, they were astonished to come upon civilizations that were so much similar to those of the Old World: there were kingdoms and kings, royal courts and their ministers and advisers, cities and marketplaces, sacred precincts and temples and priests; art, poetry, literature; commerce and industry; armies and soldiers. How was it possible, the Europeans asked themselves, that in such unknown, distant, and isolated lands with which there seemed to have never been contact, societies and civilizations had been created that were so similar to those of the Old World?

The natives even had a religion. It was a pagan religion, with many gods and goddesses. It was filled with incredible tales of wars and loves, alliances and jealousies between these gods, and complex genealogies. The Catholic priests who arrived on the scene were shocked and determined to obliterate the heathen and pagan beliefs and to smash all the incredibly artistic statues and artifacts honoring that pantheon.

But it was equally astounding to find that in spite of the confusing variety of deities, the natives spoke of *one* supreme God, one Creator of All. The Conquistadores had to confront this baffling fact from the very beginning, as Cortes and his men encountered the Aztecs and their leader Moctezuma. How was it possible that such "savages" offered prayers to this supreme god, whom they called *Quetzacoatl* ("The Plumed Serpent"), as this one:

You inhabit the heavens,
You uphold the mountains . . .
You are everywhere, everlasting.
You are beseeched, you are entreated.
Your glory is eminent.

And, to make matters even more difficult for the arriving priests intent on converting the pagans to Christianity, the "pagans" already knew of the *symbol* of the Cross! They venerated the symbol as having celestial significance; they depicted it as the emblem of Quetzalcoatl on his shield.

Quetzalcoatl with his shield with the CROSS emblem

To the east of the Aztec empire with its capital Tenochtitlan (nowadays: Mexico City) lay the lands of the Maya; and there too the Supreme God was the "Plumed Serpent," in the Mayan language called *Kukulkan*.

Was it possible that the impossible did happen—that somehow, sometime in the past, people from the Old World had come to these lands, bringing with them the religious beliefs, the social structures, and the civilizations of the Old World—but from a time too long ago to be remembered in the Old World, from an era that preceded Christianity, millennia upon millennia ago?

LEGENDS OF THE RETURNING GOD

Such thoughts occurred to the arriving Europeans not only because of the obvious similarities, but also because of the legend that was central to Aztec beliefs. This was the *Legend of the Return*. Quetzalcoatl, they said, after giving the people of prehistoric Mexico civilization, left by disappearing over the waters toward the east. But before he left he promised to return, coming back from the east.

According to the Aztec legends, Quetzalcoatl was forced by the evil God of War to leave the lands of the Aztecs (central Mexico). With a group of followers he went eastward, to the Yucatan peninsula, from whence he took off toward the eastern horizon. But he vowed to return, and gave a date: I will return, he said, on the day of my birthday, "1 Reed."

In the Aztec calendar, the cycle of years completed itself every 52 years; therefore, the year of the promised return could occur once in 52 years. In the parallel Christian calendar "1 Reed" occurred in 1363, 1415, and 1467—and again in the year 1519. That was *precisely* the year in which Cortes and his band arrived in the Aztec domain in the Aztec lands, having sailed from Cuba in command of an armada of eleven ships, some six hundred men, and many horses. As they sailed along the coast of Yucatan, they passed the Mayan lands and landed in what was the Aztec kingdom. As they were establishing their outpost, calling it Veracruz (as it is still called), they were surprised to see a procession of emissaries of the Aztec king offering them greetings and exquisite gifts. It was a welcome by the Aztecs to the Returning God who promised to return, with *his bearded followers,* in the year 1 Reed. The Aztecs, in other words, welcomed the Conquistadores because they were considered to be fulfilling the legend of the return of Quetzalcoatl!

The surprise of discovering in these lands beyond the great oceans beliefs and civilizations similar to those of Europe and the ancient Near East was multiplied when the Spaniards arrived in Peru, all the way in South America. There they discovered not only the same societal aspects of kingdoms and kings, temples and priests, and so on, but also a similarity between the legends of the gods in Mesoamerica and such legends in South America—especially in view of the assumption that the two were not in touch with each other.

There, in South America, in the Incan empire, the Supreme Creator was called *Viracocha,* a great god of Heaven and Earth who came to the Andes in ancient times. According to the legends, his main abode was on the shores of Lake Titicaca (now divided between Peru and Bolivia), where the enigmatic remains of a megalithic city called Tiahuanacu are situated and where two small islands, connected with these legends, are still called Island of the Sun and Island of the Moon.

It was from a cave there that Viracocha, creating four brothers and four sisters, gave them a magical wand and told them where to go in order to start a kingdom and civilization in South America; the city is the one that was called (then as now) Cuzco, the Incan capital.

When all that was achieved, the gods of the Sun and of the Moon,

Viracocha on the Sun Gate, Tiahuanacu (Bolivia)

The Sun Gate, Tiahuanacu

who were helping Viracocha, returned to heaven. In another version of these legends, the two helpers were children of Viracocha who were sent out to give civilization. In both versions, in the end Viracocha and his helpers met at the seashore, on the Pacific coast "from where they ascended to heaven."

Viracocha was depicted, in paintings and in sculptures (as, for example, on the famous Sun Gate in Tiahuanacu), as holding in one hand an axe and in the other hand the thunderbolt. To the Incas, the Spaniards' rifles that fired "thunderbolts" looked like confirmation that indeed Viracocha's people had returned. As in Mexico, this made the Spanish conquest so much easier.

LEGENDS OF CREATION AND THE DELUGE

Already puzzled by the similarities of the American civilizations to those of the Old World, and between those of the Aztecs, Maya, and Incas, the Europeans were even more surprised to find that in the *farthest* regions the similarities seemed to indicate some knowledge of the Bible and biblical customs!

Among the Indians of Peru, customs included a Festival of the First Fruits, as commanded in the Bible; an Expiation Feast at the end of September corresponded in its features and timing to the Jewish Day of Atonement. The rite of circumcision was kept; so was the custom of abstaining from the blood of animal meat. There was a prohibition against eating fish without scales—all major aspects of the rules for Kosher ("proper, acceptable") food in the Old Testament. In the Feast of the First Fruits, the Indians chanted the mystic words *Yo Meshica, He Meschica, Va Meschica;* to the Spanish scholar-priests who had followed the Conquistadores, the term "Meschica" sounded clearly as the term Maschi'ach—the Hebrew word for "Messiah."

Moreover, these scholar-priests discovered that among the local legends there were tales that looked as if they were learnt in a Bible class on Sunday; tales of the creation of the first human pair—an "Adam and Eve"; and tales of a Great Flood, the Deluge, that swept over the Earth and destroyed everything except for one couple.

In Mexico, legends in the Nahuatl language (the language of the Aztecs and their predecessors, the Toltecs) said that the Creator-of-All, after shaping the Heaven and the Earth, fashioned a man and a woman out of clay to begin mankind; but all the men and women on Earth were destroyed in a great flood, except for one priest and his wife who, taking along seeds and animals, floated in a hollowed-out log until the flood subsided.

Recollections of a Deluge featured in almost all the versions in Southern America, both in the Quechua language of the Incas and in the Aymara language of their predecessors. According to Father Molina (*Relacion de las fabulas y ritos de los Yngas*), who collected and brought together the various versions, the Indians "had a full account of the Deluge; they say that all people and all created things perished in it, the waters having risen above all the highest mountains in the world. No living thing survived except a man and a woman who remained in a box."

Throughout the Americas, recollections of earlier times were divided

Aztec stone calendar showing the Ages of the five Suns

into ages called "Suns." The clearest version of that was expressed in the Aztec calendar, such as the Great Calendar Stone discovered in the pre-conquest sacred precinct of the Aztecs of Mexico City. The central panel, standing for what the Aztecs believed was their own Age of the Fifth Sun, was surrounded by symbols of the past four ages, each destroyed by a different calamity: Water (the Deluge), Wind, Quakes and Storms, and the Jaguar (wild beasts).

THE LOST TRIBES OF ISRAEL?

In the search for explanations for these puzzling similarities to biblical customs and echoes of biblical tales of Creation and Deluge, it occurred to the arriving Europeans that a simple explanation could exist: That the Indians of the Americas were, somehow, descendants of the Ten

Lost Tribes of Israel—the tribes that were exiled and dispersed by the Assyrians when they conquered Judea in the seventh century B.C. That would also explain the organizational similarities (kings, royal courts), religious similarities (temples, priests), and the belief in a "Creator of All."

If not the first one to think of it, then certainly the first one to expound the theory in a single manuscript, was the Dominican Friar Diego Duran, who was brought to New Spain at the age of five. It was mainly in his second book, *Historia de las Indias de Nueva Espana,* that—after reviewing the many similarities—he stated forcefully his conclusion that "the natives of the Indies and the mainland of this new world" were "Jews and Hebrew people." These natives, he wrote, "were part of the ten tribes of Israel which Shalmaneser, King of the Assyrians, captured and took to Assyria."

Among the legends that Friar Diego Duran collected, one that impressed his readers most was the tale of "giants, not having found a way to reach the Sun, decided to build a tower so high that its summit would reach unto heaven." That the natives in the Americas would even know the story of the Tower of Babel (told in the Bible in chapter 11 of Genesis), looked like a convincing argument that indeed the Indians' ancestors were Israelites who spread to distant places after being taken to Mesopotamia (Assyria-Babylonia), where the events of the Tower of Babel had taken place (the city's name, Babylon in English, meant in the ancient language "Gateway of the Gods").

The theory of the Ten Lost Tribes became the favorite one to explain the enigmas found in the New World, and was the basic scientific theory during the sixteenth and seventeenth centuries. It was held that as the exiles kept migrating eastward, they reached the Far East and somehow crossed the Pacific Ocean, reaching the Americas. Such theories seemed to receive corroboration by other legends—throughout the Americas—that the first settlers arrived in those lands by balsa boats across the Pacific Ocean, landing at Cape Santa Helena in Ecuador. This is the place where the South American continent projects into the ocean westward, to become the closest continental point as one sails eastward in the Pacific.

Various chroniclers, among them Juan de Velasco, recorded such

Black Obelisk of Shalmaneser, king of Assyria, showing Israelite king bowing

legends, according to which before those human settlers there were "giants" on the cape, to whom the settlers built temples in which they worshipped a pantheon of twelve gods. The leader of these settlers, according to such detailed legends, was called Naymlap; he found the way across the ocean and was told where to land with the help of a green stone that could utter the words spoken by the Great God. After the people landed on the cape, the deity gave the settlers instructions—again speaking through the green stone—about the arts of farming, handicrafts, and building.

THE ERA OF "LOGIC" AND RIDICULE

What seemed to the explorers and investigators in the sixteenth and seventeenth centuries as a simple explanation for all these legends and enigmas, was to become the subject of "logical analysis" and thus of ridicule in the eighteenth and nineteenth centuries. . . .

With the advent of scientific knowledge, local folkloric tales and legends were discarded as primitive myths of no scientific value. The settling of the Americas, it came to be held by scholars, was by migrations across the Bering Strait—where Alaska stretches toward Asia—during the last Ice Age, when ice bridged the Asian and American continents. The settlers then gradually spread southward, until they reached the southernmost tip of South America.

All talk of ancient peoples—"lost" Israelites, shipwrecked Phoenicians, and the like—being able to sail across the Pacific or Atlantic Oceans was held to be foolish and childish, because logic dictated that no one could cross the oceans in primitive vessels. Even tales of pre-Columbian arrivals in the Americas, for instance by Norsemen or Irishmen, were discounted; it had to be migrants across the Bering Strait, and nothing else was acceptable.

In my writings, and especially in the book *The Lost Realms,* which deals with these matters, I questioned this "logic" with logic. If those who (according to this theory) trekked over the ice to the Americas from Asia were the *first* settlers—why would they go through the hardship of moving, with women and children, across thousands of miles of ice if they did not know what lay ahead . . . if they did not know that there were fertile lands "over there"? If no one else was there before, how could they know that they would find habitable land at all, and not just more ice and more seas?

When the Israelites left Egypt (I wrote, in 1985) and wandered in the desert for forty years, they accepted the hardships because God told them that in the end they would come to a fertile land, a land of milk and honey, for which all the wandering and trekking in the desert would prove to have been worthwhile.

So, I wrote, those who claim that the first settlers simply kept going over thousands of miles of frozen ice are either completely wrong—or they have to accept the legends that said that God, speaking through a green stone or otherwise, told the first settlers where to go. And if so, they did not foolishly spend years moving across an ice sheet, but sailed in boats. . . .

I am pleased to say that, in the last two to three years, scientists have come around to discarding the "trek across the ice sheet" theory. Archaeologists and paleoanthropologists have found remains of human settlement, more so in the south than in the north, going back to long before the presumed time of the freezing of the Bering Strait. It is now more and more accepted among scientists that *people from the Old World did arrive in the Americas by boats*—long before the Maya (who were latecomers) and the Aztecs and the Toltecs, and certainly long before the Incas (whose empire, stretching from Ecuador to Chile, began only in A.D. 1021).

But how could people cross two forbidding oceans in those early days?

The scientists still do not offer an answer. But the ancient peoples themselves did: They came across *on the command of the gods and with their help!*

IDENTIFYING THE EARLY SETTLERS

Who were the earliest carriers of civilization (as distinct from primitive, Stone Age people)? Fortunately, they have left behind evidence not only of their presence, but also their *portraits*.

Scholars now acknowledge that in Mesoamerica (which includes Mexico, Central America, and sometimes also the northernmost parts of South America), the first recognizable true civilization was of a people called Olmecs. Inhabiting mostly the area stretching from central Mexico to the borders of Yucatan, and from the coasts of the Gulf of Mexico to the shores of the Pacific in the south, their kingdom was in full bloom circa 1500 B.C. No one is sure when it started—at least a thousand years earlier. It is certain, however, that by 800 B.C. their civilization declined, to be replaced by the later Toltecs, Aztecs, and Maya.

The Olmecs left behind great cities, among them Tres Zapotes, La Venta, and San Lorenzo. There, impressive statues, pyramids, and earthworks have been found. The first Mesoamerican glyph writing began in the Olmec lands. So did the system of numeration. Moreover, the calendar system known as the Long Count began there; this is the counting system that counts the number of days that have actually passed from an enigmatic starting point in the year 3113 B.C.

In *The Lost Realms* I have suggested a solution to the puzzle of this date; we will return to look at it later in this article.

Who were the Olmecs, where did they come from, where did their civilization originate?

Their "portraits" leave no doubt as to *who* they were. From colossal stone heads to numerous smaller carvings and monuments, it is clear that they were Africans of Negroid stock. Comparison between these portraits in stone and present-day tribal types in Africa, shows that they had come from West Africa from the area known earlier as the Gold Coast and now primarily known as the country called Ghana.

Why did they come? The answer is also provided by their monuments. The Olmecs are usually depicted holding certain tools—and usually inside caves or other hollow-out spaces inside a mountain. Sometimes, their chiefs are shown using a kind of flaming device that is used to cut through the rocks or melt the stones. There can be no doubt that these depictions tell us *why* the Olmecs had come to Mesoamerica from Africa: to be *miners,* to extract a certain mineral from the depths of the earth. And the mineral or metal they were after was *gold.*

Stone-sculpted "portraits" of Olmecs

A giant Olmec stone head, the Park Museum, Villahermosa, Yucatán, Mexico

The Expedition with a giant Olmec stone head in Jalapa, Mexico

Olmecs as miners, with mining tools

THE "BEARDED ONES"

The flaming-device or flamethrower used for mining operations appears in two instances connected with the Mesoamerican gods.

One instance has been and remains most enigmatic. It relates to a number of gigantic figures carved from stone that stand atop a sacred pyramid in the city called Tollan (northwest of Mexico City), which was the ancient capital of the Toltecs (the people who preceded the Aztecs). Each of these giants is armed with such a flamethrower, held in a holster on the right-hand hip. On one of the square carved columns that held up the roof of the temple where these giants, called popularly *"Atlanteans,"** stood, the use of these flamethrowers to cut out and melt off rocks is clearly demonstrated.

The other depiction of a god actually using the flaming device was found among the stone carvings of the Olmecs. It shows the god called in the Nahuatl language Tepeyolloti, meaning "Heart of the Mountain." He was worshipped in caves or mines inside mountains. His glyph-symbol was a pierced mountain. He was depicted holding his tool—a flamethrower or stone-melter. *And he was bearded.*

The very idea of a *bearded* god seems strange, for the native Indians—throughout the Americas—did not grow facial hair. Where did they get the notion that other people could have beards, unless they had actually seen such people? Where did they get the notion of a god or gods with beards—unless that is how the gods actually looked?

As a matter of fact, it was a *bearded* Quetzalcoatl whose return the Aztecs were expecting—mistaking the bearded Spaniards led by Cortes to be the returning gods. . . .

The fact is that bearded people had indeed come to Mesoamerica, and South America, long, long before Columbus. Their portraits were also left behind, as irrefutable evidence. In most cases, they are shown together with the Olmecs; it means that they were present in Mesoamerica as early as 1500 B.C.

---

*Editor's note: Sitchin called them "Atlantes" in his published works.

"Atlanteans" armed with flamethrowers

Drawing of the stone carved columns

A closer look at the flamethrower in its holster

The "Bearded Ones" from the ancient Near East

QUETZALCOATL:
THE EGYPTIAN GOD THOTH

We can now solve the puzzle of when, why, and who settled Mesoamerica thousands of years before Columbus, and at least a thousand years before the Toltecs and Aztecs, two thousand years before the Maya.

They came from the Old World, as gold miners from West Africa—accompanied and assisted, somewhat later, by people from the ancient Near East.

They could come, and their metals could be transported, because it was the will of the gods.

And heading them all was the god of the Plumed Serpent—Quetzalcoatl, Kukulkan.

When did he first arrive in those lands? The Long Count calendar begun by the Olmecs gives us the answer: in 3113 B.C.

As I have shown in greater detail in my earlier books (*The 12th Planet, The Stairway to Heaven, The Wars of Gods and Men*), that exact year was when in Egypt the god the Egyptians called Thoth, the god of science and the calendar, was *exiled* as a result of struggles between the gods. *Quetzalcoatl, I showed, was none other than Thoth.*

One of his tasks in ancient Egypt was to be the "keeper of the secrets of the pyramids." Possessing that knowledge, he supervised the construction of Mexico's two largest pyramids in a colossal site called Teotihuacan (north of Mexico City). There, an avenue that stretches for miles as if it was a landing and takeoff runway, connects the Pyramid of the Sun and the Pyramid of the Moon.

Teotihuacan was mainly a center for the processing of minerals. The mining operations under the aegis of Quetzalcoatl/Thoth extended all the way into South America. There, in northern Peru, at a place called Chavin de Huantar, the realm of Thoth reached its southernmost extent; for there it met the realm of another Old World god—the god of storms, the God of the Thunderbolt.

WHO WAS VIRACOCHA?

That was the realm of Viracocha, the god who headed the South Americans' pantheon, the god that featured in the various Creation Tales.

Archaeological and legendary evidence leave no doubt that he too had come to South America in connection with mining operations—first gold, then tin with which to make bronze (by mixing it with copper). His domain too was dotted with pyramids, but they were more like the Mesopotamian stage-towers ("ziggurats") than the smooth-sided pyramids of Egypt.

He too brought with him his followers, but they were not West Africans. As "portraits" carved from stone clearly show, they were of Indo-European stock; I have suggested in my books that they were *Hittites* from Anatolia (today's Turkey), who were the Near East's leading expert miners.

His mining center was Tiahuanacu—the very place on the shores of Lake Titicaca that the Inca and pre-Inca legends considered the oldest city in South America. Studies based on archaeo-astronomy confirm my conclusion that the city was begun in the fourth millennium B.C.—almost 6,000 years ago.

Who was Viracocha?

His tale begins not in the Americas and not in Egypt but in ancient Sumer the place of Mankind's first known civilization; it

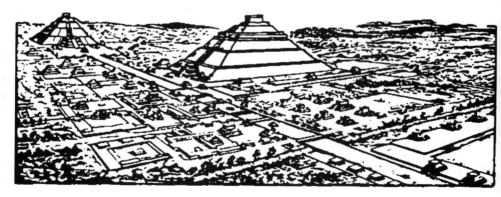

The pyramids and long avenue at Teotihuacan, Mexico

blossomed out suddenly in the south of Mesopotamia (today's Iraq) about 6,000 years ago.

Every "first" of what we deem essential for civilization—the wheel, the kiln, writing, mathematics, sciences, art, religion, etc.—every such aspect of an advanced civilization began in Sumer. Most amazing of all was the Sumerian knowledge of astronomy, for they knew that the Sun (not the Earth) is in the center, knew of (and described) all the planets we know of—even the distant Uranus, Neptune, and Pluto, and claimed that there is *one more planet* in our solar system. They called it NIBIRU, meaning "Planet of the Crossing." Its symbol was the cross; and according to the Sumerians, in its vast orbit that lasts 3,600 Earth-years, it comes near us, between Mars and Jupiter, once every 3,600 years.

The cross, the sign of Nibiru

A cylinder seal depicting a group of plowmen looking up at Nibiru, the Twelfth Planet, depicted with its cross symbol

It is at such times, the Sumerians asserted, visitors from Nibiru come and go between their planet and our planet Earth.

The Sumerians called those visitors—the ancient "gods"— ANUNNAKI, meaning "Those Who from Heaven to Earth Came." It was the Anunnaki, the Sumerians wrote on clay tablets, who had given Mankind civilization. The biblical tales of Creation, scholars now know, are only abbreviated versions of much more detailed Sumerian texts. The tales of how Earth was created, how "The Adam" was created, of the Garden of Eden, of the Deluge, of the Tower of Babel—all these tales were Sumerian records of what, according to them, had really happened on Earth. That is why I call the series of my books The Earth Chronicles.

The god called Viracocha in South America was none other than the god called by the Sumerians Ishkur ("He of the Mountains") and by the later Semites *Adad,* the god of the storms and the thunderbolts.

"EL DORADO" OF THE HEAVENS

The European conquest of the Americas, with all the avarice and cruelty that accompanied it, was motivated (after the first discoveries) by the greed for gold, the search for *El Dorado*—the place of the legendary king who had so much gold that he bathed in gold every day.

The fact is that before the Conquistadores, the "gods"—the Anunnaki—had come to the New World for the very same purpose. Thousands of years before Columbus *they* came to the Americas in search of gold, bringing with them the miners and the expert metallurgists from the Old World.

Indeed, the very reason why the Anunnaki had come to Earth itself was the need for gold. On their planet the atmosphere was dwindling, and life on Nibiru was in danger of extinction. Their scientists decided that they could survive only by creating a shield of suspended gold particles above their atmosphere. Discovering the presence of gold on Earth, the Anunnaki came here some 450,000 years ago. They first tried to obtain gold from the waters of the Persian Gulf. When this failed, they started to mine gold in southern Africa.

But then the Deluge came and everything in the ancient lands was flooded over. So a new source for the gold had to be found. This was the New World, the Americas.

The story of gods and men on Earth cannot be understood without the roles of Nibiru, the Anunnaki, and the search for gold.

The story of the Americas is part of that greater story. What happened in the Americas—long before Columbus—can also not be understood without Nibiru, the Anunnaki, and the search for gold.

As people in the Americas—and especially in the Andes or the vast Amazon valley—see UFOs in the skies, they should know that it is only a reminder that *the present and the future are echoes of the past: the time when gods, and not only men, roamed the New World.*

11
Cities Lost and Found

Selection from
The Lost Realms *(Chapter 9)*

In *The Lost Realms,* Sitchin discusses his findings as they relate to the Americas. He writes about the ancient civilizations that began near Lake Titicaca, monolithic boulders similar to those seen in Baalbek in Lebanon, evidence of African and Indo-European and Semitic people having been in the Americas in ancient times, temples aligned to the solstices and equinoxes, and sacred areas that seem to have been utilized in the practice of metallurgy. Given that gold was of utmost importance to the Anunnaki, and the abundance of it in these regions, it is not surprising that they might explore and exploit the mineral resources available.

The tales and legends passed down by the local people and preserved in drawings and other inscriptions provide descriptions of a pantheon similar to that found in other parts of the world. The stories of the Deluge, of a "Tower of Babel," and more are echoed in this region, even though more modern archaeologists are not yet convinced there was travel between the continents in those days. Here again, Sitchin's theories open a new paradigm for the events recorded in the drawings and artifacts of the day. If we believe in the technology of the Anunnaki, we can easily imagine travel between the regions in ancient times. The stories of personal aircraft available to the Anunnaki, communication devices, and perhaps sophisticated equipment that could cut and transport large stones, create a new understanding about how events in the Old World and in the New World could have been part of the same history, shared by the gods who could travel and interact with people from both regions.

THE DISCOVERY OF THE STORY OF GENESIS, in its original Mesopotamian version, depicted on the Inca temple's Holy of Holies, raises a host of questions. The first obvious one is, How—how did the Incas come to know these tales, not just in the general manner in which they have become known universally (the creation of the first couple, the Deluge), but in a manner that follows the Epic of Creation including knowledge of the complete Solar System and the orbit of Nibiru?

One possible answer is that the Incas had possessed this knowledge from time immemorial, bringing it with them to the Andes. The other possibility is that they had heard it from others whom they met in these lands.

In the absence of written records as one finds in the ancient Near East, the choice of an answer depends to some extent on how one answers another question: Who, indeed, were the Incas?

The *Relacion* of Salcamayhua is a good example of the Incas' attempt to perpetuate an exercise in state propaganda: the attribution of the revered named *Manco Capac* to the first Inca monarch, Inca Rocca, in order to make the people they had subjugated believe that the first Inca was the original "Son of the Sun," fresh out of the sacred Lake Titicaca. In fact, the Inca dynasty began some 3,500 years after that hallowed beginning. Also, the language that the Incas spoke was Quechua, the language of the people of the central-north Andes, whereas in the highlands of Lake Titicaca the people spoke Aymara. That, and other considerations, have led some scholars to speculate that the Incas were latecomers who had arrived from the east, settling in the Cuzco valley that borders on the great Amazon plain.

That, in itself, does not rule out a Near Eastern origin or link for the Incas. While attention has been focused on the depiction on the wall above the High Altar, no one has wondered why, in the midst of peoples who had made images of their gods and who placed their idols in shrines and temples, there was no idol whatsoever in the great Inca temple, nor in any other Inca shrine.

The chroniclers related that an "idol" was carried during some celebrations, but it was the image of Manco Capac, not of a god. They also relate that on a certain holy day a priest would go to a distant mountain upon which there stood a large idol of a god, and would sacrifice there a llama. But the mountain and its idol were from pre-Inca times, and the reference could well be to the temple of Pachacamac on the coast (regarding which we have already written).

Interestingly, the two customs are in line with biblical commandments from the time of the Exodus. The prohibition against making and worshipping idols was included in the Ten Commandments. And on the eve of the Day of Atonement, a priest had to sacrifice a "sin-goat" in the desert. No one has ever pointed out that the *quipos* used by the Incas to recall events—strings of different colors that had to be of wool, with knots at different positions—were in make and purpose akin to the *tzitzit,* "fringes on the corner of a blue thread," that the Israelites were commanded to attach to their garments as a way to remember the Lord's commandments. There is the matter of the rules of succession, by which the legal heir was the son by a half sister—a Sumerian custom followed by the Hebrew patriarchs. And there was the custom of circumcision in the Inca royal family.

Peruvian archaeologists have reported intriguing finds in the Amazonian provinces of Peru, including the apparent remains of stone-built cities, especially in the valleys of the Utcubamba and Marañón rivers. There are undoubtedly "lost cities" in the tropical zones; but in some instances the announced discoveries are really expeditions to known sites. Such was the case of headline news from Gran Patajen in 1985—a site visited by the Peruvian archaeologist F. Kauffmann-Doig and the American Gene Savoy twenty years earlier. There have been reports of aerial sightings of "pyramids" on the Brazilian side of the border, of lost cities such as Akakor, and Indians' tales of ruins hold-ing untold treasures. A document in the national archives in Rio de Janeiro is purportedly an eighteenth-century report recording a lost city in the Amazon jungles seen by Europeans in 1591; the document even transcribes a script found there. It was the main reason for an expedi-tion by Colonel Percy Fawcett whose mysterious disappearance in the jungles is still a subject of popular-science articles.

All this is not to say that there are no ancient ruins in the Amazon basin that remain from a trail across the South American continent from Guiana/Venezuela to Ecuador/Peru. Humboldt's reports of his travels across the continent mention a tradition that people from across the sea landed in Venezuela and proceeded inland; and the principal river of the Cuzco valley, the Urubamba, is but a tributary of the Amazon. Official Brazilian teams have visited many sites (without, however, conducting sustained excavations). At one site near the mouth of the Amazon, pottery urns decorated with incised patterns that remind one of the designs on earthenware jars from Ur (the Sumerian birthplace of Abraham) have been found. An islet called Pacoval appeared to have been artificially created, and served as a base for a number of mounds (which were not excavated). According to L. Netto, *Investigacioes sobre a Archaeologia Braziliera,* similarly decorated urns and vases "of superior quality" have been found farther up the Amazon. And, we believe, an equally important route connecting the Andes with the Atlantic Ocean did exist farther to the south.

Still, it is uncertain that the Incas themselves came this way. One of their ancestry versions attributes their beginnings to a landing on the Peruvian coast. Their language, Quechua, bears Far Eastern resem-blances both in word meanings and dialect. And they clearly belong to the Amerindian stock—the fourth branch of mankind that, we have ventured to suggest, stemmed from the line of Cain. (A guide in Cuzco, hearing of our biblical expertise, asked whether *In-ca* might have stemmed from *Ca-in* by reversing the syllables. One wonders!)

The evidence at hand, we believe, indicates that the Near Eastern tales and beliefs, including knowledge of the story of Nibiru and the Anunnaki who had come from there to Earth—the pantheon of twelve—were brought to the predecessors of the Incas from overseas. It took place in the days of the Ancient Empire; and the bearers of these tales and beliefs were also Strangers From Across the Seas, but not necessarily the same ones who brought similar tales, beliefs, and civilization to Mesoamerica.

In addition to all the facts and evidence that we had already provided, let us return to Izapa, a site near the Pacific coast where Mexico and Guatemala meet and where the Olmecs and the Maya rubbed shoulders. Recognized only belatedly as the largest site along the Pacific coast of North or Central America, it spans 2500 years of continuous occupation, from 1500 B.C. (a date confirmed by carbon dating) to A.D. 1000. It had the customary pyramids and ball courts; but it has mostly amazed archaeologists by its carved stone monuments. The style, imagination, mythical content, and artistic perfection of these carvings have come to be called "Izapan style," and it is now recognized that it was the source from which the style spread to other sites along the Pacific slopes of Mexico and Guatemala. It was art belonging to the Early and Middle Preclassic Olmec, adopted by the Maya as the site changed hands.

Archaeologists from the New World Archaeological Foundation of Brigham Young University, who have devoted decades to the excavation and study of the site, have no doubt that it was oriented toward the solstices at the time of its foundation and that even the various monuments were placed "on deliberate alignments with planetary movements" (V. G. Norman. *Izapa Sculpture*). Religious, cosmological, and mythological themes intermingled with historical subjects are expressed in the stone carvings. We have already seen one of the many and varied depictions of winged deities. Of particular interest here is a large carved stone whose face measures some thirty square feet, designated by the archaeologists Izapa Stela 5, found in conjunction with a major stone altar. The complicated scene (Fig. 87) has been recognized by various scholars as a "fantastic visual myth" concerning the "genesis of humanity" at a Tree of Life that grows by a river. The mythical-historical tale is told by an old bearded man seated on the left, and is retold by a Maya-looking man on the right (of the stela's observer).

Figure 87

The scene is filled with diverse vegetation, birds, and fish as well as human figures. Interestingly, two central figures represent men that have the face and feet of elephants—an animal completely unknown in the Americas. The one on the left is shown in association with a helmeted Olmec man, which reinforces our contention that the colossal stone heads and the Olmecs they portrayed were Africans.

The left-hand panel, when enlarged (Fig. 88a), clearly reveals details which we consider extremely important clues. The bearded man tells his story over an altar that bears the symbol of the umbilical cutter; this was the symbol (Fig. 88b) by which Ninti (the Sumerian goddess who had helped Enki create Man) was identified on cylinder seals and on monuments. When the Earth was divided among the gods she was given dominion over the Sinai peninsula, the Egyptians' source of their cherished blue-green turquoise; they called her Hathor and depicted her with cow's horns, as on this Creation of Man scene (Fig. 88c). These "coincidences" reinforce the conclusion that the Izapa stela illustrates

Figure 88

none other than the Old World tales of the Creation of Man and the Garden of Eden.

And finally there are portrayals of pyramids, smooth sided as at Giza on the Nile, depicted here at the bottom of the panel beside a flowing river. Indeed, as one examines and reexamines this millennia-old panel, one must agree that a picture is worth a thousand words.

Legends and archaeological evidence indicate that the Olmecs and the Bearded Ones did not stop at the edge of the ocean, but pushed on southward into Central America and the northern lands of South America. They may have advanced overland, for they certainly left traces of their presence at inland sites. In all probability they journeyed southward the easier way, by boats.

The legends in the equatorial and northern parts of the Andes recalled not only the arrival by sea of their own ancestors (such as Naymlap), but also two separate ones by "giants." One had occurred in ancient empire times, the other in Mochica times. Cieza de Leon described the latter thus: "There arrived on the coast, in boats made of reeds as big as large ships, a party of men of such size that, from the knee downward their height was as great as the entire height of an ordinary man." They had metal tools with which they dug wells in the living rock, but for food they raided the natives' provisions. They also violated the natives' women, for there were no women among the landing giants. The Mochica depicted these giants who had enslaved them on their pottery, painting their faces in black (Fig. 89) while those of the Mochicas were painted white. Also found in Mochica remains are clay portrayals of older men with white beards.

It is our guess that these unwanted visitors were Olmecs and their bearded Near Eastern companions who were fleeing the uprisings in Mesoamerica, circa 400 B.C. They left behind them a trail of dreaded veneration as they passed through Central America to the equatorial lands farther down in South America. Archaeological expeditions to the equatorial areas of the Pacific coast have found enigmatic monoliths that stem from that fearsome period. The George C. Heye expedition found in Ecuador giant stone heads with humanlike features but with

Figure 89

a   b

Figure 90

fangs as though they were ferocious jaguars. Another expedition found at San Agustin, a site closer to the Colombian border, stone statues portraying giants, sometimes shown holding tools or weapons; their facial features are those of the African Olmecs (Fig. 90a, b).

These invaders may have been the source of the legends current also in these lands of how Man was created, of a Deluge, and of a serpent god who demanded an annual tribute of gold. One of the ceremonies recorded by the Spaniards was a ritual dance performed by twelve men dressed in red; it was performed on the shores of a lake connected with the legend of El Dorado.

The equatorial natives worshiped a pantheon of twelve, a number of great significance and an important clue. It was headed by a triad consisting of the Creation God, the Evil God, and the Mother Goddess; and it included the gods of the Moon, the Sun, and the Rain-Thunder. Significantly too, the Moon God ranked higher than the Sun God. The deities' names changed from locality to locality, retaining however the celestial affinity. Among the strange-sounding names, though, two stand out. The head of the pantheon was called in the Chibcha dialect *Abira*—remarkably similar to the Mesopotamian divine epithet *Abir,* which meant Strong, Mighty; and the Moon God, as we have noted, was called "Si" or "Sian," which parallels the Mesopotamian name *Sin* for that deity.

The pantheon of these South American natives therefore brings inevitably to mind the pantheon of the ancient Near East and the eastern Mediterranean—of the Greeks and the Egyptians, the Hittites and the Canaanites and Phoenicians, the Assyrians and the Babylonians—all the way back to where it all began: to the Sumerians of southern Mesopotamia from whom all others had obtained the gods and their mythologies.

The Sumerian pantheon was headed by an "Olympian Circle" of twelve, for each of these supreme gods had to have a celestial counterpart, one of the twelve members of the Solar System. Indeed, the names of the gods and their planets were one and the same (except when a variety of epithets were used to describe the planet or the god's attributes). Heading the pantheon was the ruler of Nibiru, ANU whose name was synonymous with "Heaven," for he resided on Nibiru. His spouse, also a member of the Twelve, was called ANTU. Included in this group were the two principal sons of ANU: E.A. ("Whose House Is Water"), Anu's Firstborn but not by Antu; and EN.LIL ("Lord of the Command") who was the Heir Apparent because his mother was Antu, a half sister of Anu. Ea was also called in Sumerian texts EN.KI ("Lord Earth"), for he had led the first mission of the Anunnaki from Nibiru to Earth and established on Earth their first colonies in the E.DIN ("Home of the Righteous Ones")—the biblical Eden.

His mission was to obtain gold, for which Earth was a unique source. Not for ornamentation or because of vanity, but as a way to save the atmosphere of Nibiru by suspending gold dust in that planet's stratosphere. As recorded in the Sumerian texts (and related by us in *The 12th Planet* and subsequent books of The Earth Chronicles), Enlil was sent to Earth to take over the command when the initial extraction methods used by Enki proved unsatisfactory. This laid the groundwork for an ongoing feud between the two half brothers and their descendants, a feud that led to Wars of the Gods; it ended with a peace treaty worked out by their sister Ninti (thereafter renamed Ninharsag). The inhabited Earth was divided between the warring clans. The three sons of Enlil—Ninurta, Sin, Adad—together with Sin's twin children, Shamash (the Sun) and Ishtar (Venus), were given the lands of Shem and Japhet, the lands of the Semites and Indo-Europeans: Sin (the Moon), lowland Mesopotamia; Ninurta ("Enlil's Warrior," Mars), the highlands of Elam and Assyria; Adad ("The Thunderer," Mercury), Asia Minor (the land of the Hittites) and Lebanon. Ishtar was granted dominion as the goddess of the Indus Valley civilization; Shamash was given command of the spaceport in the Sinai peninsula.

This division, which did not go uncontested, gave Enki and his sons the lands of Ham—the brown/black people—of Africa: the civilization of the Nile Valley and the gold mines of southern and western Africa—a vital and cherished prize. A great scientist and metallurgist, Enki's Egyptian name was *Ptah* ("The Developer"; a title that translated into *Hephaestus* by the Greeks and *Vulcan* by the Romans). He shared the continent with his sons; among them was the firstborn MAR.DUK ("Son of the Bright Mound") whom the Egyptians called *Ra,* and NIN.

GISH.ZI.DA ("Lord of the Tree of Life") whom the Egyptians called Thoth (Hermes to the Greeks)—a god of secret knowledge including astronomy, mathematics, and the building of pyramids.

It was the knowledge imparted by this pantheon, the needs of the gods who had come to Earth, and the leadership of Thoth, that directed the African Olmecs and the bearded Near Easterners to the other side of the world.

And having arrived in Mesoamerica on the Gulf coast—just as the Spaniards, aided by the same sea currents, did millennia later—they cut across the Mesoamerican isthmus at its narrowest neck and—just like the Spaniards due to the same geography—sailed down from the Pacific coast of Mesoamerica southward, to the lands of Central America and beyond.

For that is where the gold was, in Spanish times and before.

Before the Incas and the Chimu and the Mochica, a culture named by scholars Chavin flourished in the mountains that lie in northern Peru between the coast and the Amazon basin. One of its first explorers, Julio C. Tello (*Chavin* and other works) called it "the matrix of Andean civilization." It takes us back to at least 1500 B.C.; and like that of the Olmec civilization in Mexico at the same time, it arose suddenly and with no apparent prior gradual development.

Encompassing a vast area whose dimensions are constantly expanded as new finds are made, the Chavin Culture appeared to have been centered at a site called Chavin de Huantar, near the village of Chavin (and hence the culture's name). It is situated at an elevation of 10,000 feet in the Cordillera Blanca range of the northwestern Andes. There, in a mountain valley where tributaries of the Marañón river form a triangle, an area of some 300,000 square feet was flattened and terraced and made suitable for the construction of complex structures, carefully and precisely laid out according to a preconceived plan that took into consideration the contours and features of the site (Fig. 91a). Not only do the buildings and plazas form precise rectangulars and squares; they have also been precisely aligned with the cardinal points, with east-west as the major axis. The three main buildings stood upon terraces that elevated them and leaned against the outer western wall that ran for some 500 feet. The wall that

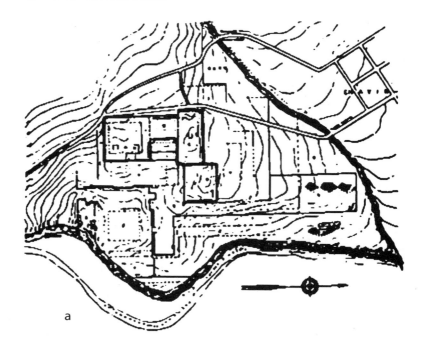

a

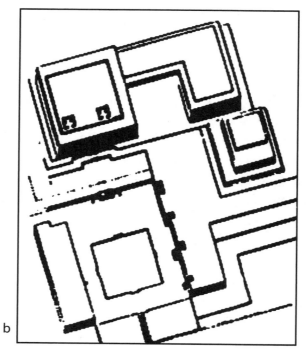

b

Figure 91

apparently encompassed the complex on three sides, leaving it open to the river that flowed on the east, rose to about forty feet.

The largest building was at the southwest corner, measured about 240 by 250 feet, and consisted of at least three floors (see an artist's bird's-eye-view reconstruction, Fig. 91b). It was built of masonry stone blocks, well shaped but not dressed, laid out in regular and level courses. As some remaining slabs indicate, the walls were faced outside with smooth, marble like stone slabs; some still retain their incised decorations. From a terrace on the east a monumental stairway led through an imposing gate up toward the main building; the gate was flanked by two cylindrical columns—a most unusual feature in South America—that together with adjoining vertical stone blocks supported a thirty-foot horizontal lintel made of a single monolith. Farther up, a double monumental stairway led to the building's top. This stairway was built of perfectly cut and shaped stones that remind one of the great Egyptian pyramids. The two stairways led to the building's top, where archaeologists have found the remains of two towers; the rest of the uppermost platform remained unbuilt.

The eastern terrace, forming part of the platform on which this edifice was built, led to (or from) a sunken plaza reached by ceremonial steps and surrounded on three sides by rectangular plazas or platforms. Just outside the southwestern corner of the sunken plaza, and perfectly aligned with the staircases of the main edifice and its terrace, there stood a large flat boulder: it had in it seven grind holes and a rectangular niche.

The exterior's precision was exceeded by the interior complexity. Within the three structures there ran corridors and mazelike passages, intermingled with connecting galleries, rooms, and staircases, or leading to dead ends and therefore nicknamed labyrinths. Some of the galleries have been faced with smooth slabs, here and there delicately decorated; all the passages are roofed with carefully selected stone slabs that have been placed with great ingenuity that prevented their collapse over the millennia. There are niches and protrusions for no apparent purpose; and vertical or sloping shafts that the archaeologists thought might have served for ventilation.

What was Chavin de Huantar built for? The only plausible purpose that its discoverers could see was that of a religious center, a kind of ancient "Mecca." This notion was strengthened by the three fascinating and most enigmatic relics found at the site. One that baffles by its complex imagery was discovered by Tello in the main building and is called the Tello Obelisk (Fig. 92a,b shows the front and back). It is engraved

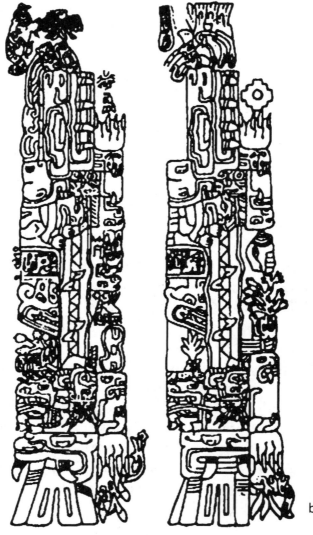

a   b

Figure 92

Figure 93

with an agglomeration of human bodies and faces but with feline hands with fangs or wings. There are animals, birds, trees; gods emitting rocketlike rays; and a variety of geometric designs. Was this a totem pole that served for worship, or an attempt by an ancient "Picasso" to convey all the myths and legends on one column? No one has yet come up with a plausible answer.

A second carved stone is called the Raimondi Monolith (Fig. 93), after the archaeologist who found it at a nearby estate; it is believed that it originally stood atop the grooved stone at the southwestern edge of the sunken plaza, aligned with the monumental stairway. It is now on exhibit in Lima.

The ancient artist carved upon this seven-foot-high granite column the image of a deity holding a weapon—a thunderbolt, some believe—in each hand. While the deity's body and limbs are essentially though not entirely anthropomorphic, the face is not. This face has puzzled scholars because it does not represent or stylize a local creature (such as a jaguar); rather, it appears to be the artist's conception of what scholars conveniently called "a mythological animal," namely one of which the artist had heard but had not actually seen.

To our eyes, however, the deity's face is that of a bull—an animal completely absent in South America but one that featured considerably in the lore and iconography of the ancient Near East. Significantly (in our opinion) it was the "cult animal" of Adad, and the mountain range in his domain, in Asia Minor, is still called to this very day the Taurus Mountains.

A third unusual and enigmatic carved stone column at Chavin de Huantar is called *El Lanzon* because of its lancelike shape (Fig. 94). It was discovered in the middle building and has remained there because its height (twelve feet) exceeds the ten-foot height of the gallery where it stands; the monolith's top therefore protrudes into the floor above it through a carefully cut square opening. The image on this monolith has been the subject of much speculation; to our eyes, again, it seems to depict an anthropomorphized face of a bull. Does it mean, then, that whoever erected this monument—obviously *before* the building was constructed, for the latter was built to accommodate the statue—worshiped the Bull God?

It was by and large the high artistic level of the artifacts rather than the complex and unusual structures that so impressed scholars and led them to consider Chavin the "matrix culture" of north-central Peru, and to believe that the site was a religious center. But that the purpose was not religious but rather utilitarian seems to be indicated by recent finds at Chavin de Huantar. These latest excavations revealed a network of subterranean tunnels hewed out of the native rock; they honeycombed the whole site, both under built as well as unbuilt parts, and served to connect several series of underground compartments arranged in a chainlike manner (Fig. 95).

Figure 94

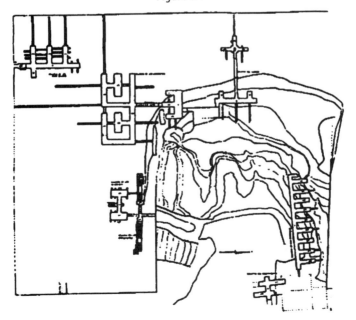

Figure 95

The openings of the tunnels perplexed their discoverers, for they seemed to connect the two river tributaries that flank the site, one (due to the mountainous terrain) above it and the other in the valley below it. Some explorers have suggested that these tunnels were so built for flood control purposes, to channel the onrushing water from the mountains as the snows melt and let it flow under instead of through the buildings. But if there was a danger of such flooding (after heavy rains rather than from melting snows), why did the otherwise ingenious builders place their structures at such a vulnerable spot?

They did so, we hold, on purpose. They ingeniously used the two levels of the tributaries to create a powerful, controlled flow of water needed for the processes that were carried out at Chavin de Huantar. For there, as at many other sites, such devices of flowing water were used in the panning of gold.

We will encounter more of these ingenious waterworks in the Andes; we have seen them, in more rudimentary forms, at Olmec sites. They were in Mexico part of complex earthworks; they were in the Andes masterpieces in stone—sometimes large sites such as Chavin de Huantar, sometimes lone remains of incredibly cut and shaped rocks, as this one seen by Squier in the Chavin area (Fig. 96), that seem to have been intended for some ultramodern machinery long gone.

It was indeed the stonework—not of the edifices but of the artistic artifacts—that seems to provide the answer to the question Who was there at Chavin de Huantar? The artistic skills and stone-sculpting styles are surprisingly reminiscent of the Olmec art of Mexico. The enchanting objects include a jaguar-cat receptacle, a feline-bull, an eagle-condor, a turtle basin; a large number of vases and other objects decorated with glyphs created of entwined fangs—a motif decorating wall slabs as well as artifacts (Fig. 97a). There were, however, also stone slabs covered with Egyptian motifs—serpents, pyramids, the sacred Eye of Ra (Fig. 97b). And as though this variety was insufficient, there were fragments of carved stone blocks that depicted Mesopotamian motifs, such as deities within Winged Disks (Fig. 97c) or (engraved on bones) images of gods wearing conical headdresses, the headgear by which Mesopotamian gods were identified (Fig. 97d).

Figure 96

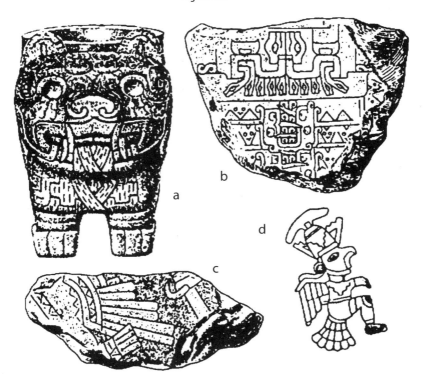

a

b

c

d

Figure 97

Figure 98

The deities wearing the conical headdresses have facial features that have an "African" look, and having been carved on bones may represent the earliest art depictions at the site. Could it be that Africans—negroid, Egyptian-Nubian—were ever at this South American site at its earliest time? The surprising answer is yes. There were indeed black Africans here and at nearby sites (especially at one called Sechin), and they left their portraits behind. At all these sites carved stones by the dozens bear depictions of those people; in most instances they are shown holding some kind of tool; in many instances, the "engineer" is depicted as associated with a symbol for waterworks (Fig. 98).

At coastal sites that lead to the Chavin sites in the mountains, archaeologists have found sculpted heads of clay, not stone, that must have represented Semitic visitors (Fig. 99); one was so strikingly similar to Assyrian sculptures that the discoverer, H. Ubbelohde-Doering (*On the Royal Highway of the Incas*) nicknamed it "King of Assyria." But it is not certain that these visitors had made it to the highland sites—at least

Figure 99

not alive: sculpted stone heads with Semitic features have been found at Chavin de Huantar—but mostly with grotesque grimaces or mutilations, stuck as trophies in the site's surrounding walls.

The age of Chavin suggests that the first wave of these Old World, both Olmec and Semitic migrants, had arrived there circa 1500 B.C. Indeed, it was in the reign of the 12th monarch of the Ancient Empire that, as Montesinos chronicled, "news reached Cuzco of the disembarking on the coast of some men of great stature . . . giants who were settling on the whole coast" and who possessed metal implements. After some time they moved inland into the mountains. The monarch sent runners to investigate and to provide him with reports of the giants' advance, lest they come too close to the capital. But as things turned out, the giants provoked the wrath of the Great God and he destroyed them. These events had taken place about a century before the standstill of the Sun that had occurred circa 1400 B.C.—i.e. circa 1500 B.C., the very time at which Chavin de Huantar's waterworks were built.

This, it must be pointed out, is not the same incident reported by Garcilaso, about giants who despoiled the land and raped the women—an occurrence in Moche times, circa 400 B.C. Indeed, it was at that time, as we have already seen, that the two commingled groups of Olmecs and Semites were fleeing Mesoamerica. Their fate, however, was no different in the northern Andes. Besides the grotesque Semitic stone heads found at Chavin de Huantar, depictions of mutilated negroid bodies are found in the whole area, and especially at Sechin.

Thus it was, after some 1,000 years in the northern Andes and almost 2,000 years in Mesoamerica, that the African-Semitic presence had come to a tragic end.

Although some of the Africans may have gone farther south, as finds at Tiahuanacu attest, the African-Semitic extension into the Andes from Mesoamerica appears to have not gone beyond the Chavin-culture area. The tales of the giants stricken by divine hand may hold more than a kernel of fact; for it is quite possible that there, in the northern Andes, two realms of two gods had met, with an unseen boundary between jurisdictions and human subordinates.

We say this because, in that very zone, other white men had been present. They were portrayed in stone busts (Fig. 100)—nobly clad, wearing turbans or headbands with symbols of authority, and decorated with what scholars call "mythological animals." These bust-statues have been mostly found at a site near Chavin named Aija. Their facial features, especially the straight noses, identify them as Indo-Europeans.

Figure 100

Their origin could have been only the land of Asia Minor and Elam to its southeast, and in time the Indus Valley farther east.

Is it possible that people from those distant lands had crossed the Pacific and come to the Andes in prehistoric times? The link that evidently existed is confirmed by depictions illustrating the feats of an ancient Near Eastern hero whose tales were told and retold. He was Gilgamesh, ruler of Uruk (the biblical Erech) who had reigned circa 2900 B.C.; he went in search of the hero of the Deluge story whom the gods had granted (according to the Mesopotamian version) immortality. His adventures were told in the *Epic of Gilgamesh,* which was translated in antiquity from Sumerian into the other languages of the Near East. One of his heroic deeds, the wrestling with and defeat of two lions with his bare hands, was a favorite pictorial depiction by ancient artists, as this one on a Hittite monument (Fig. 101a).

Amazingly, the same depiction appears on stone tablets from Aija

Figure 101

(Fig. 101b) and a nearby site, Callejon de Huaylus (Fig. 101c) in the northern Andes!

These Indo-Europeans have not been traced in Mesoamerica or Central America, and we must assume that they came across the Pacific straight to South America. If legends be the guide, they preceded the two waves of African "giants" and Mediterranean Bearded Ones, and could have been the earliest settlers of which the tale of Naymlap recounts. The traditional landing site for that arrival has been the peninsula of Santa Elena (now Ecuador) which, with its nearby La Plata island, juts out into the Pacific. Archaeological excavations have confirmed early settlements there, beginning with what is called a Valdivian Phase circa 2500 B.C. Among the finds reported by the renowned Ecuadorian archaeologist Emilio Estrada (*Ultimas Civilizaciones Pre-Historicas*) were stone statuettes with the same straight-nose features (Fig. 102a) as well as a symbol on pottery (Fig. 102b) that was the Hittite hieroglyph for "gods" (Fig. 102c).

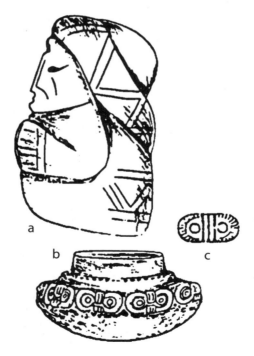

Figure 102

It is noteworthy that the megalithic structures in the Andes, as we have already seen at Cuzco, Sacsahuaman, and Machu Picchu, all lie south of the unseen demarcation line between the two divine realms. The handiwork of the megalithic builders—Indo-Europeans guided by their gods?—which began south of Chavin (Fig. 96), has left its mark all the way south into the valley of the Urubamba river and beyond—everywhere, indeed, where gold was collected and panned. Everywhere, rocks were fashioned as though they were soft putty into channels, compartments, niches, and platforms that from a distance look like stairways to nowhere; tunnels lead into mountainsides; fissures have been enlarged into corridors whose walls have been smoothed or shaped in precise angles. Everywhere, even at sites where the inhabitants could obtain all their water needs from the river below, elaborate water funneling and channeling were created higher up to make water from spring, tributary, or rain sources flow in a desired direction.

West-southwest of Cuzco, on the way to the town of Abancay, lie the ruins of Sayhuiti-Rumihuasi. As at other such sites it is situated near the junction of a river and a smaller stream. There are remains of a retaining wall, the remnant of large-sized structures that had once stood there; as Luis A. Pardo has pointed out in a study devoted to the site (*Los Grandes Monolitos de Sayhuiti*) the name means in the native tongue "Truncated Pyramid."

The site is known for its several monoliths and especially one called the Great Monolith. The name is appropriate since this huge rock, which from a distance appears as an immense bright egg resting on the hillside, measures about fourteen by ten by nine feet. While its bottom part has been carefully shaped as half an ovoid, the upper part has been carved out to represent in all probability a scale model of some unknown area. Discernible are miniature walls, platforms, stairways, channels, tunnels, rivers, canals; diverse structures, some representing edifices with niches and steps between them; images of various animals indigenous to Peru; and human figures of what look like warriors and, some say, gods.

Some see in this scale model a religious artifact, honoring the deities that they discern upon it. Others believe it represents a section of

Peru that encompasses three districts, extending to the south to Lake Titicaca (which they identify with a lake carved on the stone) and the very ancient site of Tiahuanaco. Was this, then, a map carved in stone—or perhaps a scale model of a grand artificer who planned the layout and structures to be erected?

The answer may lie in the fact that, winding through this scale model, are grooves, an inch to two inches wide. They all originate in a "dish" located at the monolith's highest point and slope down, winding and zigzagging, to the lowest edge of the sculptured model, reaching there round discharge holes. Some consider these grooves to have served for the pouring by priests of potions (coca juices) as offerings to the gods represented on the rock. But if it was the gods themselves who were the architects, what was their purpose?

The telltale grooves are also a feature of another immense rock outcropping that has also been cut and shaped with geometric precision (Fig. 103), its surface and sides made into steps, platforms, and cascading niches. One side has been cut to form small "dishes" on the upper level; they are connected to a larger receptacle from which a deep channel leads down, separating midway into two grooves. Whatever liquid they carried poured into the rock, which was hollowed out and could be entered through an entryway in the back.

Figure 103

Other remains on the site, probably broken off from larger slabs, puzzle by the complex and geometrically precise grooves and hollows cut into them; they can be best likened to dies or matrixes for the casting of some ultramodern instruments.

One of the better known sites, just east of Sacsahuaman, is called Kenko—a name which in the native tongue means "Twisting Channels." The main tourist attraction there is a huge monolith standing on a podium that may have represented a lion or other large animal standing on its hind legs. In front of the monolith is a six-foot-high wall built of beautiful ashlars, surrounding the monolith in a circle. The monolith stands in front of an immense natural rock and the circular wall reaches and ends at the rock as a pincer. In the back, the rock has been cut, carved, and shaped into several levels connected by staggered platforms. Zigzagging channels have been cut on the rock's artificially sloping sides and the rock's interior has been hewed out to create labyrinthine tunnels and chambers. Nearby, a cleft in the rock leads to a cavelike opening that has been hollowed out with geometric precision to form stone features that some describe as thrones and altars.

There are more of these sites around Cuzco-Sacsahuaman, all along the Sacred Valley and reaching to the southeast, where a lake bears the name Golden Lake. A site named Torontoy includes among its precisely cut, megalithic stone blocks one that has thirty-two angles. Some fifty miles from Cuzco, near Torontoy, an artificial water flow was made to cascade between two walls and over fifty-four "steps," all cut out of the living rock; significantly, the site is called Cori-Huairachina, "Where Gold is Purified."

Cuzco meant "The Navel" and indeed Sacsahuaman appears to have been the largest, most colossal and central of all these sites. One aspect of this centrality may be evidenced by a place called Pampa de Anta, some ten miles west of Sacsahuaman. There, the sheer rock has been carved into a series of steps that form a large crescent (hence the rock's name *Quillarumi*, "Moon Stone"). Since there is nothing to view from there except the eastern skies, Rolf Müller (*Sonne, Mond und Steiner über dem Reich der Inka*) concluded that it was some kind of observatory, situated so as to reflect astronomical data to the promontory at Sacsahuaman.

But what was Sacsahuaman itself, now that the notion of its having been built by the Incas as a fortress is completely discredited? The perplexing labyrinthine channels and other seemingly haphazard cutouts into which the natural rocks were shaped begin to make sense as a result of new archaeological excavations begun several years ago. Though far from uncovering more than a small part of the extensive stone structures in the plateau that extends behind the smooth Rodadero rock, they have already revealed two major aspects of the site. One is the fact that walls, conduits, receptacles, channels, and the like have been created both out of the living rock and with the aid of perfectly shaped large ashlars, many of the polygonal kind of the Megalithic Age, to form a series of water-channeling structures one above the other; rain or spring waters could thus be made to flow in a regulated manner from level to level.

The other aspect is the uncovering of a huge circular area enclosed by megalithic ashlars, that by all opinions served as a reservoir. Also uncovered was a sluice-chamber built of megalithic ashlars, that lies underground at a level permitting the running off of the water from the circular reservoir. As children who come to play there have demonstrated, the channel leading away from this sluice-chamber leads to the *Chingana* or "Labyrinth" carved out of the native rock behind and below this circular area.

Even before the whole complex that had been built on this promontory is uncovered, it is by now clear that some mineral or chemical compounds had been poured down the Rodadero, giving its back smooth side the discoloration resulting from such use. Whatever it was—gold-bearing soil?—was poured down into the large circular reservoir. From the other side, water was force-flowed. It all looks like a large-scale gold-panning facility. The water was finally flowed off through the sluice-chamber, and out and away through the labyrinth. In the stone vats, what remained was gold.

What then did the megalithic, colossal zigzagging walls, at the edge of the promontory, protect or support? To this question there is still no clear answer, except to surmise that some kind of massive platform was required for the vehicles—airborne, we must presume—that were used to haul in the ores and take away the nuggets.

One site that may have served, or was intended to serve, a similar transportation function, located some sixty miles northwest of Sacsahuaman, is Ollantaytambu. The archaeological remains are atop a steep mountain spur; they overlook an opening between the mountains that rise where the Urubamba-Vilcanota and Patcancha rivers meet. A village that gave its name to the ruins is situated at the bottom of the mountain; the name, meaning "Restplace of Ollantay," stems from the time an Inca hero prepared there a stand against the Spaniards.

Several hundred stone steps of crude construction connect a series of terraces of Inca make and lead to the principal ruins on the summit. There, in what has been presumed to have served as a fortress, there are indeed remains of Inca-walled structures built of fieldstones. They look primitive and ugly beside pre-Inca structures from the Megalithic Age.

The megalithic structures begin with a retaining wall built of the beautifully fashioned polygonal stones as one finds at the previously described megalithic remains. Passing through a gateway cut of a single stone block one reaches a platform supported by a second retaining wall, similarly constructed of polygonal stones but of a larger size. On one side an extension of this wall becomes an enclosure with twelve trapezoid openings—two serving as doorways and ten being false windows; perhaps this is why Luis Pardo (*Ollamtaitampu, Una ciudad megalitica*) called this structure "the central temple." On the other side of the wall there stands a massive and perfectly shaped gate (Fig. 104) that in its

Figure 104

time (though not now) served as the way up to the main structures.

The greatest mystery of Ollantaytambu is there: a row of six colossal monoliths that stand on the topmost terrace. The gigantic stone blocks are from eleven to almost fourteen feet high, average six or more feet in width and vary in thickness from about three to over six feet (Fig. 105). They stand joined together, without mortar or any other bonding material, with the aid of long dressed stones that had been inserted between the colossal blocks. Where the thickness of the blocks fell short of the greatest thickness (of over six feet), large polygonal stones fitted together, as at Cuzco and Sacsahuaman, to create an even thickness. In front, however, the megaliths stand as a single wall, oriented exactly southeast, with faces that have been carefully smoothed to obtain a slight curvature. At least two of the monoliths bear the weathered remains of relief decorations; on the fourth one (counting from the left) the design is clearly that of the Stairway symbol; all archaeologists agree that the symbol, which had its origin at Tiahuanacu at Lake Titicaca, signified the ascent from Earth to Heaven or, in reverse, a descent from Heaven to Earth.

Figure 105

Figure 106

Jambs and protrusions on the sides and faces of the monoliths and step-like cuts at the top of the sixth one suggest that the construction was not completed. Indeed, stone blocks of various shapes and sizes lie strewn about. Some have been cut and shaped and given perfect corners, grooves and angles. One provides a most significant clue: a deep T shape has been cut into it (Fig. 106). All the scholars, having found such cuts in gigantic stone blocks at Tiahuanacu, had to agree that this groove was intended to hold together two stone blocks with a *metal* clamp: as a precaution against earthquakes.

One must therefore wonder how scholars can continue to attribute these remains to the Incas, who did not possess any metal except gold, which is too soft and thus totally unsuitable to hold together colossal stone blocks shaken by an earthquake. Naive too is the explanation that Inca rulers built this colossal place as a gigantic bathhouse, for bathing was one of their cherished pleasures. With two rivers running just at the foothills, why haul immense blocks—some weighing as much as 250 tons—to build a bathtub up the hill? And all that without iron tools?

More serious is the explanation for the row of six monoliths that they were part of a planned retaining wall, probably to support a large platform atop the mountain. If so, the size and the massivity of the stone blocks bring to mind the colossal stone blocks used to construct the unique platform at Baalbek, in the Lebanon mountains. In *The Stairway to Heaven* we described and examined at length that megalithic platform, and concluded that it was the "landing place" that had been the first destination of Gilgamesh—a landing place for the "aerial ships" of the Anunnaki.

The many similarities we find between Ollantaytambu and Baalbek include the origin of the megaliths. The colossal stone blocks of Baalbek were quarried miles away in a valley, then incredibly lifted, transported, and put in place to fit with other stones of the platform. At Ollantaytambu too the giant stone blocks were quarried on the mountainside on the opposite side of the valley. The heavy blocks of red granite, after they had been quarried, hewed, and shaped, were then transported from the mountainside, across two streams, and up the Ollantaytambu site; then carefully raised, put precisely in place, and finally fused together.

Whose handiwork was Ollantaytambu? Garcilaso de la Vega wrote that it was "from the very first epoch, before the Incas." Blas Valera stated, "from an era that anteceded the epoch of the Incas . . . the era of the pantheon of the gods of pre-Inca times." It is time that modern scholars agree.

It is also time to realize that these gods were the same deities to whom the construction of Baalbek has been attributed by Near Eastern legends.

Was Ollantaytambu intended to be a stronghold, as Sacsahuaman might have been, or a landing place, as Baalbek had been?

In our previous books we have shown that, in determining the site of their spaceport and "landing places," the Anunnaki first anchored a landing corridor on some outstanding geographical feature (such as Mount Ararat). The flight path within this corridor was then inclined at a precise 45 degrees to the equator. In postdiluvial times, when the spaceport was in the Sinai peninsula and the landing place for airborne craft at Baalbek, the grid followed the same pattern.

The *Torreon* at Machu Picchu has, besides the two observation windows in the semicircular section, another enigmatic window (Fig. 107) that has an inverted stairway opening at its bottom and a wedgelike slit at its top. Our own studies show that a line from the Sacred Rock through the slit to the Intihuatana will run at a precise angle of 45 degrees to the cardinal points, thus establishing for Machu Picchu its principal orientation.

This 45 degree orientation determined not only the layout of

Figure 107

Machu Picchu, but also the location of major ancient sites. If one draws on a map of the region a line connecting the legendary stops made by Viracocha from the Island of the Sun in Lake Titicaca, the line will pass Cuzco and continue to Ollantaytambu—precisely at a 45 degree angle to the equator!

A series of studies and lectures by Maria Schulten de D'Ebneth, summed up in her book *La Ruta de Wirakocha,* showed that the 45 degree line on which Machu Picchu is located fits a grid pattern along the sides of a square tilted at 45 degrees (so that the corners, not the sides, point toward the cardinal points). She confessed that she was inspired to search for this ancient grid by the *Relacion* of Salcamayhua. Relating the tale of the three windows, he drew a sketch (Fig. 108a) to illustrate the narrative, and gave each window a name: Tampu-Tocco, Maras-Tocco, and Sutic-Tocco. Maria Schulten realized that these are place names. When she applied the tilted square to a map of the Cuzco-Urubamba area, with its northwestern corner at Machu Picchu (alias Tampu-Tocco), she discovered that all the other places fell into the correct positions.

She drew lines showing that a 45 degree line originating at Tiahuanacu, combined with squares and circles of definite measurements, embraced all the key ancient sites between Tiahuanacu, Cuzco, and Quito in Ecuador, including the all-important Ollantaytambu (Fig. 108b).

No less important is another finding by her. The subangles that she had calculated between the central 45 degree line and sites located away from it, such as Pachacamac's temple, indicated to her that the Earth's

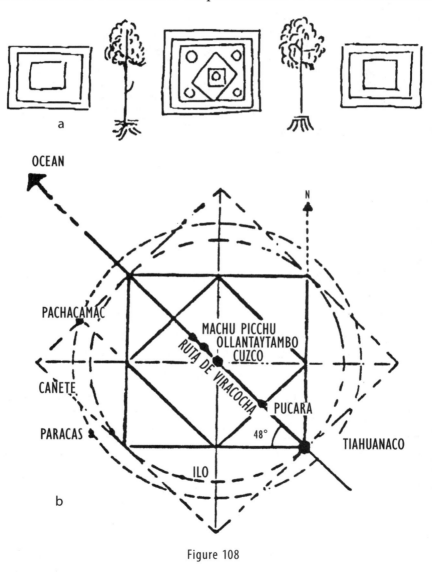

Figure 108

tilt ("obliquity") at the time this grid was laid out was close to 24° 08'. This means the grid was planned (according to her) 5,125 years before her measurements were done in 1953; in other words, in 3172 B.C.

It is a determination that confirms our own conclusion that the megalithic structures belong to the Age of Taurus, the era between 4000 B.C. and 2000 B.C. And, by combining modern studies with the data provided by the chroniclers, it affirms what the legends kept reiterating:

It all began at Lake Titicaca.

12

The Emergence of
There Were Giants
Upon the Earth

Unpublished Articles, Written in 1991

The last of his books that was published before Zecharia Sitchin's passing in 2010, *There Were Giants Upon the Earth,* had been in the works in the author's mind for a long time. Indeed, as we have learned, the mention of the "giants" in Genesis chapter 6 was the spark that started the young Sitchin on his study of ancient civilizations and ancient languages: "There were giants upon the Earth in those days and also thereafter, when the sons of the gods came unto the daughters of men and had children by them—those who were the mighty men which were of old, men of renown."

The Book of Genesis is not the only source of information on ancient giants. All over the globe, in the New World as well as the Old, stories of giants linger on. Some of the better-known accounts involve the giants of the Greek myths as well as their counterparts in Indian mythology. Other examples include South American legends, which recount men of giant stature landing on those shores in the first and second millennia A.D.

Evidence of giants in the New World exists not only in these legends but also in the huge statues of Tollan, Mexico, in which actual giants are depicted—as well as images of giants rendered in paintings in Peru. The presence of giants in the New World may be further deduced from the presence of megalithic structures composed of large blocks of stone, some weighing more than 100 tons, in and around Cuzco, the ancient Incan capital. Their counterparts exist in the Old World as well, some of them weighing over 1,000 tons! How were these huge stones transported and so precisely engineered to create perfect structures of stone? Further investigation into the megaliths of South America reveals that, when viewed from the air, the megalithic sites fall into a straight line leading to the Pacific Ocean, thus paralleling the ancient myth of the god Viracocha, who was said to have disappeared over the waters of the Pacific.

The two-part article that follows summarizes some of Sitchin's findings on the topic of giants. As you will see, it links the presence of giants with accounts of the mysterious gods from space, the Anunnaki, who came to Earth long ago.

PART 1

Was there a time when there were giants upon the Earth?

This is not a silly question or one that belongs to fairy tales or children's books. Surprisingly, the search for an answer will take us back to ancient times and to the affairs of divine and heroic beings. Moreover: the answer will open the door to understanding what had *really* happened on our planet.

The folklore and mythology of almost all the nations are replete with tales of giants and their deeds. For a long time these tales were treated indeed as fairy tales or legends evolved by primitive peoples; but there has been mounting evidence—including physical evidence—that indicates that these tales of giants or deeds explainable only by attributing them to giants represent collective memories of events that, although they happened long ago, have remained imprinted on people's minds. This is true both for the peoples of the Old World as well as for the New World.

The Legends of the Greeks

In Western lore the best-known tales of giants are found in Greek mythology; they take us back to the time when there were gods upon the Earth. Such early Greek writings as the *Theogony* by Hesiod as well as the *Odes* of Pindar recollect the early "giants" as varied offspring of a line of gods that were at first heavenly and then became terrestrial. Interestingly—but not by chance alone—these writings emulate the tales of the beginning of the Old Testament and start their tale with *Chaos,* following which *Gaea* ("Earth") and *Uranus* ("Starry Heaven") have come into being. Of their union there came forth the twelve *Titans*—six males and six females who intermarried and had numerous offspring. The Greeks thought of the Titans as being of great size and extraordinary power, a race of gods who linked the heavens with the Earth. We use the term "titanic" to this day to denote something of great size, something truly "gigantic."

Never satiated sexually, the lusty Uranus continued to produce offspring even though some had various deformities or unusual features. First of the monsters were the three *Cyclopes* ("Orb Eyed"), so called because they had only one eye, as an orb, in their foreheads. The Greek belief that they were giants in size has been retained in our languages by the use of the term "cyclopean" to denote something truly immense. These were followed by the three *Hekatoncheires* meaning "The Ones with a Hundred Arms," male gods of giant size from whose shoulders there sprang a hundred arms and fifty heads.

When Gaea got tired of the sexual excesses of Uranus, she persuaded her son Cronos to cut off the genitals of Uranus—to castrate his own father. Hesiod describes how the cruel deed was done as Uranus came to Gaea at nighttime, "longing for love." Cronos was hiding, waiting for the right moment. Then, "with the great long sickle with jagged teeth . . . he swiftly cut off his father's genitals and cast them away into the surging sea."

But the blood of Uranus impregnated Gaea and resulted in more offspring. Among them were the *Gigantes,* the very gods from whose name the term "giants" has entered Man's memories as well as lexicons.

All these diverse gods—some evil, some good, some loyal to their mother, some to their father—ended up as adversaries. These conflicting loyalties turned into true wars of the gods in the time of the third generation of the gods—who were by then on Earth. When Zeus, the youngest son of Cronos, sought to seize the leadership of the gods away from the older Titans, the Gigantes sided with the Titans but the Cyclopes and Hekatoncheires sided with Zeus. They armed Zeus with a "Thunder Stone" whose flashing glare blinded the opposing Titans and whose "Wind Storm" made the earth quake.

In the final battle Zeus faced *Typhoeus* ("Typhon"), the winged-snake god. The weapons they used against each other had all the attributes of *Star Wars* technology, including nuclear thunderbolts and laser beams. This last battle, which ended with the supremacy of Zeus, was fought mostly in the air, with the two gods fighting each other from "aerial chariots." Here I will not go into more details and descriptions (those interested will find more on the subject in *The Wars of Gods and Men,* the third book of The Earth Chronicles series). What is pertinent here is to note that the final battle between the gods took place, according to Greek traditions, in the environs of Mount Casius; most scholars locate it in the mountains of Lebanon. Let us keep this location in mind as we continue.

Tales of the Indo-Europeans

Let us jump thousands of miles eastward, to the Indian subcontinent.

There we find Hindu myths and legends that are almost identical to the Greek descriptions of the battles of the gods and the genealogy of the gods.

The tales, rendered in the Sanskrit language—the mother-tongue of the Indo-European branch of languages—are found in the Vedas. These are sacred scriptures that, according to Hindu tradition, are "not of human origin," having been composed by the gods themselves in a previous age. They were brought to the Indian subcontinent by

Indo-European migrants, sometimes called "Aryans," some 3,500 years ago as memorized oral texts and were written down word for word some time later. Together with auxiliary texts called *Puranas* ("ancient writings") and the epic tales of the Mahabharata and the Ramayana, they constitute the sources for the Hindu-Aryan tales of Heaven and Earth, of gods and giants.

As in the Greek tales, these "myths," as the scholars like to call them, begin with the celestial or planetary gods, then tell of the second and third generations of these heavenly beings who had come to Earth. The parallels with Greek mythology are well established. Paralleling the Greek Cronos, meaning "The Crowned One," is the chief of "The Shiny Ones" called *Kas-Yapa* ("He of the Throne"). The parallel of Zeus is *Dyaus-Pitar,* "Sky Father." The Greek name "Zeus" is clearly derived from "Dyaus"; the Romans have retained for this deity the full name Dyaus-Pitar in their name for him, *Jupiter.*

The divine battles are described in the Vedas in verses that are almost identical to the Greek ones, and there is no doubt that both versions deal with the same events and the same "gods" of Heaven and Earth. In the Hindu versions the last battle is between Indra and the monstrous Vritra.

They fight from *Vimanas,* aerial "cars" that could traverse great distances with incredible speed. They use beam-emitting and earth-shattering weapons. And as in the Greek tales, the final victor is Indra, alias Zeus.

Who copied from the other? Scholars are convinced that the Greek and Hindu versions are not copies of each other, but that both stem from the same, earlier source. They attribute these earlier recollections of past events to an earlier group of people called *Hurrians* (the biblical Horites), who inhabited the upper reaches of the Euphrates River. The first Indo-Europeans to borrow these legends and beliefs were an ancient people called Hittites, who at one time, some 3,500 years ago, ruled what is today Turkey and northern Syria and Lebanon from their capital in the highlands of Asia Minor.

Their tales were fortunately written down, on clay tablets or sometimes carved on stone; fortunately, scholars have been able to decipher this writing. The finds by archaeologists include what they call "mythological texts." And in them we find tales of wars between the gods, and the final battles between the god of thunder and lightning, *Teshub* ("The Wind Blower") and a monster that grew and grew to cyclopean size.

Thus, as far back as Greek, Hindu, Hittite, Horrite, and all Indo-European accounts are concerned, there had indeed been a time when there were giants upon the Earth—the time when the gods who had come from the Heaven began to have offspring on Earth.

Giants in the New World

Such recollections of gods and giants are not limited to the Old World. They also abound in the lore of the peoples of the New World, the Americas.

In the lands of the Aztecs and Maya in Mesoamerica and of the Incas in South America, there have persisted recollections of giants who had come to those lands from across the waters. They are depicted as warriors, possessing metal implements and awesome weapons. Some were benevolent; others not. I deal extensively with these recollections and their meaning in the fourth book of The Earth Chronicles series, titled *The Lost Realms*.

The Aztecs, for example, recorded on their stone calendars four ages or "Suns" which preceded their own time. The first age, they told, came to an end by a Great Flood that engulfed the Earth. It was followed by the "Golden Age." Some versions of these legends say that the first era, or according to others the second era, was the age of the "White Haired Giants."

Local legends, recorded by the Spaniards soon after the conquest of Mexico, included traditions of a time when "men of great stature appeared and took possession of the country . . . And these giants, not having found a way to reach the Sun, decided to build a tower so high that its summit would reach to heaven."

The two themes, of a Great Flood and of a Tower whose top reached unto the heavens, remind us of course of the biblical tales of the Deluge and the Tower of Babel. These are clues to which we shall return.

It is now known that the Aztecs acquired their traditions and beliefs from the Toltecs, an earlier people who had settled in the Valley of Mexico after long migrations, including an arrival from across the seas. Centuries before the Aztecs, the Toltecs had built their capital and religious center at Tollan, a place filled with step-pyramids. Tollan, archaeologists now know, was also the model for the well-known Maya site called Chichen-Itza in Yucatan, where many of Tollan's pyramids, other structures, and symbolism were copied.

It was at Tollan that the recollection of giants found physical expression in the sculpting of a number of colossal stone statues of those giants. Some of these colossal stone figures, most rising to some fifteen feet, have been restored and re-erected atop the step pyramid that was once dedicated to the Feathered or Winged Serpent god. Each one of these giants is armed with what appears to be a beam-gun. Though similarly attired and equipped, each gigantic statue bears a different face, suggesting that these are actual portraits in stone of specific individuals. None bear features that resemble any known race on Earth. These giants were indeed the gods of myth and legend, strange people from a strange place.

In *The Lost Realms,* I identify *Quetzalcoatl,* the Plumed or Winged Serpent God who taught the Mesoamericans how to build pyramids and the secrets of mathematics and the calendar, as the god called by the Egyptians *Thoth* (Hermes to the Greeks). Thoth was deemed the god of mathematics and the calendar and the keeper of the secrets of building pyramids. The two great pyramids of Giza in Egypt are paralleled in many ways by two great pyramids in the Valley of Mexico, at a place called Teotihuacan, which means "The Place/City of the Gods." They are called nowadays the Pyramid of the Sun and the Moon Pyramid, for no valid reason; and their construction is attributed by legends to "the gods" who had gathered there when the Sun stood still; it is a recollection of an event that corroborates biblical tales.*

---

*Editor's note: Please see Appendix 1 for more on the day the sun stood still.

The Giants of South America

Such physical evidence in support of legends—great pyramids whose construction is attributed to gods/giants and actual "stone portraits" of such giants—extends beyond Mesoamerica.

The lands in South America bordering Meso- and Central America also recall times when they had witnessed the arrival of "giants." Some of the legends pinpoint Cape Santa Elena in Ecuador as the landing site. In Ecuador and adjoining Colombia, archaeologists have found numerous gigantic stone statues in veneration of those enigmatic "giants."

Farther down the Pacific Coast of South America, myth and legend—as well as many depictions and stone monuments—provide physical evidence in support of the tales of gods and giants. It is now well known that the Incas, whom the Spaniards encountered in the Andes when they arrived in Peru in the 1530s, were not the first advanced civilization in those lands. On the coastal areas they were immediately preceded by the Chimu civilization (A.D. 1000 to A.D. 1400) and before that by the civilization of the Moche people (400 B.C. to A.D. 1000). The legends of those earlier peoples recall a time when "there arrived on the coast, in boats made of reeds as big as large ships, a party of men of such great size that, from the knee downward their height was as great as the entire height of an ordinary man." This seems to be a description fitting the height of the enigmatic giants depicted in stone at Tollan, but whether or not it was they who were the giants arriving by boats on the South American coast no one can say. What we do learn from the local traditions, as recorded by Spanish chroniclers right after the conquest, is that those giants had metal tools, which they used to dig wells in the rocky ground. "But for food they raided the natives' provisions; they also violated the natives' women, for there were no women among the landing giants."

Drawings on Mochica pottery show scenes of these giants being served by the human natives; they also depict the giants as warriors engaged in battle, wearing oddly shaped helmets, armed with metal weapons, and sometimes equipped with wings.

Later Inca legends recalled the arrival of such giants, who despoiled the land; but the highland population was spared their invasion because the giants somehow provoked "the wrath of the Great God" who destroyed them with fire from the heavens.

Links with the Bible

The recollection and *belief* of divine punishment coming in the form of fire from the skies is not unique to the Americas. We find it much earlier, in the Bible. When the enemies of the Prophet Elijah tried to capture him, "there came fire down from the heaven and burnt up" his enemies (II Kings 1:10–14). Much better known is the destruction of Sodom and Gomorrah at the time of Abraham, when the Lord "rained upon Sodom and Gomorrah brimstone and fire from the Lord, out of heaven."

We have noted earlier the similarities in American legends dealing with giants to the biblical tales of the Deluge and of the Tower of Babel. We shall see, in the continuation of this article, that these were not coincidences: In fact, the similarities come from very close links with the lands of the Bible.

PART 2

Earlier I warned the reader that the question, "Was there a time when there were giants upon the Earth?" was not a matter for fairy tales or children's books; I wrote that the answer will take us "back to ancient times and to the affairs of divine and heroic beings."

Moreover, I promised that "the answer will open the door to understanding what had *really* happened on our planet."

And indeed, this review of myths and tales about "giants" has taken us to ancient Greece and to wars among the gods that bring to mind future "Star Wars." We visited the ancient Hindu pantheon and so its links with the Greek pantheon and gods and goddesses armed with "Thunder Throwers and Heavenly Fire." We went back to the source of these Indo-European tales, and found their links to the Hittites of Asia Minor.

Then, traversing the oceans to the Americas, we found in the New

World the same recollections of giant gods—not just in verbal legends, but also in *actual depictions*: Colossal statues at Tollan in Mexico, paintings of giants in northern Peru.

Moreover, we found that the American recollections about the giants link them to distinct biblical tales: The memory of a global Deluge, and the Story of the Tower of Babel. There is much more to these tales and these links with the Bible.

The Megalithic Age

In the highlands of Peru and what is nowadays Bolivia, tales of giants are connected with colossal stone structures that are so immense and precise that the natives cannot conceive of their builders being anything but giants. Indeed, these are structures that even modern engineers could not duplicate, achieve, or even figure out how they were erected in antiquity.

Some of these remains, though by far not the largest, can still be seen in Cuzco, the ancient Inca capital. Neither the Conquistadores, who dismantled what they could to suit their own needs, nor the frequent earthquakes in the area, could destroy these walls that date to pre-Inca times, to what archaeo-astronomers have determined must have been a time between 4000 and 2000 B.C., namely at least 4,000 years ago and probably much earlier. These remaining walls are built of polygonal stones dressed and cut with such ingenuity that their many sides and angles fit perfectly into the adjoining stone blocks. The stones fit into each other so that, without mortar, they had stood firmly for millennia; no one has yet succeeded in even thrusting the point of a knife between these stones.

The promontory called Sacsahuaman above Cuzco is the location of even more amazing megalithic structures, probably even older than the pre-Incan stone walls in Cuzco. At Sacsahuaman someone has erected three parallel rows of zigzagging stone walls made of colossal megaliths, some weighing well over 100 tons each. The giant stones were brought over by the mysterious builders from great distances, over mountains and across valleys and rivers. Each colossal stone boulder was given a smooth slightly convex face and was cut into polygonal shapes. Here again the giant boulders were shaped into numerous sides and angles so as to perfectly fit into the adjoining megaliths—again without mortar, again with such precision that not a blade could be inserted between the stones. Thus these three walls, one rising somewhat higher than the other, have withstood time, earthquakes, and manmade erosion for millennia.

Who has erected these walls, which no modern engineering technology can duplicate? Local lore attributes the construction to "the giants." Why, what for? No one knows, but we will offer a plausible guess after other megalithic structures in the Andes are examined.

Another site with amazing megaliths is called Ollantaytambu. There, atop a mountain to the northwest of Cuzco, the same mysterious builders have erected a high wall made up of six megaliths. As at Sacsahuaman, the purpose seems to have been to create a massive platform that could withstand heavy weights. Stone blocks, perfectly shaped and dressed to form granite beams and other structural components as one would use nowadays wood or concrete, lie about the mountaintop. How the stone blocks were cut and shaped with incredible precision is only one of the enigmas. An even greater puzzle stems from the fact that where these stone blocks were quarried is known, for some of them were still at the quarry: on the mountainside on the opposite side of the gushing Urubamba River that separates the quarry from Ollantaytambu. How were these immense stone blocks carried over and then placed so precisely?

Continuing to the northwest along the winding Urubamba River— the whole area is called the Sacred Valley—lies the "lost city" of Machu Picchu, discovered by Hiram Bingham in 1911. Inca rulers had escaped there at various times, including when they finally revolted against the Spaniards. But in addition to Inca structures, crudely built of field stones, there stand in Machu Picchu amazing megalithic structures, which again display an incredible size, polygonality, and the need for transporting them from a very great distance across mountains that rise as huge skyscrapers. They all belong to the Megalithic Age, when gods, not men, had roamed the land.

The First Metropolis in the Americas

The mystery of the megalithic structures in Peru, especially at the locations mentioned above, begins with the wonderment regarding *how* they were erected; but that at once leads to the question *by whom,* and then by the search for a reason, *what for?*

There are legends and tales of the beginning in the Andes that link Cuzco, Machu Picchu, and the whole Sacred Valley of the Incas to the southern shore of Lake Titicaca, which is now in Bolivia. It is the largest navigable lake at such an elevation anywhere in the world. The legends say that in great antiquity, gods, led by one whom they call *Viracocha,* meaning "Creator of All," came to the southern shores of Lake Titicaca and built there a great city, an immense metallurgical center. The legends recollect a Great Flood, the Deluge, and the re-population of the highlands from a saved human couple. Thereafter, Viracocha gave to some selected leaders a golden wand and told them in which direction to go, to build a city-of-men where the wand would sink into the ground; the eventual place thus selected was Cuzco.

South American researchers, until recently the only ones to take these legends seriously, have found that all the sites along the legendary route indeed lie on a straight line that begins at the shores of Lake Titicaca and continues through Cuzco, Sacsahuaman, Ollantaytambu, and Machu Picchu, and onward to the Pacific coast where—according to these legends—Viracocha finally disappeared over the waters. All these megalithic places, then, were built according to a master plan that required seeing and surveying the Andes from the skies. . . .

It is worth noting here that the progress of archaeology has been known for the numerous instances in which legendary cities whose very existence was for long taken to be mere fantasy have proven to be real places. This has been true for many of the kingdoms and ancient cities mentioned in the Bible. A well-known instance concerns the city of Troy, which was deemed, as the whole tale of the Iliad, to be fanciful fiction. But it proved to be a real city due to the determination of a single man, Heinrich Schliemann, who was not even an archaeologist.

The same holds true for the legendary city on the shores of Lake Titicaca, called Tiahuanaco. It proved to be a real place due to the belief

296 The Emergence of *There Were Giants Upon the Earth*

and determination of one man, also not an archaeologist but an engineer by profession, Arthur Posnansky. For decades working almost single-handed, he uncovered there a vast city with pyramidlike structures, an observatory with precise alignments, intricate waterworks, and facilities for processing metals. A large monolith known as the Gate of the Sun still stands majestically at what once was just a corner of a great enclosure. Intricately engraved and carved, it is cut out of one large stone block weighing more than 100 tons and, as elsewhere, originating from a quarry tens of miles away.

The top of the Gate of the Sun—a name given this monument by the Spaniards—has been carved with unusual images, symbols, and signs; they are believed to constitute a calendar in stone. To the surprise of many but not to mine, it is a calendar that is an accurate copy of the calendar first introduced in Mesopotamia, on the other wide of the world. . . . The carvings are dominated by the image of Viracocha, holding the golden wand in one hand and the lightning bolt in the other—an image of the god that has been copied endlessly by the Andean peoples in their art. On the Gate of the Sun, as well as on numerous woven shawls with which the mummified dead were wrapped, Viracocha is shown accompanied by his attendants or "rank and file" gods, all shown with wings to indicate their ability to fly in earth's skies. Tiahuanaco, or *Tianaku* as the locals prefer to pronounce it, spread in its time of greatness to the shores of Lake Titicaca.

Known as Puma Punku, the part of the city that hugged the Lake's shores was, according to the attempts at reconstruction, a kind of "Venice" of the New World—a place with extensive quays and piers from which numerous canals led landward, connecting the lake through the piers and the canals to gigantic metal processing and storing facilities. Some of the service structures were constructed of stone walls and floors that were cut and carved out of single gigantic boulders—again brought over from incredible distances. No less amazing than these stone remains are numerous stone blocks of the hardest andesite that were cut in intricate and precise shapes. The only explanation for them is that they served as dies for metal casting or forming. By whom? The natives' constant answer has been "the gods, the giants."

In *The Lost Realms* I offer more evidence for my conclusion that Tianaku was what its name meant in Near Eastern languages: *Tin City*, the metallurgical capital in the New World that provided the tin and bronze to the Old World when the civilizations there ran out of tin.

Could there have been active trading between the two parts of the world millennia ago? Could traders from the Mediterranean and miners from Asia Minor—Semites and Indo-Europeans—have come to the Andes 3,500 years *before the Incas?* Those who still cannot accept the unavoidable conclusion have to find some other explanation for the statues of men—with both clean cut Indo-European as well as bearded Semitic features—that have been found in the Andes.

Indeed, inescapable too is the conclusion that Viracocha was none other than the Old World's God of the Mining Lands whom the Near Eastern peoples called "The Thunderer" or "The Storm God" on account of the lightning bolt that was his weapon. He was *Adad* to the Canannites, *Teshub* to the Hittites. At some Hittite sites in Asia Minor (today's Turkey), he was depicted—as at Tianaku—accompanied by winged attendants.

Links with the Lands of the Bible

Legends as well as physical evidence thus link the Americas with the Lands of the Bible—and even with the Bible itself, for some of the biblical accounts of Creation found not only verbal but even graphical emulation in the New World.

When the Spaniards arrived in the New World, they were astounded not only by these similarities but also by similarities in customs (such as circumcision or the offering of first fruits, both biblical commandments). They were also astounded by similarities in terminology (*Manco,* meaning "King," being a variant of the Semitic *malko,* as an example), making them certain that the American Indians were descendants of the Ten Lost Tribes of Israel.

These notions have come into ridicule in following centuries by scholars who had insisted that the Americas developed in total isolation, that there was no contact whatsoever between the Old World and the New World—if for no other reason then simply because ancient man could not have possibly navigated across the Pacific or Atlantic Oceans. Well, now they all know better, because the archaeological evidence— even if we ignore legends, customs, languages—has increasingly shown in recent years that there had been such contacts, and they were not occasional such as by shipwrecks—but constant, frequent, and deliberate.

And just as the megalithic structures in the Americas have been attributed by the local inhabitants to "the giants," so have they been in the ancient Near East. Indeed, one of the leading explorers of these Andean sites in the nineteenth century, Ephraim Squier, has compared them to the unique stone platform at Baalbek in the mountains of Lebanon. There, stone blocks shaped with great precision and weighing over 1,000—yes, one *thousand*—tons each, were quarried miles away, then carried over mountains and valleys to be placed precisely atop and along each other, without mortar, to create an immense solid stone platform the likes of which is not found anywhere else. Canaanite texts identify the place as the stronghold of Adad, the place from which he took off skyward to "ride the clouds." In the well-known Epic of Gilgamesh, the tale of a Sumerian king who went in search of immortality, the platform of Baalbek is clearly called "the Landing Place."

The Canaanites, as the Assyrians and Babylonians before them, called these gods who roamed the skies *Ilu,* which meant "the Lofty Ones." Was this just a term of veneration and awe, a figurative adjective, or did the term actually denote the height and size of these gods, their being giants?

Whether in Hittite depictions or Assyrian ones, we find that when a king and a god are shown together, the god towers over the human being. So the question, Were there *giants* upon the Earth, ends up with the question, Were there *gods* upon the Earth, and if so—who were they? Did the megalithic structures on both sides of the world require physical giants able to lift and transport the colossal stone blocks, or were they simply people of an advanced civilization and a technology that mankind did not possess then and does not possess even now? In other words, were the "giants" in truth visitors to Earth from another planet?

The Giants of the Bible

The farther back in time, into prehistory, that we go it seems that we can rely less on archaeological finds and physical evidence, and have to depend more on vague recollections that scholars treat as "mythology." But I have asked myself at the beginning of my writings, "What *if*"—what if the "myths" are not fanciful superstitions, but are based on a record of what had actually happened on Earth?

Fortunately, a reliable, respected, and venerated source exists in which such "myths" have been recorded, collected, and written down in very precise language. It is a source that cannot be ignored; it is called the Bible, the Old Testament.

We have already seen that the many events recorded in the biblical tale of Creation, in the Book of Genesis, have found expression in the Americas. We have noted how the tale of the Deluge, the great flood that had swept over the Earth, is a central feature of all the mythologies everywhere. It is thus perhaps not odd at all that it is in the biblical version of the Deluge story that we find the most important information regarding the "giants" of that long-ago time.

The biblical account of the Deluge, of Noah and the Ark, begins in chapter 6 of Genesis. However, the tale of the Deluge is preceded by several very enigmatic verses. They are clearly an extract, a remainder from a much more detailed text or chapter; and they deal with the conditions on Earth on the eve of the Deluge. It is among these verses that we find the intriguing one, so often used by preachers and philosophers— the verse that states that at that time there were giants upon the Earth. Here is how the enigmatic verses are commonly translated:

> And it came to pass
> when men began to multiply upon the face of the Earth
> and daughters were born unto them,
> That the sons of the gods
> saw the daughters of men that they were suitable,
> and they took themselves wives
> of whomever they chose . . .
> There were giants upon the Earth

in those days and also thereafter,
when the sons of the gods
came unto the daughters of men
and had children by them—
those who were the mighty men.

As I have pointed out not only in my very first book, *The 12th Planet,* but already as a schoolboy studying the Bible in its original Hebrew, the term the Bible uses for what is translated "giants" is *Nefilim,* which literally means "Those Who Have Come Down," from the heavens to Earth. Translators have assumed it to mean "giants" because elsewhere in the Bible it is mentioned that the *Nefilim* were also known as *Anakim;* and in the tale about the giant Goliath it was stated that he was a descendant of *Anak;* hence the line of thought that if Anak was a giant, then the Nefilim (plural) who were also Anakim (plural) were of giant size.

But even if the people in question were of great size, why did the Bible refer to them as the "Sons of the gods," a group distinctly different from the descendants of Man, and describe them as "Those Who Had Come Down" from the heavens to Earth?

Devoting some thirty years of my life in search of the Nefilim, I have found that the mythologies of all ancient civilizations, be it in the Old World or the New World, stem from the texts written on clay tablets by the Sumerians, the people to whom the first known civilization is attributed. It blossomed out, suddenly and unexpectedly, in Mesopotamia (today's Iraq), some 6,000 years ago. And its basic belief and message was that, in much earlier times, people from another planet called Nibiru came to Earth in search of gold—gold not for jewelry, but to use as gold particles to protect their dwindling atmosphere.

The Sumerians called those visitors to Earth *Anunnaki,* literally meaning "Those Who from Heaven to Earth Came." They depicted them frequently as Winged Beings, to indicate their ability to take to the air, and also drew pictures of the aerial vehicles of the Anunnaki. It was this name, *Anunnaki,* from which the Book of Genesis borrowed to create the term *Anakim* in the Bible. They were the Sons of the Gods who had married the daughters of Man on the eve of the Deluge; they were the *Nefilim.*

Are we to believe these Sumerian texts and all the mythologies that ensued? Are we to accept the statements in the Bible?

If not, how can we explain the colossal megalithic structures that only "giants" could build?

13
Calendar Tales

Selection from
When Time Began *(Chapter 8)*

How did our present-day calendar come about and what was the motivation for its creation in the first place? Was it a tool for farmers to refer to in order to ensure an abundant harvest? Or was it created to mark the festive days of worship of Earth's early religions? As mankind evolved, so did many different types of calendars, some based on the actions of the sun and some based on the cycles of the moon. In addition to a calendar developed by the church, a secular calendar also evolved in Egypt in approximately 2800 B.C.

In this insightful article, Sitchin traces the development of these early calendars and examines their varied functions before launching into a discussion of how both the zodiac and the Egyptian calendar developed in Sumer as "inventions of the Gods." He also discusses how innovations of these calendars were motivated by the shifting dynamics between the brothers Marduk/Ra and Ningishzidda/Thoth as well as the ever-changing relationships Ra and Thoth had with their other brothers, all of whom were constantly vying amongst themselves for power and supremacy.

A particularly fascinating feature of our present-day calendar is the division of the year into weeks comprised of seven days. From whence did this derive? The lord Enlil was associated with the number seven and, according to Sitchin, Earth was known as the seventh planet to the Sumerians. Thus the number seven was of extreme importance to them, as reflected by its use in the calendar as it evolved. The precise determination of soltices, equinoxes, and eclipses was also of great importance, so much so that ancient temples and monuments were constructed to show the timing of these events.

THE STORY OF THE CALENDAR is one of ingenuity, of a sophisticated combination of astronomy and mathematics. It is also a tale of conflict, religious fervor, and struggles for supremacy.

The notion that the calendar was devised by and for farmers so that they would know when to sow and when to reap has been taken for granted too long; it fails both the test of logic and of fact. Farmers do not need a formal calendar to know the seasons, and primitive societies have managed to feed themselves for generations without a calendar. The historic fact is that the calendar was devised in order to predetermine the precise time of festivals honoring the gods. The calendar, in other words, was a religious device. The first names by which months were called in Sumer had the prefix EZEN. The word did not mean "month"; it meant "festival." The months were the times when the Festival of Enlil, or the Festival of Ninurta, or those of the other leading deities were to be observed.

That the calendar's purpose was to enable religious observances should not surprise one at all. We find an instance that still regulates our lives in the current common, but actually Christian, calendar. Its principal festival and the focal point that determines the rest of the annual calendar is Easter, the celebration of the resurrection, according to the New Testament, of Jesus on the third day after his crucifixion. Western Christians celebrate Easter on the first Sunday after the full moon that occurs on or right after the spring equinox. This created a problem for the early Christians in Rome, where the dominant calendrical element was the solar year of 365 days and the months were of irregular length and not exactly related to the Moon's phases. The determination of Easter Day therefore required a reliance on the Jewish calendar, because the Last Supper, from which the other crucial days of Eastertide are counted, was actually the *Seder* meal with which the Jewish celebration of Passover begins on the eve of the fourteenth day of the month Nissan, the time of the full Moon. As a result, during the first centuries of Christianity Easter was celebrated in accordance with the Jewish calendar. It was only when the Roman emperor Constantine, having adopted Christianity, convened a church council, the Council of Nicaea, in the year 325, that the continued dependence on the Jewish calendar was severed, and Christianity, until then deemed by the gentiles as merely another Jewish sect, was made into a separate religion.

In this change, as in its origin, the Christian calendar was thus an expression of religious beliefs and an instrument for determining the dates of worship. It was also so later on, when the Moslems burst out of Arabia to conquer by the sword lands and people east and west; the imposition of their purely lunar calendar was one of their first acts, for it had a profound religious connotation: it counted the passage of time from the *Hegira,* the migration of Islam's founder Mohammed from Mecca to Medina (in 622).

The history of the Roman-Christian calendar, interesting by itself, illustrates some of the problems inherent in the imperfect meshing of solar and lunar times and the resulting need, over the millennia, for calendar reforms and the ensuing notions of ever-renewing Ages.

The current Common Era Christian calendar was introduced by Pope Gregory XIII in 1582 and is therefore called the Gregorian Calendar. It constituted a reform of the previous Julian Calendar, so named after the Roman emperor Julius Caesar.

That noted Roman emperor, tired of the chaotic Roman calendar, invited in the first century B.C. the astronomer Sosigenes of Alexandria, Egypt, to suggest a reform of the calendar. Sosigenes's advice was to forget about lunar timekeeping and to adopt a solar calendar "as that of the Egyptians." The result was a year of 365 days plus a leap year of 366 days once in four years. But that still failed to account for the extra 11 ¼ minutes a year in excess of the quarter-day over and above the 365 days. That seemed too minute to bother with; but the result was that by 1582 the first day of spring, fixed by the Council of Nicaea to fall on March 21, was retarded by ten days to March 11th. Pope Gregory corrected the shortfall by simply decreeing on October 4, 1582, that the next day should be October 15. This reform established the currently used Gregorian calendar, whose other innovation was to decree that the year begin on January first.

The astronomer's suggestion that a calendar "as that of the Egyptians" be adopted in Rome was accepted, one must assume, without undue difficulty because by then Rome, and especially Julius Caesar, were quite familiar with Egypt, its religious customs, and hence with its calendar. The Egyptian calendar was at that time indeed a purely solar calendar of 365 days divided into twelve months of thirty days each. To these 360 days an end-of-year religious festival of five days was added, dedicated to the gods Osiris, Horus, Seth, Isis, and Nephthys.

The Egyptians were aware that the solar year is somewhat longer than 365 days—not just by the full day every four years, as Julius Caesar had allowed for, but by enough to shift the calendar back by one month every 120 years and by a full year every 1,460 years. The determining or sacred cycle of the Egyptian calendar was this 1,460-year period, for it coincided with the cycle of the heliacal rising of the star Sirius (Egyptian *Sept,* Greek *Sothis*) at the time of the Nile's annual flooding, which in turn takes place at about the summer solstice (in the northern hemisphere).

Edward Meyer (*Ägyptische Chronologie*) concluded that when this Egyptian calendar was introduced, such a convergence of the heliacal rising of Sirius and of the Nile's inundation had occurred on July 19th. Based on that Kurt Sethe (*Urgeschichte und älteste Religion der Ägypter*) calculated that this could have happened in either 4240 B.C. or 2780 B.C. by observing the skies at either Heliopolis or Memphis.

By now researchers of the ancient Egyptian calendar agree that the solar calendar of 360 + 5 days was not the first prehistoric calendar of that land. This "civil" or secular calendar was introduced only after the start of dynastic rule in Egypt, i.e., after 3100 B.C.; according to Richard A. Parker (*The Calendars of the Ancient Egyptians*) it took place circa 2800 B.C. "probably for administrative and fiscal purposes." This civil calendar supplanted, or perhaps supplemented at first, the "sacred" calendar of old. In the words of the *Encyclopaedia Britannica,* "the ancient Egyptians originally employed a calendar based upon the Moon." According to R.A. Parker (*Ancient Egyptian Astronomy*) that earlier calendar was, "like that of all ancient peoples," a calendar of twelve *lunar* months plus a thirteenth intercalary month that kept the seasons in place.

That earlier calendar was also, in the opinion of Lockyer, equinoctial and linked indeed to the earliest temple at Heliopolis, whose orientation was equinoctial. In all that, as in the association of months with religious festivals, the earliest Egyptian calendar was akin to that of the Sumerians.

The conclusion that the Egyptian calendar had its roots in predynastic times, before civilization appeared in Egypt, can only mean that it was not the Egyptians themselves who invented their calendar. It is a conclusion that matches that regarding the zodiac in Egypt, and regarding both the zodiac and the calendar in Sumer: they were all the artful inventions of the "gods."

In Egypt, religion and worship of the gods began in Heliopolis, close by the Giza pyramids; its original Egyptian name was *Annu* (as the name of the ruler of Nibiru) and it is called *On* in the Bible: when Joseph was made viceroy over all of Egypt (Genesis chapter 41), the Pharaoh "gave him Assenath, the daughter of Potiphera, the [high] priest of On, for a wife." Its oldest shrine was dedicated to *Ptah* ("The Developer") who, according to Egyptian tradition, raised Egypt from under the waters of the Great Flood and made it habitable by extensive drainage and earthworks. Divine reign over Egypt was then transferred by Ptah to his son *Ra* ("The Bright One") who was also called *Tem* ("The Pure One"); and in a special shrine, also at Heliopolis, the Boat of Heaven of Ra, the conical *Ben-Ben,* could be seen by pilgrims once a year.

Ra was the head of the first divine dynasty according to the Egyptian priest Manetho (his hieroglyphic name meant "Gift of Thoth"), who compiled in the third century B.C. Egypt's dynastic lists. The reign of Ra and his successors, the gods Shu, Geb, Osiris, Seth, and Horus, lasted more than three millennia. It was followed by a second divine dynasty that was begun by Thoth, another son of Ptah; it lasted half as long as the first divine dynasty. Thereafter a dynasty of demigods, thirty of them, reigned over Egypt for 3,650 years. Altogether, according to Manetho, the divine reigns of Ptah, the Ra dynasty, the Thoth dynasty, and the dynasty of the demigods lasted 17,520 years. Karl R. Lepsius (*Königsbuch der alten Ägypter*) noted that this time span represented exactly twelve Sothic cycles of 1,460 years each, thereby corroborating the prehistoric origin of calendrical-astronomical knowledge in Egypt.

Based on substantial evidence, we have concluded in *The Wars of Gods and Men* and other volumes of The Earth Chronicles that Ptah was none other than Enki and that Ra was Marduk of the Mesopotamian pantheon. It was to Enki and his descendants that the African lands were granted when Earth was divided among the Anunnaki after the Deluge, leaving the E.DIN (the biblical land of Eden) and the Mesopotamian sphere of influence in the hands of Enlil and his descendants. Thoth, a brother of Ra/Marduk, was the god the Sumerians called Ningishzidda.

Much of the history and violent conflicts that followed the Earth's division stemmed from the refusal of Ra/Marduk to acquiesce in the division. He was convinced that his father was unjustly deprived of lordship of Earth (what the epithet-name EN.KI, "Lord Earth," connoted); and that therefore he, not Enlil's Foremost Son Ninurta, should rule supreme on Earth from Babylon, the Mesopotamian city whose name meant "Gateway of the Gods." Obsessed by this ambition, Ra/Marduk caused not only conflicts with the Enlilites, but also aroused the animosity of some of his own brothers by involving them in these bitter conflicts as well as by leaving Egypt and then returning to reclaim the lordship over it.

In the course of these comings and goings and ups and downs in Ra/Marduk's struggles, he caused the death of a younger brother called Dumuzi, let his brother Thoth reign and then forced him into exile, and made his brother Nergal change sides in a War of the Gods that resulted in a nuclear holocaust. It was in particular the on-again, off-again relationship with Thoth, we believe, that is essential to the Calendar Tales.

The Egyptians, it will be recalled, had not one but two calendars. The first, with roots in prehistoric times, was "based upon the Moon." The later one, introduced several centuries after the start of pharaonic rule, was based on the 365 days of the solar year. Contrary to the notion that the latter "civil calendar" was an administrative innovation of a pharaoh, we suggest that it too, like the earlier one, was an artful creation of the gods; except that while the first one was the handiwork of Thoth, the second one was the craftwork of Ra.

One aspect of the civil calendar considered specific and original to it was the division of the thirty-day months into "decans," ten-day periods each heralded by the heliacal rising of a certain star. Each star (depicted as a celestial god sailing the skies, Fig. 100) was deemed to

Figure 100

give notice of the last hour of the night; and at the end of ten days, a new decan-star would be observed.

It is our suggestion that the introduction of this decan-based calendar was a deliberate act by Ra in a developing conflict with his brother Thoth.

Both were sons of Enki, the great scientist of the Anunnaki, and one can safely assume that much of their knowledge had been acquired from their father. This is certain in the case of Ra/Marduk, for a Mesopotamian text has been found that clearly states so. It is a text whose beginning records a complaint by Marduk to his father that he lacks certain healing knowledge. Enki's response is rendered thus:

> My son, what is it you do not know?
> What more could I give to you?
> Marduk, what is it that you do not know?
> What could I give you in addition?
> Whatever I know, you know!

Was there, perhaps, some jealousy between the two brothers on this score? The knowledge of mathematics, of astronomy, of orienting sacred structures was shared by both; witness to Marduk's attainments in these sciences was the magnificent ziggurat of Babylon, which, according to the *Enuma elish,* Marduk himself had designed. But, as the above-quoted text relates, when it came to medicine and healing, his knowledge fell short of his brother's: he could not revive the dead, while Thoth could. We learn of the latter's powers from both Mesopotamian and Egyptian sources. His Sumerian depictions show him with the emblem of the entwined serpents (Fig. 101a), the emblem originally of his father Enki as the god who could engage in genetic engineering— the emblem, we have suggested, of the double helix of DNA (Fig. 101b). His Sumerian name, NIN.GISH.ZID.DA, which meant "Lord of the Artifact of Life," bespoke recognition of his capacity to restore life by reviving the dead. "Lord healer, Lord who seizes the hand, Lord of the Artifact of Life" a Sumerian liturgical text called him. He was prominently featured in magical healing and exorcism texts; a *Maqlu* ("Burnt

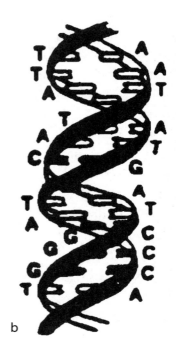

Figure 101a and 101b

Offerings") series of incantations and magical formulas devoted a whole tablet, the seventh, to him. In one incantation, devoted to drowned mariners ("the seafaring folk who are utterly at rest"), the priest invokes the formulas of "Siris and Ningishzidda, the miracle workers, the spellbinders."

Siris is the name of a goddess otherwise unknown in the Sumerian pantheon, and the possibility that it is a Mesopotamian rendition of the star's name Sirius comes to our mind because in the Egyptian pantheon Sirius was the star associated with the goddess Isis. In Egyptian legendary tales, Thoth was the one who had helped Isis, the wife of Osiris, to extract from the dismembered Osiris the semen with which Isis was impregnated to conceive and bear Horus. This was not all. In an Egyptian inscription on an artifact known as the Metternich Stela, the goddess Isis describes how Thoth brought her son Horus back from the dead after Horus was stung by a poisonous scorpion. Responding to her cries, Thoth came down from the skies, "and he was provided with magical powers, and possessed the great power which made the word become indeed." And he performed magic, and by nighttime it drove the poison away and Horus was returned to life.

The Egyptians held that the whole *Book of the Dead,* verses from which were inscribed on the walls of pharaonic tombs so that the deceased pharaoh could be translated into an Afterlife, was a composition of Thoth, "written with his own fingers." In a shorter work called by the Egyptians the *Book of Breathings,* it was stated that "Thoth, the most mighty god, the lord of Khemennu, cometh to thee; he writeth for thee the Book of Breathings with his own fingers, so that thy *Ka* shall breathe for ever and ever and thy form endowed with life on Earth."

We know from Sumerian sources that this knowledge, so essential in pharaonic beliefs—knowledge to revive the dead—was first possessed by Enki. In a long text dealing with Inanna/Ishtar's journey to the Lower World (southern Africa), the domain of her sister who was married to another son of Enki, the uninvited goddess was put to death. Responding to appeals, Enki fashioned medications and supervised the treatment of the corpse with sound and radiation pulses, and "Inanna arose."

Evidently, the secret was not divulged to Marduk; and when he complained, his father gave him an evasive answer. That alone would have been enough to make the ambitious and power-hungry Marduk jealous of Thoth. The feeling of being offended, perhaps even threatened, was probably greater. First, because it was Thoth, and not Marduk/Ra, who had helped Isis retrieve the dismembered Osiris (Ra's grandson) and save his semen, and then revived the poisoned Horus (a great-grandson of Ra). And second, because all that led—as the Sumerian text makes clearer—to an affinity between Thoth and the star Sirius, the controller of the Egyptian calendar and the harbinger of the life-giving inundation of the Nile.

Were these the only reasons for the jealousy, or did Ra/Marduk have more compelling reasons to see in Thoth a rival, a threat to his supremacy? According to Manetho, the long reign of the first divine dynasty begun by Ra ended abruptly after only a short reign of three hundred years by Horus, after the conflict that we have called the

First Pyramid War. Then, instead of another descendant of Ra, it was Thoth who was given lordship over Egypt and his dynasty continued (according to Manetho) for 1,570 years. His reign, an era of peace and progress, coincided with the New Stone (Neolithic) Age in the Near East—the first phase of the granting of civilization by the Anunnaki to Mankind.

Why was it Thoth, of all the other sons of Ptah/Enki, who was chosen to replace the dynasty of Ra in Egypt? A clue might be suggested in a study titled *Religion of the Ancient Egyptians* by W. Osborn, Jr., in which it is stated as follows regarding Thoth: "Though he stood in mythology in a secondary rank of deities, yet he always remained a direct emanation from, and part of, Ptah—the *firstborn* of the primeval deity" (emphasis is ours). With the complex rules of succession of the Anunnaki, where a son born to a half sister became the legal heir ahead of a firstborn son (if mothered not by a half sister)—a cause of the endless friction and rivalry between Enki (the firstborn of Anu) and Enlil (born to a half sister of Anu)—could it be that the circumstances of Thoth's birth somehow posed a challenge to Ra/Marduk's claims for supremacy?

It is known that initially the dominating "company of the gods" or divine dynasty was that of Heliopolis; later on it was superseded by the divine triad of Memphis (when Memphis became the capital of a unified Egypt). But in between there was an interim *Paut* or "divine company" of gods headed by Thoth. The "cult center" of the latter was Hermopolis ("City of Hermes" in Greek) whose Egyptian name, *Khemennu,* meant "eight." One of the epithets of Thoth was "Lord of Eight," which according to Heinrich Brugsch (*Religion und Mythologie der alten Aegypter*) referred to eight celestial orientations, including the four cardinal points. It could also refer to Thoth's ability to ascertain and mark out the eight standstill points of the Moon—the celestial body with which Thoth was associated.

Marduk, a "Sun god," on the other hand, was associated with the number ten. In the numerical hierarchy of the Anunnaki, in which Anu's rank was the highest, sixty, that of Enlil fifty and of Enki forty (and so on down), the rank of Marduk was ten; and that could have been the origin of the decans. Indeed, the Babylonian version of the

Epic of Creation attributes to Marduk the devising of a calendar of twelve months each divided into three "celestial astrals":

> He determined the year,
> designating the zones:
> For each of the twelve months
> he set up three celestial astrals,
> [thus] defining the days of the year.

This division of the skies into thirty-six portions as a means of "defining the days of the year" is as clear a reference as possible to the calendar—a calendar with thirty-six "decans." And here, in *Enuma elish,* the division is attributed to Marduk, alias Ra.

The Epic of Creation, undoubtedly of Sumerian origin, is known nowadays mostly from its Babylonian rendition (the seven tablets of the *Enuma elish*). It is a rendition, all scholars agree, that was intended to glorify the Babylonian national god Marduk. Hence, the name "Marduk" was inserted where in the Sumerian original text the invader from outer space, the planet Nibiru, was described as the Celestial Lord; and where, describing deeds on Earth, the Supreme God was named Enlil, the Babylonian version also named Marduk. Thereby, Marduk was made supreme both in heaven and on Earth.

Without further discovery of intact or even fragmented tablets inscribed with the original Sumerian text of the Epic of Creation, it is impossible to say whether the thirty-six decans were a true innovation by Marduk or were just borrowed by him from Sumer. A basic tenet of Sumerian astronomy was the division of the celestial sphere enveloping the Earth into three "ways"—the Way of Anu as a central celestial band, the Way of Enlil of the northern skies, and the Way of Ea (i.e., Enki) in the southern skies. It has been thought that the three ways represented the equatorial band in the center and the bands demarcated by the two tropics, north and south; we have, however, shown in *The 12th Planet* that the Way of Anu, straddling the equator, extended 30° northward and southward of the equator, resulting in a width of 60°; and that the Way of Enlil and the Way of Ea similarly extended for 60° each, so that the three covered the complete celestial sweep of 180° from north to south.

If this tripartite division of the skies were to be applied to the calendrical division of the year into twelve months, the result would be thirty-six segments. Such a division—resulting in decans—was indeed made, in Babylon.

In 1900, addressing the Royal Astronomical Society in London, the orientalist T.G. Pinches presented a reconstruction of a Mesopotamian astrolabe (literally: "Taker of stars"). It was a circular disk divided like a pie into twelve segments and three concentric rings, resulting in a division of the skies into thirty-six portions (Fig. 102). The round symbols next to the inscribed names indicated that the reference was

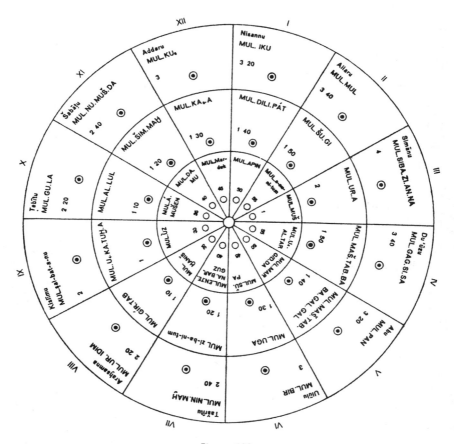

Figure 102

to celestial bodies; the names (here transliterated) are those of constellations of the zodiac, stars, and planets—thirty-six in all. That this
division was linked to the calendar is made clear by the inscribing of
the months' names, one in each of the twelve segments at the segment's
top (the marking I to XII, starting with the first month Nisannu of the
Babylonian calendar, is by Pinches).

While this Babylonian planisphere does not answer the question
of the origin of the relevant verses in *Enuma elish,* it does establish
that what was supposed to have been a unique and original Egyptian
innovation in fact had a counterpart (if not a predecessor) in Babylon—
the place claimed by Marduk for his supremacy.

Even more certain is the fact that the thirty-six decans do not fea-
ture in the first Egyptian calendar. The earlier one was linked to the
Moon, the later one to the Sun. In Egyptian theology, Thoth was a
Moon God, Ra was a Sun God. Extending this to the two calendars,
it follows that the first and older Egyptian calendar was formulated by
Thoth and the second, later one, by Ra/Marduk.

The fact is that when the time came, circa 3100 B.C., to extend the
Sumerian level of civilization (human Kingship) to the Egyptians, Ra/
Marduk—having been frustrated in his efforts to establish supremacy
in Babylon—returned to Egypt and expelled Thoth.

It was then, we believe, that Ra/Marduk—not for administrative
convenience but in a deliberate step to eradicate the vestiges of Thoth's
predominance—reformed the calendar. A passage in the *Book of the
Dead* relates that Thoth was "disturbed by what hath happened to the
divine children" who have "done battle, upheld strife, created fiends,
caused trouble." As a consequence of this Thoth "was provoked to anger
when they [his adversaries] bring the years to confusion, throng in and
push to disturb the months." All that evil, the text declares, "in all they
have done unto thee, they have worked iniquity in secret."

This may well indicate that the strife that led to the substitution of
Thoth's calendar by Ra/Marduk's calendar in Egypt took place when
the calendar (for reasons explained earlier) needed to be put back on
track. R. A. Parker, we have noted above, believes that this change
occurred circa 2800 B.C. Adolf Erman (*Aegypten und Aegyptisches*

Leben im Altertum) was more specific. The opportunity, he wrote, was the return of Sirius to its original position, after the 1,460-year cycle, on July 19, 2776 B.C.

It should be noted that that date, circa 2800 B.C., is the official date adopted by the British authorities for Stonehenge I.

The introduction by Ra/Marduk of a calendar divided into, or based upon, ten-day periods may have also been prompted by a desire to draw a clear distinction, for his followers in Egypt as well as in Mesopotamia, between himself and the one who was "seven"—the head of the Enlilites, Enlil himself. Indeed, such a distinction may have underlain the oscillations between lunar and solar calendars; for the calendars, as we have shown and ancient records attested, were devised by the Anunnaki "gods" to delineate for their followers the cycles of worship; and the struggle for supremacy meant, in the final analysis, who was to be worshiped.

Scholars have long debated, but have yet to verify, the origin of the week, the slice of the year measured in lengths of seven days. We have shown in earlier books of The Earth Chronicles that seven was the number that represented our planet, the Earth. Earth was called in Sumerian texts "the seventh," and was depicted in representations of celestial bodies by the symbol of the seven dots because journeying into the center of our Solar System from their outermost planet, the Anunnaki would first encounter Pluto, pass by Neptune and Uranus (second and third), and continue past Saturn and Jupiter (fourth and fifth). They would count Mars as the sixth (and therefore it was depicted as a six-pointed star) and Earth would be the seventh. Such a journey and such a count are in fact depicted on a planisphere discovered in the ruins of the royal library of Nineveh, where one of its eight segments (Fig. 103) shows the flight path from Nibiru and states (here in English translation) "deity Enlil went by the planets." The planets, represented by dots, are seven in number. For the Sumerians, it was Enlil, and no other, who was "Lord of Seven." Mesopotamian as well as biblical names, of persons (e.g., *Bath-sheba*, "Daughter of Seven") or of places (e.g., *Beer-Sheba*, "the well of Seven"), honored the god by this epithet.

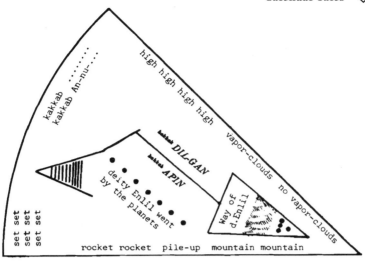

Figure 103

The importance or sanctity of the number seven, transferred to the calendrical unit of seven days as one week, permeates the Bible and other ancient scriptures. Abraham set apart seven ewe lambs when he negotiated with Abimelech; Jacob served Laban seven years to be able to marry one of his daughters, and bowed seven times as he approached his jealous brother Esau. The High Priest was required to perform various rites seven times; Jericho was to be circled seven times so that its walls should tumble down; and calendrically, the seventh day had to be strictly observed as the Sabbath and the important festival of Pentecost had to take place after the count of seven weeks from Passover.

Though no one can say who "invented" the seven-day week, it is obviously associated in the Bible with the earliest times—indeed, when Time itself began: witness the seven days of Creation with which the Book of Genesis begins. The concept of a seven-day delineated period of counted time, a Time of Man, is found in the biblical as well as the earlier Mesopotamian Deluge tale, thereby attesting to its antiquity. In the Mesopotamian texts, the hero of the flood is given seven days' advance warning by Enki, who "opened the water clock and filled it" to make sure his faithful follower would not miss the deadline. In those versions the Deluge is said to have begun with a storm that "swept the country for seven days and seven nights." In the biblical version the Deluge also began after a seven-day advance warning to Noah.

The biblical tale of the flood and its duration reveals a far-reaching understanding of the calendar in very early times. Significantly, it shows familiarity with the unit of seven days and of a division of the year into fifty-two weeks of seven days each. Moreover, it suggests an understanding of the complexities of a lunar-solar calendar.

According to Genesis, the Deluge began "in the second month, on the seventeenth day of the month" and ended the following year "in the second month, on the twenty-seventh day of the month." But what on the face of it would appear to be a period of 365 days plus ten, is not so. The biblical tale breaks down the Deluge into 150 days of the avalanche of water. 150 days during which the water receded, and another forty days until Noah deemed it safe to open the Ark. Then, in two seven-day intervals, he sent out a raven and a dove to survey the landscape; only when the dove no longer came back did Noah know it was safe to step out. According to this breakdown, it all added up to 354 days (150 + 150 + 40 + 7 + 7). But that is not a solar year; that is precisely a lunar year of twelve months averaging 29.5 days each ($29.5 \times 12 = 354$) represented by a calendar—as the Jewish one still is—alternating between months of 29 and 30 days.

But 354 days is not a full year in solar terms. Recognizing this, the narrator or editor of Genesis resorted to intercalation, by stating that the Deluge, which began on the seventeenth day of the second month, ended (a year later) on the twenty-seventh of the second month. Scholars are divided in regard to the number of days thus added to the lunar 354. Some (e.g., S. Gandz, *Studies in Hebrew Mathematics and Astronomy*) consider the addition to have been eleven days—the correct intercalary addition that would have expanded the lunar 354 days to the full 365 days of the solar year. Others, among them the author of the ancient *Book of Jubilees,* consider the number of days added to be just ten, increasing the year in question to only 364 days. The significance is, of course, that it implies a calendar divided into fifty-two weeks of seven days each ($52 \times 7 = 364$).

That this was not just a result of adding 354 + 10 as the number of days, but a deliberate division of the year into fifty-two weeks of seven days each, is made clear in the text of the *Book of Jubilees*. It states (chapter 6) that Noah was given, when the Deluge ended, "heavenly tablets" ordaining that

> All the days of the commandment
> will be two and fifty weeks of days
> which will make the year complete.
> Thus it is engraven and ordained
> on the heavenly tablets;
> there shall be no neglecting for a single
> year or from year to year.
> And command thou the children of Israel
> that they observe the years according to
> this reckoning:
> three hundred and sixty-four days;
> these shall constitute a complete year.

The insistence on a year of fifty-two weeks of seven days, adding up to a calendrical year of 364 days, was not a result of ignorance regarding the true length of 365 full days in a solar year. The awareness of this true length is made clear in the Bible by the age (*"five* and sixty and three hundred years"*) of Enoch until he was lofted by the Lord. In the nonbiblical *Book of Enoch* the "overplus of the Sun," the five epagomenal days that had to be added to the 360 days (12 × 30) of other calendars, to complete the 365, are specifically mentioned. Yet the *Book of Enoch,* in chapters describing the motions of the Sun and the Moon, the twelve zodiacal "portals," the equinoxes and the solstices, states unequivocally that the calendar year shall be "a year exact as to its days: three hundred and sixty-four." This is repeated in a statement that "the complete year, with perfect justice" was of 364 days—fifty-two weeks of seven days each.

The *Book of Enoch,* especially in its version known as Enoch II, is believed to show elements of scientific knowledge centered at the time in Alexandria, Egypt. How much of that can be traced back to the teachings of Thoth cannot be stated with any certainty; but biblical as well as Egyptian tales suggest a role for seven and fifty-two times seven beginning in much earlier times.

Well known is the biblical tale of Joseph's rise to governorship over Egypt after he had successfully interpreted the pharaoh's dreams of, first, seven fat-fleshed cows that were devoured by seven lean-fleshed cows, and then of seven full ears of corn swallowed up by seven dried-out ears of corn. Few are aware, however, that the tale—"legend" or "myth" to some—had strong Egyptian roots as well as an earlier counterpart in Egyptian lore. Among the former was the Egyptian forerunner of the Greek Sibylline oracle goddesses; they were called the Seven Hathors, Hathor having been the goddess of the Sinai peninsula who was depicted as a cow. In other words, the Seven Hathors symbolized seven cows who could predict the future.

The earlier counterpart of the tale of seven lean years that followed seven years of plenty is a hieroglyphic text (Fig. 104) that E. A. W. Budge (*Legends of the Gods*) titled "A legend of the god Khnemu and of a seven year famine." Khnemu was another name for Ptah/Enki in his role as fashioner of Mankind. The Egyptians believed that after he had turned over lordship over Egypt to his son Ra, he retired to the island of Abu (known as Elephantine since Greek times because of its shape), where he formed twin caverns—two connected reservoirs—whose locks or sluices could be manipulated to regulate the flow of the Nile's waters. (The modern Aswan High Dam is similarly located above the Nile's first cataract).

According to this text, the Pharaoh Zoser (builder of the step-pyramid at Saqqara) received a royal dispatch from the governor of the people of the south that grievous suffering had come upon the people "because the Nile hath not come forth to the proper height for *seven years*." As a result, "grain is very scarce, vegetables are lacking altogether, every kind of thing which men eat for their food hath ceased, and every man now plundereth his neighbor."

Hoping that the spread of famine and chaos could be avoided by a direct appeal to the god, the king traveled south to the island of Abu. The god, he was told, dwells there "in an edifice of wood with portals

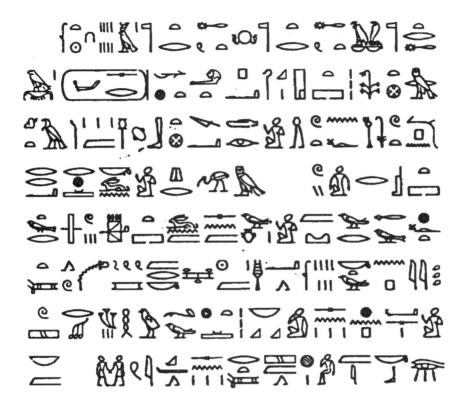

Figure 104

formed of reeds," keeping with him "the cord and the tablet" that enable him to "open the double door of the sluices of the Nile." Khnemu, responding to the king's pleadings, promised "to raise the level of the Nile, give water, make the crops grow."

Since the annual rising of the Nile was linked to the heliacal rising of the star Sirius, one must wonder whether the tale's celestial or astronomical aspects recall not only the actual shortage of water (which occurs cyclically even nowadays) but also to the shift (discussed above) in the appearance of Sirius under a rigid calendar. That the whole tale had calendrical connotations is suggested by the statement in the text that the abode of Khnemu at Abu was astronomically oriented: "The god's house hath an opening to the southeast, and the Sun standeth immediately opposite thereto every day." This can only mean a facility for observing the Sun in the course of moving to and from the winter solstice.

This brief review of the use and significance of the number seven in the affairs of gods and men suffices to show its celestial origin (the seven planets from Pluto to Earth) and its calendrical importance (the seven-day week, a year of fifty-two such weeks). But in the rivalry among the Anunnaki, all that assumed another significance: the determination of who was the God of Seven (*Eli-Sheva* in Hebrew, from which *Elizabeth* comes) and thus the titular Ruler of Earth.

And that, we believe, is what alarmed Ra/Marduk on his return to Egypt after his failed coup in Babylon: the spreading veneration of Seven, still Enlil's epithet, through the introduction of the seven-day week into Egypt.

In these circumstances the veneration of the Seven Hathors, as an example, must have been anathema to Ra/Marduk. Not only their number, seven, which implied veneration of Enlil; but their association with Hathor, an important deity in the Egyptian pantheon but one for whom Ra/Marduk had no particular liking.

Hathor, we have shown in earlier books of The Earth Chronicles, was the Egyptian name for Ninharsag of the Sumerian pantheon—a half sister of both Enki and Enlil and the object of both brothers' sexual attention. Since the official spouses of both (Ninki of Enki, Ninlil of Enlil) were not their half sisters, it was important for them to beget a son by Ninharsag; such a son, under the succession rules of the Anunnaki, would be the undisputed Legal Heir to the throne on Earth. In spite of repeated attempts by Enki, all Ninharsag bore him were daughters; but Enlil was more successful, and his Foremost Son was conceived in a union with Ninharsag. This entitled Ninurta (Ningirsu, the "Lord of Girsu" to Gudea) to inherit his father's rank of fifty—at the same time depriving Enki's firstborn, Marduk, of rulership over the Earth.

There were other manifestations of the spread of the worship of seven and its calendrical importance. The tale of the seven-year drought takes place at the time of Zoser, builder of the Saqqara pyramid. Archaeologists have discovered in the area of Saqqara a circular "altar-top" of alabaster whose shape (Fig. 105) suggests that it was intended to serve as a sacred lamp to be lighted over a seven-day

Figure 105

period. Another find is that of a stone "wheel" (some think it was the base of an omphalos, an oracular "navel stone") that is clearly divided into four segments of seven markers each (Fig. 106), suggesting that it was really a stone calendar—a lunar calendar, no doubt—incorporating the seven-day week concept and (with the aid of the four dividers) enabling a lunar monthly count ranging from twenty-eight to thirty-two days.

Calendars made of stone had existed in antiquity, as evidenced by Stonehenge in Britain and the Aztec calendar in Mexico. That this one was found in Egypt should be the least wonder, for it is our belief that the genius behind all of those geographically spread stone calendars was one and the same god: Thoth. What may be surprising is this calendar's embracing the cycle of seven days; but that too, as another Egyptian "legend" shows, should not have been unexpected.

What archaeologists identify as games or game boards have been

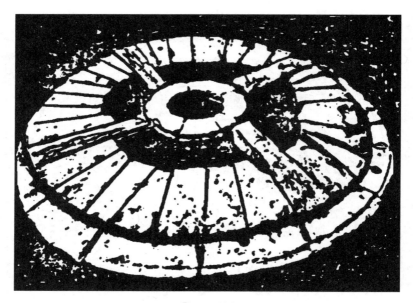

Figure 106

found almost everywhere in the ancient Near East, as witness these few
illustrations of finds from Mesopotamia, Canaan, and Egypt (Fig. 107).
The two players moved pegs from one hole to another in accordance
with the throw of dice. Archaeologists see in that no more than games
with which to while away the time; but the usual number of holes,
fifty-eight, is clearly an allocation of twenty-nine to each player—and
twenty-nine is the number of full days in a lunar month. There were
also obvious subdivisions of the holes into smaller groups, and grooves
connected some holes to others (indicating perhaps that the player
could jump-advance there). We notice, for example, that hole 15 was
connected to hole 22 and hole 10 to 24, which suggests a "jump" of one
week of seven days and of a fortnight of fourteen days.

Nowadays we employ ditties ("Thirty days hath September") and
games to teach the modern calendar to children; why exclude the possibility that it was so also in antiquity?

That these were calendar games and that at least one of them, the
favorite of Thoth, was designed to teach the division of the year into
fifty-two weeks, is evident from an ancient Egyptian tale known as
"The Adventures of Satni-Khamois with the Mummies."

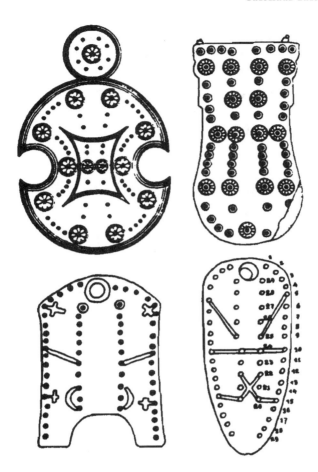

Figure 107

It is a tale of magic, mystery, and adventure, an ancient thriller that combines the magical number fifty-two with Thoth and the secrets of the calendar. The tale is written on a papyrus (cataloged as Cairo-30646) that was discovered in a tomb in Thebes, dating to the third century B.C. Fragments of other papyruses with the same tale have also been found, indicating that it was part of the established or canonical literature of ancient Egypt that recorded the tales of gods and men.

The hero of this tale was Satni, a son of the pharaoh, "well instructed in all things." He was wont to wander in the necropolis of Memphis, studying the sacred writings on temple walls and researching ancient "books of magic." In time he himself became "a magician who had no equal in the land of Egypt." One day a mysterious old man told him of a tomb "where there is deposited the book that the god Thoth had written with his own hand," and in which the mysteries of the Earth and the secrets of heaven were revealed. That secret knowledge included divine information concerning "the risings of the Sun and the appearances of the Moon and the motions of the celestial gods [the planets] that are in the cycle [orbit] of the Sun"; in other words—the secrets of astronomy and the calendar.

The tomb in question was that of Ne-nofer-khe-ptah, the son of a former king. When Satni asked to be shown the location of this tomb, the old man warned him that although Nenoferkheptah was buried and mummified, he was not dead and could strike down anyone who dared take away the Book of Thoth that was lodged at his feet. Undaunted, Satni searched for the subterranean tomb, and when he reached the right spot he "recited a formula over it and a gap opened in the ground and Satni went down to the place where the book was."

Inside the tomb Satni saw the mummies of Nenoferkheptah, of his sister-wife, and of their son. The book was indeed at Nenoferkheptah's feet, and it "gave off a light as if the sun shone there." As Satni stepped toward it, the wife's mummy spoke up, warning him to advance no farther. She then told Satni of her own husband's adventures when he had attempted to obtain the book, for Thoth had hidden it in a secret place, inside a golden box that was inside a silver box that was inside a series of other boxes within boxes, the outermost ones being of bronze and iron. When her husband, Nenoferkheptah, ignored the warnings and the dangers and grasped the book, Thoth condemned him and his wife and their son to suspended animation: although alive, they were buried; and although mummified, they could see, hear, and speak. She warned Satni that if he touched the book, his fate would be the same or worse.

The warnings and the fate of the earlier king did not deter Satni. Having come so far, he was determined to get the book. As he took another step toward the book, the mummy of Nenoferkheptah spoke up. There was a way to possess the book without incurring the wrath of Thoth, he said: to play and win the Game of Fifty-Two, "the magical number of Thoth."

Challenging fate, Satni agreed. He lost the first game and found himself partly sunk into the floor of the tomb. He lost the next game, and the next, sinking down more and more into the ground. How he managed to escape with the book, the calamities that befell him as a result, and how he in the end returned the book to its hiding place, makes fascinating reading but is unessential to our immediate subject: the fact that the astronomical and calendrical "secrets of Thoth" included the Game of Fifty-Two—the division of the year into fifty-two seven-day portions, resulting in the enigmatic year of only 364 days of the books of Jubilees and Enoch.

It is a magical number that vaults us across the oceans, to the Americas, returns us to the enigma of Stonehenge, and parts the curtains on the events leading to, and resulting from, the first New Age recorded by Mankind.

14

The Twelfth Planet—
The Key to the UFO Enigma

*Lecture at the Dialogue with the
Universe International Conference, Frankfurt,
West Germany, October 26–29, 1989*

Embracing Zecharia Sitchin's cosmology requires a belief in life on other planets and an acknowledgment of the fact that this extraterrestrial life has undoubtedly visited Earth in the past. To those who have not read Sitchin's books, this might seem a bit crazy. Our modern culture tends to dismiss the veracity of the UFO phenomenon as well as studies related to it. As a result, many people prefer to distance themselves from any discussion of extraterrestrial life and the possibilities that it entails.

That said, a great many people the world over do believe that UFOs exist. This is attested to by the number of conferences that are held every year on the subject. One such conference was held in October 1989 at which my Uncle Zecharia gave a lecture, which is what you will read next. The text selected for this chapter is an abridged version of that lecture. Although it contains much material that you may already be familiar with, it underscores the point that Nibiru, the home planet of the Anunnaki, has a cyclical orbit wherein it returns to Earth every 3,600 years.

Sitchin goes on to demonstrate that biblical accounts and the well-known Sumerian Epic of Gilgamesh tell of seeing visitors from the skies who looked like human beings but were not human—instead they were artificial, or machinelike. He surmises that they were robots created by the ancients to assist them in myriad ways.

There are reports of similar sightings today, prompting Sitchin readers to ask the question: "Are we then seeing in the UFOs the spaceships or scout ships of the Anunnaki?" According to Sitchin's theories, Mars had been used as a transfer station of the Anunnaki in the past, as evidenced by the many mysterious structures on and features of that planet. Its reduced atmosphere made it easier for a spaceship to blast off with a heavy load of cargo, and it was easier to intercept Earth from Nibiru by first going to Mars.

Sitchin posits that the orbit of Nibiru is due to place that planet in close proximity to Earth within the next few centuries. Read this fascinating account for yourself, and see what you decide about the future of planet Earth and the possibility that we will have visitors from afar one day in the not too distant future.

AS I STAND UP TO ADDRESS YOU, it seems to me that we are looking at each other with a certain curiosity. As UFO enthusiasts, you are no doubt wondering what my subject, "The 12th Planet," has to do with unidentified flying objects. And I, on my part, am asking myself what brings so many of you to such a gathering. It is obvious that if we are to believe the press and radio and television, you are a small minority of people who believe in the impossible.

I also belong to such a minority, although I have no claim to having seen a UFO or to having been abducted. But I have come all the way from New York to tell you that the mystery of UFOs *has* a solution. I cannot offer you a trip in a UFO, but I can, and I shall, take you on a journey that is no less thrilling. It is a journey to the future by way of the past.

Although I am not a UFO expert, I can tell you that the UFO phenomenon is not a mirage. Although the official circles still ridicule the phenomenon, the fact is that the *Wall Street Journal* published a page-one report on the mysterious circles that appeared in a field in England. And even the distinguished *New York Times* found it necessary to put the report from Voronezh, of the supposed landing there of a UFO, on its front page.

In other words, they still ridicule—but in their hearts they think: *Who knows?*

Well, let me take you on a voyage to the past and tell you what *I* know.

To take you on this journey involves the investigation of a planet that appears between Mars and Jupiter. It is a rather large planet, not as large as Jupiter but larger than Mars. This, ladies and gentlemen, is the twelfth member of the solar system, the subject of the Sumerian's most ancient cosmogony.

The Sumerians called this planet *Nibiru,* which meant "Planet of Crossing," and its symbol was the Cross. Nibiru, they said, comes to the vicinity of Earth every 3,600 years, when it passes between Mars and Jupiter, as is depicted in the cylinder seal I have shown you.*

And when it does so, the Sumerians said, the Anunnaki, the people who reside on that planet, come and go between Nibiru and Earth. And it is they who told us all that we know.

The name *Anunnaki* means "Those Who from Heaven to Earth Came." It is exactly what the biblical term *Nefilim* means. In the Sumerian Anunnaki, my friends, I have found the answer to my childhood question: Who were the Nefilim?

The story of Nibiru and how it came to be a member of the solar system is told in a very ancient text that recorded the Sumerian cosmogony. Archaeologists found the text in a more or less complete form written on seven clay tablets in Old Babylonian script. This text is called by scholars *Enuma Elish,* after its opening words. The Babylonians changed the name of Nibiru to "Marduk," to honor their national god. But how

---

*Editor's note: Please see Fig. 45 on page 89.

and what happened remained the same. Scholars call it a "myth." They call all the Sumerian texts of what happened in the beginning, of how the Earth was created, how Man was created, "myths." The only basic difference between me and all other scholars is that I *do not* consider these tales as "myth." I consider them as true records of the past.

Enuma Elish describes quite scientifically and step by step how the solar system was created. At first there were the sun and its "messenger" whom we call Mercury, and a large planet called *Tiamat* "Mother of Life." Then the next series of Planets appeared in pairs: Venus and Mars on one side of Tiamat, Jupiter and Saturn, Uranus and Neptune on the other side. Pluto was a "messenger" or Moon of Saturn. Earth did not yet exist. And our Moon was the largest one of eleven Moons that Tiamat had.

About half a billion years after the solar system reached this stage, an invader appeared from outer space—a planet thrown out by another star system. This was Nibiru/Marduk.

Dramatically, we read how Marduk was drawn into the solar system by the gravitational pull of the outer planets, more and more its orbit bent inwards toward Tiamat and finally the two met in a series of collisions.

As a result of that "celestial battle," Tiamat broke up into two parts. One part was smashed to bits and pieces, and became the asteroid belt, (which is indeed situated between Mars and Jupiter). The other, intact half was pushed into a new orbit, and became the smaller planet, *Earth,* pulled with it to the new orbit was the chief satellite of Tiamat— "Kingu," our Moon.

And what happened to Nibiru/Marduk? As I have mentioned, it was caught in a vast elliptical orbit of 3,600 years around the Sun. And once in 3,600 years it returns to the same spot where the asteroid belt is today, to what the Sumerians called "The Place of the Celestial Battle."

How did the Sumerians know all that? Those who had come to Earth from Nibiru told us—so the Sumerians said.

Is it possible, is it believable that someone from another planet, flying in interplanetary space toward Earth, was the source of all the knowledge that we call "civilization"—and especially the incredible and amazing knowledge of the heavens, of astronomy?

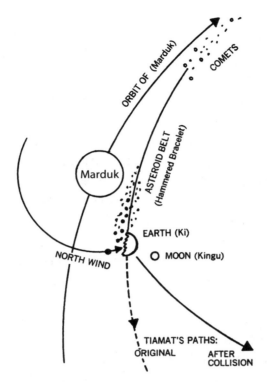

The collision of Marduk and Tiamat

Scholars who read the Sumerian texts, as I do, *but* treat them as "myths," have no explanation, no answer.

The same scholars who cannot explain the fantastic astronomical knowledge of the Sumerians have also never been able to explain why Earth was called by them "the seventh planet." If you ask our astronomers about Earth, they will tell you that it is the *third* planet: Mercury is the first, Venus is the second, Earth is the third from the Sun, but this very puzzle is the clue to the answer: for Earth *is indeed the seventh planet*—if one begins counting from the *outside*. Going inward: Pluto would be the first, Neptune the second, Uranus the third; Saturn the fourth, Jupiter the fifth, Mars the sixth—and *Earth the seventh!*

I can tell you at this point that a leading American astronomer who has read my books told me: "If there was no other evidence in your books, this one fact alone, that Earth was called 'the seventh,' convinces me that you are right." I would ask you to keep this designation of

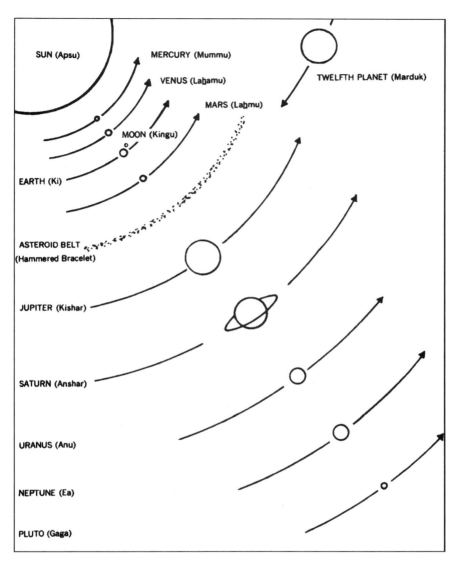

Counting from the outside, toward the sun, we see that Earth
is the seventh planet from Pluto

Earth in mind. Because according to this count, Mars should have been depicted as the "sixth" planet and, on the other side of Earth, Venus should have been depicted as an "eighth" planet. This is exactly how they were depicted, and this, as we shall soon see, is a most important clue to the UFO enigma.

This is one of many reasons why I have been treating the Sumerian texts not as "myths" but as sources of factual information about what had really happened on Earth in antiquity.

The Sumerian texts recorded what the visitors from Nibiru/Marduk had told them. The story, they said, begins about 450,000 years ago. On Nibiru/Marduk, a high civilization had developed, capable of space travel. If we think of what has been happening on Earth in a few centuries, since the Industrial Revolution, we can understand what had happened on Nibiru. There, they were losing their atmosphere and all life was in danger. Through a series of events that is detailed in my second book, *The Stairway to Heaven,* they discovered that there was gold on Earth. Their scientists decided that they could protect their atmosphere by suspending gold particles above the atmosphere. A group of fifty Anunnaki, led by their chief scientist, splashed down in the Persian Gulf. They waded ashore and built their first settlement. In time they expanded their cities to five. One was a metallurgical center. Another was a spaceport. They called their spaceport *Sippar,* meaning "Bird City."

They had, of course, to use spaceships to come from Nibiru to Earth, even if from as near as the zone of Mars. The Sumerians, whose writing began by using pictographs, called the pilots and the spaceships *DIN-GIR,* and here is how they drew it: As a spaceship with a module in front. When you separate the syllables, *DIN* by itself and *GIR* by itself, this is what you get: A spaceship from which a landing module has separated!

After the waters of the Great Flood destroyed everything that was on Earth, the Anunnaki built their post-Deluge spaceport in the Sinai peninsula. An Egyptian drawing depicted what had existed there, in the

DIN-GIR

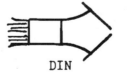

DIN   GIR

An illustration of DIN-GIR with the landing module intact.

An illustration of DIN-GIR with the landing module separated from the main craft.

Sinai: A rocketship in an underground silo, with the landing module sticking out, resting above ground. The rocket is made of several parts or stages; in the bottom one, we see two astronauts or mechanics working various dials.

Of the many illustrations in my books, let me show you another two of rockets. One is of a three-stage rocket, standing ready to be launched. Another is of a rocketlike device standing on a platform that brings to mind the construction of the Eiffel Tower. This latter one is in a protected part of a god's temple. We know from Sumerian texts

Ancient astronauts are seen in the bottom of this spacecraft
in this archaic Egyptian drawing

A Sumerian temple with a typical feature of the day:
a rocket on its launchpad

that the principal gods or the leaders of the Anunnaki had such protected compounds in their temples, each with its "bird" resting on a
launch-platform.

There are texts, quoted in my books, which describe these enclo-
sures and the flying vehicles placed therein. There are also texts that
describe not only how the Anunnaki, the so-called ancient gods, took
off heavenward but also how they flew about in Earth's skies. There was
found a life-size statue of the goddess Ishtar—at an excavated site on the
Euphrates River—called Mari, which shows her dressed as an astronaut.
Her equipment—a neck-box, an oxygen hose, a helmet equipped with
earphones—can be clearly seen from the sketch. The same Ishtar also
flew about in the skies of Earth; in such instances she was dressed as a
pilot, as we can see from this wall sculpture.

The Expedition examining the aeronautical equipment of the Flying Goddess,
Archaeological Museum, Aleppo, Syria

Sketches and representations
of the goddess Ishtar, dressed
as an astronaut

Two male Anunnaki astronauts as Eagle-men,
dressed in their official parade uniform

In case you will think that all the astronauts and flyers in antiquity
were female, I am showing you two male Anunnaki astronauts in their
official parade uniform, as that of Eagle-men. And in case you wonder
why astronauts should be associated with eagles, I will show you the
emblem of the Apollo 11 astronauts who were the first to land on the
moon. You may recall that when the landing module touched down
on the Moon's surface, they announced to Mission Control center in
Houston: "The *eagle* has landed!"

The eagle emblem of the Apollo 11 astronauts

Were these astronauts and flyers, were their rocketships and airships, hidden from the view of mankind in antiquity? Not at all.

We can see an ancient depiction that clearly shows a rocketship flying in the skies. At a site across the river Jordan opposite Jericho, at a place called Tell Ghossul, excavators have found stone dwellings going back thousands of years. The whitewashed walls were covered with beautiful murals. Among the amazing drawings were these of what looks like bulbous craft with extended legs and "eyes" that were undoubtedly lighting devices. That is the place where the Prophet Elijah was taken up. And is this a depiction of the "Vertical Liftoff" aircraft that the Prophet Ezekiel had seen?

Is it, my friends, the UFO that Jacob had seen?

Does it not lead us all to what I had stated in the beginning, that if

An ancient depiction at Tell Ghossul reveals what may be vertical
liftoff aircraft that are part of the biblical story of Elijah

you believe in the Bible, you must have an open mind about the UFO phenomenon?

Let us pause now and take a look where we have been.

We have been to the creation of Earth and the cataclysmic "Celestial Battle" that took place some four billion years ago.

We have witnessed the capture of the invader, the planet called Nibiru by the Sumerians and "Marduk" by the Babylonians, and it's becoming the twelfth member of our solar system.

We have established its orbit, a comet-like orbit that takes 3,600 years and that brings it back to our vicinity when it passes between Jupiter and Mars.

We have discovered all that through the amazing knowledge of the Sumerians, six thousand years ago. And we have concluded that what they knew could indeed have been known only in the manner stated by them: Those who had come to Earth from Nibiru told them so.

And in this way we cannot escape the conclusion that the biblical Nefilim, who were one and the same as the Sumerian Anunnaki, did in fact exist, did in fact visit the Earth.

We have seen the ancient depictions of their various vehicles: spacecraft, landing craft, airborne craft, rocketlike flying machines, multistage flying machines, flying machines that look like spheres—with or without extended legs—and cigarlike flying machines.

Is this not the answer to the first puzzling question about UFO sightings, the first reason for the doubts about them: Their *variety*. There was a variety in antiquity; why not now?

So the answer to the first enigma about the UFOs of today lies in what the ancient peoples have written and described!

Let us take up now the next enigma about UFOs. Why are their occupants reported to be in various shapes and sizes, and always *human-like but not actually human?*

I asked you to pay attention to how the Anunnaki had looked. Undoubtedly you have noticed that they look very human. In fact, they look very much like us. I have shown you even how they looked when they were dressed as "Bird-Men," the forerunners of the "Angels" of biblical stories. Perhaps I should remind you of a very interesting biblical story concerning Abraham. Just before the destruction of Sodom and Gomorrah, as he was sitting at the entrance to his tent, he "lifted his eyes and saw three men." These are the Bible's words: *Three Men*. Nevertheless, he recognized at once that they were divine beings. The same happened when two of them went to Sodom: the nephew of Abraham at once recognized who they were. And when the people of Sodom gathered around the nephew's house, the "angels" used a magical wand to direct at the people such a bright light that it blinded all of them.

I wish to show you one of the Sumerian illustrations which reminds me of this story in the Bible. Is it not one of them?—who looks like

A divine being as illustrated by the Sumerians

a "man" yet is not a man because of his helmet or face mask and his magical wand?

So, although they were from another planet, although they could dress as astronauts or pilots or as "angels," they basically looked like us. This should not be surprising, because according to the Bible *we look like them,* so they look like us. . . .

But this is not what the UFO reports of our time describe. Are the people who say they saw the occupants of the UFOs lying, are they imagining things?

Again I must stress that I myself have not seen a modern UFO nor have I seen their occupants. But I am not surprised by the reports and descriptions. In fact, I can and I will show you some of the ancient depictions which illustrate peculiar "beings" very much like the reports we hear nowadays!

The answer to who is being currently reported again lies in what has been seen in antiquity. These "beings" or "humanlike" occupants are definitely *not* the Anunnaki. So who were they in the past?

My answer to you is: Humanoids, robots!

There is a well-known Sumerian tale, the Epic of Gilgamesh, which describes his companion as an *artificial man.* There are recorded incidents of encounters with machinelike beings.

So this is the solution that I propose to the enigma of the descriptions—the varying descriptions—of humanlike beings in the observed UFOs.

Next, let us look at the question of *why* these UFOs come *and from where.* I think that unless and until these questions are answered, the whole UFO theory is without a basis. It floats in the air without a theory behind it.

To me there is no question that if, as so many report, UFOs do come to our planet and fly about in our skies, the only logical theory would be that we see now what our ancestors have seen in ancient times, in biblical times, perhaps even in the time of Jesus.

We see flying vehicles that can only be explained in terms of a) the Anunnaki, alias Nefilim, and b) in terms of the existence of Nibiru, the twelfth member of our solar system.

Could there be such a planet? The answer is a definite *yes.* Many

A depiction of what may be an extraterrestrial
humanoid of long ago

astronomers are convinced, for reasons which are too long to explain now, that there is another planet beyond Pluto.

Is there such a Planet? The answer again is *yes.* Not only because of the ancient evidence, but also because I have reason to believe that astronomers, especially with the aid of the Infrared Astronomical telescope launched in 1983, have *located* this planet.

And there is no doubt that it is on its way back to us.

Are we then seeing in the UFOs the spaceships of the Anunnaki?

No—*not—yet.*

What then are we seeing?

Here is my provocative answer: If the UFO reports are correct, we are seeing *scout ships,* operated and manned not by the Anunnaki themselves but by humanoids—by robots!

But if they do not yet come from Nibiru itself, where do they come from?

I will offer to you another provocative solution: *They come from Mars.*

As you know, Mars was probed more than any other neighboring planet, especially by the American Mariner and Viking spacecraft. These probes included the lowering of landers to the surface of Mars, to search for signs of life. At the time it was reported that no signs of life were found. But those results have been questioned and revised since then. . . .

What is undoubted is that life could have existed on Mars because at some time in the past Mars had an atmosphere denser than it is now, and more important: it had *water*. The evidence for *flowing water* is conclusive, as some of the following pictures will show.

The best theory of scientists is that due to changes in the angle of the axis of Mars (which happens also on Earth), the climate changes considerably every 50,000 years or so. So it is quite possible that some time in the past, a few thousand years ago or more than that, it was possible to exist on Mars—let us say, to *have a base on Mars.*

Will it surprise you to hear that some scholars believe that NASA photographs of Mars show evidence of such a base?

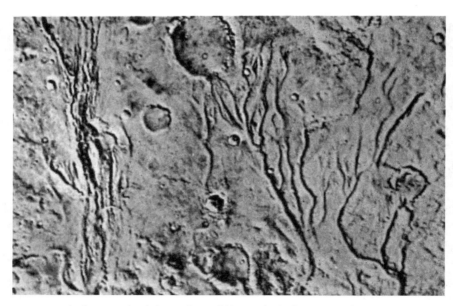

A photograph of the surface of Mars, which illustrates what may
have been ancient rivers on its surface

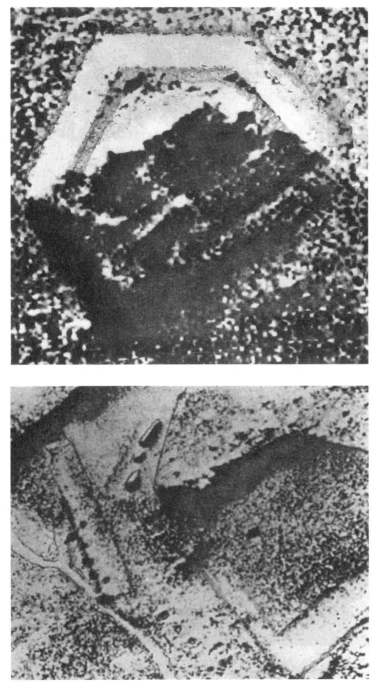

NASA photographs of what may be a base on Mars

In the past few years much attention was given to what has come to be known as *the face on Mars*. It is a rock, a natural rock that appears—I stress the word "appears"—to have been *artificially* carved out and sculpted to look like a human face—a face of a man with some kind of a helmet on his head. That the rock exists and that it looks like a human face there is no doubt, as evidence these two enlargements from *two different* photos taken by the Viking spacecraft at different times.

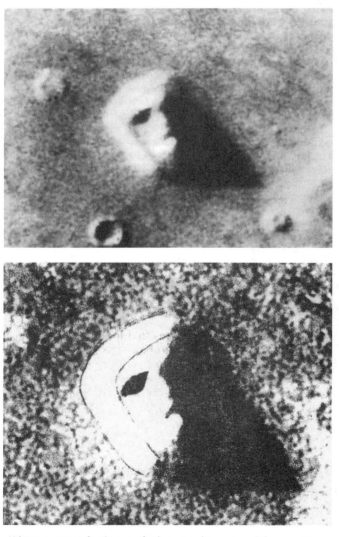

Viking spacecraft photos of what may be a carved face on Mars

Now, what does this image prove? If it is what it seems to be, then it means that someone familiar with the shape of a human face *was on Mars* sometime in the past. Could men from Earth have done it? I doubt it. Even the Sumerians gave the credit for the ability to fly, to the Anunnaki, not to themselves.

Were then the Anunnaki on Mars?

I say a definite *yes* not only because this would be the only logical explanation, but because I have in my hand the evidence to prove it. These are not only Sumerian text-references to Mars and what is on it. This is an actual illustration on a cylinder seal, which I invite you now to look at. You can see on the left hand side what is undoubtedly one of the Anunnaki "gods." Where he is, is clearly indicated by the symbol of the seven dots—the planet whose number is seven. It was, you will remember, the celestial number for Earth. The crescent of the Moon beside the Earth symbol is further evidence of where the "god" is.

Might this illustration be of an Anunnaki god on the left waving, from the planet Earth, to a Fish-Man on Mars?

He is waving his hand in greeting to someone on the other side of the heavens. This someone is dressed as an astronaut, not as an Eagle-man but as a Fish-man, which is how the earliest group that came to Earth were depicted. And where is this astronaut? He is at the planet with six angles, the planet whose number was six—*Mars!*

So whoever of the Anunnaki was on Earth, sent greetings to whoever was on Mars. And, the way they were going to meet is also shown: With the aid of a spacecraft, which is in the heavens between Mars and Earth.

It is my suggestion that the Anunnaki visited not only our planet Earth, but also had a station, a transfer point, on Mars.

I additionally suggest that the remains of their structures on Mars are still there. In fact, they were seen and photographed by the Viking spacecraft. Let me show you, first, a general view of the area in which the "face" was found. You will see that not far from the "face" are peculiar remains. Some writers have referred to them as "the city." Here is another shot of the area, taken at another Viking overflight. Some believe that certain ruins here are remains of pyramidical structures.

I'm more interested in the ruin that you can see here. It still retains two sides, which are straight—and one of the rules in archaeology is that "there are no straight lines in nature." Furthermore, the two sides form a perfect angle. And even more than that: One can notice a two-level shaping of the edges of tile structure, as if the roof had a kind of a ballustrade.

At the edge of what some call "the city" there is a most interesting structure. Its remains clearly show that it had a very thick wall surrounding it, and the walls met at a very distinct angle.

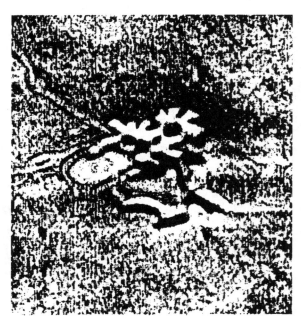

Ruins on Mars, which some writers have called "the city"

There are other structures, clearly artificially built, in other areas on Mars. Here is one of them. We see straight lines. Even more intriguing, we see some kind of a zigzag, as if this was a warehouse with loading piers. *It is impossible for this to be just a natural rock.*

If there had been a base on Mars before, could it be that the Anunnaki have re-established it, this time using it for their scout ships with the robots operating them?

Earlier this year, two Soviet Phobos spacecraft mysteriously went dead as they neared the planet Mars and its two satellites. We may yet learn what caused the unexplained incidents.

Until we hear more, one thing is clear: to understand the present we must understand the past. And by understanding the past, we will discover the future.

Postscript

As we peruse Zecharia Sitchin's writing, his published volumes, his lectures, and his articles, an alternative story of our origins on Earth takes shape. It is derived neither from creationism nor evolution, but both, and more. Sitchin's readers often ask me what he believed regarding religion and God. If the Elohim in the Hebrew Bible are the Anunnaki, then how can we reconcile that with religion?

Sitchin was a believer in God (with a capital G) and was Jewish. His faith was strengthened by his research on the Anunnaki. In many ways, what he learned supported his belief that the stories in the Bible, our Lessons for Life (the Torah), are historical facts and not myth or legend or simile. The Anunnaki believed in a "Creator of All" and Sitchin thought that the biblical Elohim, the Anunnaki, were emissaries of that Creator and that their actions were part of the Creator's greater plan.

Sitchin learned to read various types of cuneiform and researched and learned the ancient languages. They were Semitic languages and, as such, he felt they were very similar to the Hebrew that was *his* primary language. It was important to him to be able to read and translate the languages for himself so that the nuance of meaning was not lost by a poor or incomplete translation. He traveled frequently to museums and ancient monuments and sacred places in the Middle East, Europe, and the Americas so that he could see original artifacts firsthand. In some cases, he had to fight to be able to see something that the museum curators were reluctant to show him.

Ancient toy elephant on display at the Jalapa Museum
in Mexico, perhaps providing evidence of contact
between the Old World and the New

In Mexico's Jalapa Museum, for instance, a wooden toy elephant was on display on one of Sitchin's museum visits but hidden away on another. How could the people in that part of the world know of an African animal if there had been no contact between Central America and Africa in ancient times? There was reluctance on the part of the museum and the Mexican government to acknowledge possible pre-Columbian African roots of the Mexican people and perhaps that's why the elephant was on display in one instance and gone the next. Sometimes knowledge is politically inconvenient.

Another artifact, a sculpture showing what seemed to be a head-less astronaut in a space capsule, was not on display in the Istanbul Museum in Turkey for a different reason. The museum curator was reluctant to show it and did not want it to be in the general display. This time it was because he thought it must be a forgery. Why? Usually artifacts of the same type—cylinder seals, utensils, pottery, and clay tablets, for instance—are found in large numbers but in this case, the artifact was unique; it was believed to be the only one of its kind. Additionally, how was it possible that spaceships and astronauts existed in that long-ago era?

Sitchin managed, at least for a time, to see that the artifact went on

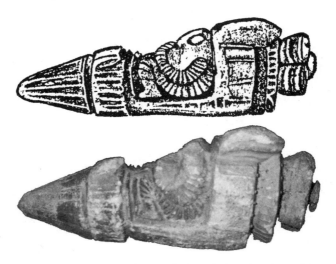

"The headless spaceman" artifact in the Istanbul Archaeological Museum

display. He did this by showing the curator that although it might be the only such item that had been found in Europe or the Middle East, dozens of similar images in drawings in the Americas showed people in a similar position, dressed in a like fashion.

The story that Sitchin uncovered—or, as he would say "reported"—from the ancient writings, artifacts, and drawings provides a believable alternate explanation of Earth's origins. My uncle was, after all, a reporter for many years in Israel before he began writing books. He also was one of the few scholars able to actually read the clay tablets and interpret ancient Sumerian and Akkadian. The story he uncovered became his legacy—in the form of the seven volumes that became The Earth Chronicles series and the accompanying seven books that supported that series—all based on the texts and pictorial evidence recorded by the ancient civilizations of the Near East. His controversial theories on the Anunnaki origins of humanity have been translated into more than twenty languages and featured on radio and television programs around the world.

My uncle's first published book, *The 12th Planet,* provides an overview of his belief system. It draws upon the Epic of Creation (*Enuma Elish*) and other sources to discuss the creation of our solar system, Earth, other planets, the celestial battle, the Anunnaki, Nefilim, Nibiru, and the creation of humankind.

The Stairway to Heaven, the second volume of The Earth Chronicles series, discusses evidence of a gateway between Heaven and Earth and mankind's search for a source of eternal life. Alexander the Great and Gilgamesh are but two individuals who sought immortality. The instructions written in the Book of the Dead to guide pharaohs to immortality are also discussed in this book.

Volume three, *The Wars of Gods and Men,* discusses some of the rivalries and wars fought between the Anunnaki leaders, including ones in which they enlisted mankind's participation. It suggests that nuclear weapons were used on Earth 4,000 years ago.

Book four, *The Lost Realms,* brings the stories of the Americas to light, explaining why the Aztec thought they were welcoming a returning god when the Spanish conquistadores arrived in the New World. The Anunnaki needed gold. They found it in abundance in Mesoamerica and they left behind facilities for processing it and for making tin.

When Time Began, the fifth volume, discusses the calendar, time, and Stonehenge and other monuments and temples that were related to keeping sophisticated and precise timings of solstices, equinoxes, and eclipses. It explains why the zodiac mattered.

The sixth volume, *The Cosmic Code,* discusses codes found in the Bible and other sacred writings and also explains the code of our DNA. Hidden codes, magic numbers, and prophecy are included.

The final volume, *The End of Days,* which Sitchin considered the core volume of The Earth Chronicles, answers the question of when Nibiru—and the Anunnaki—will be near Earth again. It brings together prophecies, calculations, astrology, and more to answer this most commonly asked question by Sitchin readers. Here is an excerpt from *The End of Days:* "Will they return? When will they return? These questions have been asked of me countless times, 'they' being the Anunnaki gods whose saga has filled my books. The answer to the first question is yes; there are clues that need to be heeded, and the prophecies of the Return need to be fulfilled. The answer to the second question has preoccupied Mankind ever since the watershed events in Jerusalem more than two thousand years ago. But the question is not only 'if' and 'when.' What will the Return signal; what will it bring with it?"

The companion volumes of *Genesis Revisted* and *Divine Encounters* delve deeper into particular aspects of the greater narrative. *The Lost Book of Enki* uses existing tablets and other documents to fill in the gaps in the story of the Anunnaki on Earth, as told in the voice of Enki. It is partially fictionalized, but based on facts and existing writings. Its poetic voice is astounding. This book is the one-volume summary of the storyline of the Anunnaki, told in one cohesive narrative.

The autobiographical *The Earth Chronicles Expeditions* and *Journeys to the Mythological Past* tell the entertaining and educational stories of Sitchin's travels to view artifacts in person, including while leading tours for interested readers. These stories also provide new information, for example, on the pyramids of Giza.

His final book, *There Were Giants Upon the Earth,* published in his 90th year—and just six months before his death—reads like a detective story and shows the true detective that Sitchin was. In this final book, Sitchin reaches the conclusion that two extraordinary tombs are the last resting place of an Anunnaki goddess and her demigod spouse, and he identifies the genealogical ancestry that dates back to those who were the first to land on Earth from Nibiru.

I brush the surface in summarizing some of the contents of each of these books; there is much more contained in them than I can describe in my few sentences here. I include the brief summaries above because some readers might be interested in reading more of Sitchin's oeuvre and thus will benefit from knowing where specific discussions may be found. I also want to underscore the point that there is a wealth of knowledge at the interested reader's disposal. The information in Sitchin's books is based on evidence, research, and scholarship. It might contradict older or long-established sources, but that's because Sitchin wanted to interpret the information himself instead of accepting a standard translation that might have missed or misinterpreted a possible meaning.

Here is a case in point: Sitchin often quotes Genesis chapter 6. Verse 2 reads, in part: "the sons of gods seeing the daughters of man, that they were fair. . . ." The word in Hebrew that was translated as "fair" also means "compatible," and Sitchin interpreted this to mean genetically compatible, which expands the meaning of the passage quite a bit. Instead of the daughters of man being merely pretty, it meant that they were capable of having intercourse and creating offspring.

It is in these kinds of interpretations that we discover much more in Sitchin's writings than we do in the traditional interpretations and translations of the ancient documents and artifacts. His books were not quickly written volumes intended to create an income. They were the result of a lifetime of research and carefully selected facts, supported by physical evidence, so as to leave no doubt that there was gravitas behind his claims. He wanted to educate and share important information. He was careful with his words, as I've already mentioned, and would not discuss theories or answer questions on incompletely researched subject areas, even if they were closely associated with topics he was mulling over at the time. Even with his brother, my father, who provided aeronautical calculations for him, he was close-lipped. If he said it, he believed it, because there was ample evidence to support it. If there wasn't, he changed the subject and would not engage in a further line of questioning on the topic.

For my part, I find it fascinating that people all over the world recognize the story of a deluge, the building of a tower to reach Heaven, and a pantheon of twelve gods with consistently similar personality traits. I don't think that the story of Nibiru and the Anunnaki could be just a myth of ancient people, similar to a novel or other tale for amusement, because it contains too many tangential stories, too much detail of the jealousies, romances, deceits, and daily activities of the main characters for this to be just a mere story. It's too complex and thematically developed, and it has its own internal logic.

The technology of the Anunnaki is something I can also imagine, given that I grew up in the age of personal computers, cellphones, and more. I have seen all of these technological advances become smaller, faster, and able to communicate better and farther and to hold vast amounts of knowledge. This knowledge is available to me with a few keystrokes on my smartphone, and perhaps in the reflection of my glasses. Is my smartphone similar to the "Me" discussed in some of Sitchin's writing? The "Me" was never fully explained in the sources Sitchin used for research, but it appeared to be something as small as a deck of cards that had great amounts of knowledge.

Another question about the ancients that pertains to their use of technology is this: How did they quarry and transport large boulders over long distances and then arrange them with such incredible precision into perfectly designed structures? Some of these boulders are too large to lift with today's technology. Did the Anunnaki have some sort of laser that could melt rock so that it could be cut to precise angles? Did they have a gravity device that could then lift the cut stones and transport them large distances and place them so precisely that no mortar was needed?

Perhaps this was everyday technology to the Anunnaki.

We find in looking at the past that there was much knowledge then that our scientists are discovering anew today. How did the Sumerians know about planets orbiting the Sun? How did they know about the color and size of the outer planets, or for that matter, that they even existed at all?

The Anunnaki told them.

Each time that an ancient piece of knowledge mentioned in one of Zecharia Sitchin's books was newly rediscovered by modern scientists, my uncle was elated and hopeful of the day when his theories would be widely acknowledged as true. The ancient people accepted that the Anunnaki could fly, communicate over long distances, knew about the solar system and astronomy, and had vast amounts of knowledge available to them. Why can't modern man understand this as well?

I look forward to the day when my uncle's theories are well-known and accepted. The day when we again are in full possession of ancient knowledge and know where it came from would be a very happy day for him. I suspect that when this happens, however, he might not receive credit for being the first to share his incredible knowledge; information that he had uncovered and then backed up by well-referenced and documented evidence. The attainment of credit and acclaim were not the reasons he wrote the books he wrote. He did so because it was important to him to do so—to share with the world what he had discovered. I could not be more proud of him.

JANET SITCHIN

Jericho

Letter to the
New York Times,
Published March 17, 1990

In the Old Testament there is a story of a time when the sun stood still and it was daylight for more than a day. Similarly, in the Americas, at the same time, there are legends of a day when the sun did not rise for more than a day. These events, on opposite sides of the world, corroborate each other, as Sitchin writes here in response to a *New York Times* article from February 22, 1990. The original published letter, written on March 1 and published on March 17, 1990, is shown on page 358, left column.

TO THE EDITOR:

"Believers Score in Battle Over the Battle of Jericho" (news article, Feb. 22), which reports new archeological evidence that corroborates the biblical tale of the shattering of Jericho's walls, also indirectly offers corroboration of an even more incredible biblical report from the same time.

The correlation between archeological evidence and biblical tale for the walled city of Jericho has been made possible by dating the Israelite conquest of the land of Canaan (later known as Palestine) to

THE NEW YORK TIMES, SATURDAY, MARCH 17, 1990

Letters

How Jericho Fell and Alexandria Burned

To the Editor:
"Believers Score In Battle Over the Battle of Jericho" (news article, Feb. 22), which reports new archeological evidence that corroborates the biblical tale of the shattering of Jericho's walls, also indirectly offers corroboration of an even more incredible biblical report from the same time.

The correlation between archeological evidence and biblical tale for the walled city of Jericho has been made possible by dating the Israelite conquest of the land of Canaan (later known as Palestine) to circa 1400 B.C., rather than centuries later. Soon thereafter, we read in the Bible, the Israelites attained another major victory when the sun stood still at Gibeon — rising but not setting for a whole day. Because scholars have been unable to explain the phenomenon, it has been disbelieved.

However, at about that same time, circa 1400 B.C., according to Aztec lore in Mexico, the sun failed to rise for a whole day in the City of the Gods, Teotihuacan (north of Mexico City). Likewise, it failed to rise for 20 hours in the Andes, according to Inca legends.

Since a day that does not end and a night that does not end are the same phenomenon in opposite parts of the world, the dating of the Israelite conquest at 1400 B.C., now corroborated by archeology at Jericho, would also confirm the tale of the sun's standing still in Gibeon.   ZECHARIA SITCHIN
New York, March 1, 1990
The writer's latest book is "The Lost Realms," on ancient civilizations and prehistoric events.

Academic Folklore

To the Editor:
One detail in "Believers Score in Battle Over the Battle of Jericho"

ite and perhaps Aryan. There never was an ethnic group called Hyksos. The existence of a tribe by this name is a bit of academic folklore, perpetuated by authors who prepare their books primarily by consulting other books, without a fresh review of the primary evidence.

The confusion caused by modern writers in this instance is similar to the confusion caused by their use of Vikings as an ethnic term: Old English "wicing" and Old Norse "vikingr" were common nouns meaning pirate and never appear as ethnic designations in medieval sources, although modern books about these Danish, Norwegian and Swedish adventurers speak of Vikings as though they constituted a single ethnic group   EARL ANDERSON
Cleveland, March 2, 1990
The writer is dean of the College of Arts and Sciences at Cleveland State University.

Don't Blame Caesar

To the Editor:
Against the background of dramatic upheavals in the world's political condition, it may seem pedantry to object to the casual perpetuation of an ancient myth in your Feb. 13 article about Egypt's attempt to create a new Library of Alexandria. You state that "the Alexandria Library assumed great fame until, in 48 B.C., the

rose up, and Caesar found him sieged with only his relativel army to defend him. He reali the reinforcements he sent fc be in certain danger from tl Egyptian fleet docked in the h Alexandria. Because he did r the resources to seize and r fleet, he ordered it burned.

The fire quickly spread fi burning ships to the wooden b surrounding the dock area, bt tainly never reached the st marble buildings (at two sit housed the famous library. books were burned, they wer stored in the warehouses n docks, perhaps awaiting ship Rome. No books in the library I

Caesar was a scholar, a wr lover of books. He would suri grieved the accidental destru the great library. Yet in Caesi account of the siege of Alexa book III of his "Civil War" nothing. Seneca, writing al years after the event does, first time, allege that 40,00 were burned at Alexandria i time. Even assuming he is n to Caesar, this number is only fraction of the library's es holdings. Most ancient autho no mention of any destructio great library by fire.

With Eastern Europe in m phosis, with Nelson Mandela f may understandably ask wha matter whether or not Julius caused the destruction of th Library at Alexandria?

To that question there are r facile answers. But long after momentous events fade from recorded memory, queries al Alexandrian Library and its tion will still be made and n fully answered. And that will b

---

circa 1400 B.C., rather than centuries later. Soon thereafter, we read in the Bible, the Israelites attained another major victory when the sun stood still at Gibeon—rising but not setting for a whole day. Because scholars have been unable to explain the phenomenon, it has been disbelieved.

However, at about that same time, circa 1400 B.C., according to Aztec lore in Mexico, the sun failed to rise for a whole day in the City of the Gods, Teotihuacan (north of Mexico City). Likewise, it failed to rise for 20 hours in the Andes, according to Inca legends.

Since a day that does not end and a night that does not end are the same phenomenon in opposite parts of the world, the dating of the Israelite conquest at 1400 B.C., now corroborated by archeology at Jericho, would also confirm the tale of· the sun's standing still in Gibeon.

ZECHARIA SITCHIN
NEW YORK, MARCH 1, 1990

APPENDIX II
Old Egyptian Road
Preserves Bible Link

Letter to the **New York Times,**
Published May 19, 1994

On May 8, 1994, the *New York Times* published an article reporting on the discovery of the world's oldest paved road, located in
Egypt near Lake Qarun. Zecharia Sitchin shed some more light
on the area and the purpose of this "road" in his letter to the
editor, written on May 9 and published on May 19, 1994.

TO THE EDITOR:

A May 8 news report that the world's oldest paved road has
been found in Egypt states that studies of an ancient road near Lake
Qarun, 43 miles southwest of Cairo, suggest that it served to transport quarried stones. Historical fact and local lore, however, connect
the place to the biblical Joseph and his achievement of feeding Egypt
during the seven lean years. My recent visit to the area supports this
link and raises the possibility that the road served to transport food,
rather than stones.

Lake Qarun is the shrunken remains of a much larger lake that
Greek and Roman geographers called Lake Moeris. It lies in and
waters a great natural depression called Al Fayum. Surrounded by an

THE NEW YORK TIMES
May 19 1994

ιs, it has
les from
ιssayed,
;ion had
·gan. As
ιd store
ng, they
history.
;hington

ν said it
ιs it was
ear fuel
um in it.
tors has
inspec-
·eadings
had oc-
r, if the
he work
εfueling,
resump-

a verifi-
for U.S.
ces and
· patient
be in a
εa?

surance
:i not to
against
ιat this
·ols and
sured.
's plan,
venting
mprove
er their
d Medi-
mpared
ryone a

nisstep,
to fill a
has co-
of Ten-
howev-
← unin-

―――

rogate decision making to vindicate
the patient's interest in self-determi-
nation. The Quinlan decision was followed by other court decisions across
the country affirming the right of
terminally ill patients to refuse life-
supporting medical treatment.

thus becomes an integral part of the
right to live: as twin axes of a single
organic process, both implicate the
most intimate and ultimate personal
decisions.
ORIN S. SNYDER
New York, May 9, 1994
The writer is a lawyer.

Old Egyptian Road Preserves Bible Link

To the Editor:
A May 8 news report that the
world's oldest paved road has been
found in Egypt states that studies of
an ancient road near Lake Qarun, 43
miles southwest of Cairo, suggest
that it served to transport quarried
stones. Historical fact and local lore,
however, connect the place to the
biblical Joseph and his achievement
of feeding Egypt during the seven
lean years. My recent visit to the area
supports this link and raises the possibility that the road served to transport food, rather than stones.
Lake Qarun is the shrunken remains of a much larger lake that
Greek and Roman geographers
called Lake Moeris. It lies in and
waters a great natural depression
called Al Fayum. Surrounded by an
arid desert, it served in antiquity and
still serves as Egypt's breadbasket
because at some time it was artificially connected to the Nile River by
a canal. To this day, the canal is
called Bahr Yusof, the Waterway of
Joseph. According to local lore, Joseph built the canal and created the
artificial lake in 1,000 days, which is
what alf yum means in Arabic.
Touring the area in search of evidence for the Israelite presence in
Egypt, I could clearly see the extent
of the ancient lake by the abrupt end
of the lush vegetation. The adjoining

Bob Gale

dry land contains the remains of what
Herodotus called Labyrinth — some
3,000 subterranean chambers that
stored grain through ground-level
openings, which can still be seen. In
the midst of the storage area rises the
pyramid of the pharaoh Amenemhat
(Ammenemes) III — the "Moeris" of
the lake's ancient name.
The Bahr Yusof canal is still working, and it is still watering the
lake.
ZECHARIA SITCHIN
New York, May 9, 1994
*The writer is the author of "When
Time Began" and other books on ancient civilizations.*

U.S. Peacekeepers Echo Anti-Serb Confusion

To the Editor:
Your May 11 article on the United
States force with the United Nations
in Macedonia states: "The resent-
ments voiced by Macedonians are not

To Change China

To the Editor:
Calls to revoke China's most fa-
vored nation trading status with the
United States as a way of changing
China's human rights practices neg-
lect to point out that our country
routinely bestows the most favorable

seen nothing wrong with
sanctioning prolonged suf
great expense to family
and society, we try to keep
ple alive by surgery, drugs
to machines. Why?
Perhaps it is our arrogan
be immortal, our culture's
with youth and beauty or o
spirituality in a material v
forces us to focus on the e:
as the only one.
I think it would be dan
assume that Dr. Jack Kevo
any ill intentions in using h
ity in assisted suicides. Dr
concerned about the legal
tions of assisted suicide, b
spoken with the families of
have sought Dr. Kevorkian
Perhaps a generation fro:
may look upon assisted su:
more humane alternative to
drawn-out, artificial and ι
way of keeping sick and
people alive.
EM
New York, Ma
•

Hospice Care

To the Editor:
Your May 3 article on th
kian verdict reports that so
rors described the not guil
as appropriate because D
kian's interest in relievin;
tient's suffering was noble
jurors acknowledged that h
may not have been appropr
The public debate has ig:
alternatives to suicide ava
the terminally ill. The prim.
native to suicide, one that
same mission of alleviation
ing, is hospice care, which n
that the physical pain and di
that may accompany a ter
ness are often accompanied
tional, spiritual and perhap
nancial suffering.
In hospice, the affected in
and their informal support
are entitled to comprehens
ices (home or hospital) to 1
the quality of life remainir
has been little discussion of
or not Dr. Kevorkian's "clie:
even aware of this option.
Hospice programs prov

---

arid desert, it served in antiquity and still serves as Egypt's breadbasket
because at some time it was artificially connected to the Nile River by
a canal. To this day, the canal is called Bahr Yusof, the Waterway of
Joseph. According to local lore, Joseph built the canal and created the
artificial lake in 1,000 days, which is what alf yum means in Arabic.

Touring the area in search of evidence for the Israelite presence in Egypt, I could clearly see the extent of the ancient lake by the abrupt end of the lush vegetation. The adjoining dryland contains the remains of what Herodotus called Labyrinth—some 3,000 subterranean chambers that stored grain through ground-level openings, which can still be seen. In the midst of the storage area rises the pyramid of the pharaoh Amenemhat (Ammenemes) III—the "Moeris" of the lake's ancient name.

The Bahr Yusof canal is still working, and it is still watering the lake.

ZECHARIA SITCHIN,
NEW YORK, MAY 9, 1994

Index

BOOKS OF RELATED INTEREST

There Were Giants Upon the Earth
Gods, Demigods, and Human Ancestry: The Evidence of Alien DNA
by Zecharia Sitchin

The Lost Book of Enki
Memoirs and Prophecies of an Extraterrestrial God
by Zecharia Sitchin

The Complete Earth Chronicles

The 12th Planet (Book I)
The Stairway to Heaven (Book II)
The Wars of Gods and Men (Book III)
The Lost Realms (Book IV)
When Time Began (Book V)
The Cosmic Code (Book VI)
The End of Days (Book VII)

by Zecharia Sitchin

DNA of the Gods
The Anunnaki Creation of Eve
and the Alien Battle for Humanity
by Chris H. Hardy, Ph.D.

Slave Species of the Gods
The Secret History of the Anunnaki
and Their Mission on Earth
by Michael Tellinger

INNER TRADITIONS • BEAR & COMPANY
P.O. Box 388
Rochester, VT 05767
1-800-246-8648
www.InnerTraditions.com

Or contact your local bookseller